How to Do Things with Myths

How to Do Things with Myths
A Performative Theory of Myths and How We Got There

Ivan Strenski

SHEFFIELD UK   BRISTOL CT

Published by Equinox Publishing Ltd
UK: Office 415, The Workstation, 15 Paternoster Row, Sheffield, South Yorkshire S1 2BX
USA: ISD, 70 Enterprise Drive, Bristol, CT 06010

www.equinoxpub.com

First published 2025
© Ivan Strenski 2025
All rights reserved. No part of this publication may be reproduced or transmitted in any form or by any means, electronic or mechanical, including photocopying, recording or any information storage or retrieval system, without prior permission in writing from the publishers.

British Library Cataloguing-in-Publication Data
A catalogue record for this book is available from the British Library.

ISBN-13 978 1 80050 476 9 (hardback)
         978 1 80050 477 6 (paperback)
         978 1 80050 478 3 (ePDF)
         978 1 80050 539 1 (ePub)

Library of Congress Cataloging-in-Publication Data

Names: Strenski, Ivan, author.
Title: How to do things with myths : a performative theory of myths and how we got there / Ivan Strenski.
Other titles: Performative theory of myths and how we got there
Description: Sheffield, South Yorkshire : Equinox Publishing Ltd., 2025. | Includes bibliographical references. | Summary: "How to Do Things with Myths: A Performative Theory of Myths and How We Got There assembles a radically updated collection of the author's oft-cited publications on myth. Together, they tell how theories of myth have changed and led to a novel 'performative' theory of myth"-- Provided by publisher.
Identifiers: LCCN 2024004900 (print) | LCCN 2024004901 (ebook) | ISBN 9781800504769 (hardback) | ISBN 9781800504776 (paperback) | ISBN 9781800504783 (pdf) | ISBN 9781800505391 (epub)
Subjects: LCSH: Myth. | Performative (Philosophy)
Classification: LCC BL304 .S76 2024 (print) | LCC BL304 (ebook) | DDC 398.2--dc23/eng/20240328
LC record available at https://lccn.loc.gov/2024004900
LC ebook record available at https://lccn.loc.gov/2024004901

Typeset by S.J.I. Services, New Delhi, India

*To the memory of Robert A. Segal, for a lifetime of collegiality,
and
to an unknown referee,
for gently rejecting my attempt to publish an article titled
"Introduction aux mythes."
Thanks to this referee's candor, I think I learned how to do better.
And
to Lionel St. Joseph.*

Contents

1. Introduction: Myths, Performatives, Performances, and Performers ... 1
2. "*Sola Scriptura*": Max Müller's Theory of Myths ... 16
3. French Connections: Durkheimian Ritualism Replaces Müller's Hegemony of Myth ... 39
4. Henri Hubert: Durkheim's Mythologist ... 54
5. What Lévi-Strauss May or May Not Owe to Henri Hubert ... 68
6. Müller's Legacy, Broken: Malinowski and the Pragmatist Concept and Theory of Myths ... 88
7. Taking Responsibility for the Concept and Theory of Myth ... 120
8. Conceptual Problems for Robert A. Segal and Jonathan Z. Smith ... 146
9. Henri Hubert Undoes Aryanist Political Myths ... 173
10. The Myth of Moscow, Third Rome: What It Seeks to Do ... 188

Notes ... 207

Bibliography ... 235

Index ... 252

Chapter 1

Introduction: Myths, Performatives, Performances, and Performers

Why Seeing Myths as Performatives Matters

In 1962, Oxford philosopher J. L. Austin published the singularly important *How to Do Things with Words*. In it, Austin shows how iterations of words are often far more than simply static *representations* or *stand-ins* for ideas. In several ways, their iteration constitutes *acts*. They *perform* various tasks—"do things"—in a field of discourse. For instance, a priest pronouncing the word "baptize" as they pour water over an infant's head while saying "I baptize you in the name of the Father…" *performs* a liturgical act of initiating a new member into the Christian community. Its iteration does not primarily *represent* or *symbolize* the concept of baptism. It *does* something. In Austin's language, by means of such an "iteration" a baptism is *performed*. Austin's theory came to be known as the "performative" theory of language. One may also refer to this theory of language as a sub-class of *pragmatic* or *pragmatist* ones, in that it regards words as "acting," "functioning," "practical," or in terms of what they "do."

The present volume aims to articulate a project analogous to Austin's by recommending a performative theory of myths. Although a *performative* theory of myths resembles Bronislaw Malinowski's classic pragmatist theory of myth, it differs significantly. Because of Malinowski's positivism, Malinowski's theory of myths eventually rested on behaviorist or phenomenalist epistemological grounds. For Malinowski, only gross observability could establish claims as "scientific." For Malinowski, what a myth *did* therefore had to be identified with observable behaviors, even down to the level of certain critical physiological reactions, such as increased heart rate or vigorous perspiration! *A Scientific Theory of*

Culture represents Malinowski's most refined *positivist* statement of how myths *act*.[1]

Malinowski's pragmatic theory also presumed as normal the "crisis" situation of life on the edge. Cultures are delicately assembled and maintained. Collapse is possible for the slightest of reasons. As Malinowski sees them, myths serve indispensable roles in maintaining cultures. Without certain myths, cultures would simply disintegrate. Malinowski, thus, left little room for cultures to maneuver or adapt. On the other hand, performance theory sees cultures as more adaptable than Malinowski did. If myths fail to do a certain job, some other cultural device might step in to play the same role. Contrary to Malinowski's view, the performances in a performative theory of myths can, in principle, range over a wide variety of human practices and discourses, even including "useless" dramatic performances or impractical artistic installations. For a *performative* theory of myth, it is enough that myths simply "do" things — without further qualification. Myths are not absolutely necessary or irreplaceable. But myths can and are useful for doing certain tasks in culture.

In these days, when myths play a prominent part in our politics, seeing them in their performative roles seems particularly timely. Myth-laden propaganda has increasingly come into its own with the rapid spread of digital communications technology. Deployed effectively, such political myths boost national pride, elevate expectations of messianic collective destiny, or appeal to apocalyptic narratives of national salvation. Negatively, they raise conspiratorial suspicions about ethnic or racial loyalties, Fifth Columns, and other subversive elements. It is because of the broad and powerful effect of the *performance* of myths in political cultures that this volume proposes principal attention to the performative nature of myths.

The appreciation of myths as performative comes in part from dissatisfaction with seeing myths only as static texts, scriptures, iterations, narratives, literatures, and such. Americanist anthropologist Jane Desmond reminds us of how much the presumption of text as static has dominated the humanistic disciplines. There, we, typically,

> ...analyze events, documents, and cultural products primarily through reference to other events, documents, and cultural products, we situate these as "texts" to be read through a variety of interpretive methods.

That is, we read potential effects of and through the textual structures in a specific historical moment.[2]

Humanist studies thus seem as if they have gotten stuck in a sixteenth-century Lutheran *sola scriptura* rut by attending only to immobile sacred texts, immutable physical documents, and the like. Desmond wants instead to recommend that humanists supplement the study of documents and texts with ethnography, history, or fieldwork because "direct contact is essential to understanding the meanings people make in their worlds and the actions, beliefs, and ideational, social, and environmental structures that shape those worlds."[3] The reason? Only by "peopling our analyses" will we be "able to see cultural products as embedded in networks of cultural and social processes—in action."[4] For Desmond, as for the present author, this entails "a more performative understanding of daily life."[5] Therefore, to the extent we seek to understand how and why things *happen* in culture, a performative theory of myth becomes increasingly desirable.

How to Do Things with Myths tries to show how one can "people" myths by showing how they *act performatively*, for instance, in politico-religious contexts. A particularly articulate manifesto, here, for *performative* approaches comes, again, from Jane Desmond. My purpose is to extend Desmond's sensibility to myths:

> I feel strongly that we must engage more fully with the performative dimensions of everyday life: how people make meaning out of the ideas, texts, practices, and beliefs available to them and how they continually reshape those practices and reconstruct their lives and the lives of the communities to which they belong. These active practices of construction and reconstruction always take place in a complex force field of possibilities enabled and limited by historical, political, and economic dimensions, as well as social formations.[6]

Accordingly, readers will note two features of how I approach both myths and theories of myth. First, I try to show to how myths *do* things in particular contexts. As part of political cultures, I show how myths play their roles in sustaining or opposing certain political arrangements. Second, I try to locate theorizing about myth in the concrete historical contexts of their origins and use. Using Desmond for my own purposes, I agree with the spirit of her assertion that "it is not enough to analyze" a myth or theory of myth "without simultaneously trying to understand not only the social, political, economic, and ideological conditions of its possibility but also the meanings people attach to it, their agency, and the uses they make of it as a way of making their world."⁷

Showing how myths do things in particular contexts often passes for what sociologists call "*legitimation.*" Here, a myth is invoked to do some task—to justify or grant *legitimacy* to certain institutions or practices. Just as likely, given other conditions, myths may do the reverse and *delegitimize* institutions or practices just as easily. Specifically, I show how myths *perform* certain tasks in the political, religious, or social fields of discourse, whether in Russia, Third Republic France, modern India, the Hebrew Bible, or other venues. There, we will see how myths figure in thinkers trying to "do things" by appealing, whether explicitly or not, to certain select narratives. What matters most here, is not what the myths *depict*, *represent*, or *symbolize* in their iteration (or narration) but how myths *perform*—how they *do* things in the world.

Myths as Texts: Friedrich Max Müller

Pragmatic or performative theories of myth are relatively novel. Regrettably, when Bronislaw Malinowski broke the theoretical ice and first theorized myths pragmatically, he did so in terms of a crass materialism. He viewed myths as exerting biological causal effects, playing down the ways culture, in a broader sense, influences political or social behavior. For Malinowski, it was as if only observable behaviors—twitching nerves or heightened blood pressure—showed what myths could do. Before Malinowski, students of myths tended toward an "intellectualist" view of myths as literatures, narratives, poems, explanations, or commonly, stories about the gods. Given the immense prestige of Luther's legacy, myths were often measured against—sometimes favorably and sometimes not—the biblical narrative. By extension, Luther's doctrinal recommendation that *sola scriptura*—only the Bible—should guide Christian life became the model for humanists conceiving and studying myths as well. Scholars, therefore, typically assumed that all the world's religions were equally well anchored in their various "scriptures," as were Judaism or Christianity. Later, with the discovery by ethnographers of societies without writing, the paradigm of the Bible anchoring entire religions was extended to mythologies which, in turn, were commonly regarded as "pagan bibles." The myths of ancient Greece and Rome, for instance, told tales of fantastic characters of god-like proportions, much as the Bible related tales of the creation of Adam from dust, or Eve from Adam's rib. In the same way, myths or fabulous tales of a talking snake led humanity's parents into original sin. If the divine Zeus/Jupiter hurled thunder bolts, the goddess, Demeter, looked out for the fecundity of crops; Pluto, then, ruled the underworld, etc.

Lutheran Indologist Friedrich Max Müller (1823-1900) was a prominent heir to Reformation biblicism in the study of myth and the first true, dedicated theorist of myth. In effect, Müller made Luther's *sola scriptura* his guide in the study of myths. To Müller, the ancient Indian narratives of *devas'* marvelous acts were legitimate *religious* documents—indeed, pagan bibles. Even when they had to be recovered as "forgotten bibles," they were nonetheless *foundational* for ancient Hindus just as the Bible was for Christians and Jews.[8] Müller's Biblicist convictions eventuated in a life's work of translating and editing a fifty-volume library of Asian religious texts, known as *The Sacred Books of the East*. Anthologies of religious "literature" like *The Sacred Books of the East* and its ilk provided the sole sources of data on the mythologies of the world for decades until ethnographers began publishing their findings toward the end of the nineteenth century.

Müller distinguished himself by writing about myths as *linguistic* phenomena. Significantly, he saw language as representational, statically standing for objective referents in the world. As a species of language, Müller assumed that myths too represented or stood for objective referents in the world or beyond. Müller did not, then, see myths as active agents capable of *performing* tasks or even being broadly "pragmatic." Thus, when it came to interpreting the Indic mythologies in the Vedas, Müller regarded them as stories *representing* the Hindu gods. Vedic myths thus made up a good portion of a Hindu "Bible," just as tales of Samson and Delilah, Moses dividing the Red Sea, Joshua's trumpets bringing down the walls of Jericho, etc. stood for divine actions in the Hebrew Bible.

But since Müller held that ancient Indian mythologies *represented* objective realities, Müller ran into theological difficulties—to which he, nevertheless, tried to respond as a liberal Christian. The Vedic myths, for instance, sang the praises of *"agni."* In so doing, the Vedic hymns literally referred reverentially, even worshipfully, to "fire." To Müller, this seemed to mean that the Vedic folk literally worshipped a natural object—fire! But Müller could not be completely sure what this meant. Did the Vedic folk mean common, natural fire—*agni*—or the *god* of fire, *Agni*? Müller really could not be sure because the ancient Indian orthography lacked capitals. When they wrote 'fire,' their orthography did not distinguish the natural phenomenon "fire" from some transcendent, disembodied divine, upper-case "Fire" or "Agni," analogous to Yahweh or Allah. But despite uncertainty about Vedic intentions, Western scholars (Müller included) theologized the Vedas along Western lines. He concluded that the word *"agni"* named a *god*, *"Agni"*—an assumption constituting nothing short of a gratuitous Christian theological imposition upon the Vedas. At the same time, Müller could not shake his own religious preferences. In some way needing further explanation, Vedic myths did promote the worship of a natural phenomenon, like fire. Müller's answer was to argue that the myths of the Vedas revealed a religion in the process of an *evolution* that had not yet reached lofty Christian levels of refinement. To Müller this indicated that Vedic myths represented the effects of a "disease of language," in that they confused natural forces named in myths with supernatural ones—gods. So influential, however, was Müller's Biblicist assumption about myths that it typified, in part, a movement among religion scholars that I call "maxmüllerism." Not only was religion typified by the myth-making faculty, but the essence of religion itself lay in myth, understood in the narrative or scriptural features of a religion not in its rituals or liturgies, ethical codes, or concrete arrangements of sacred space or time.

Much of the discourse about myth was carried on by Müller's "Science of Religion" throughout the nineteenth century, as it was under the banner of *Religionswissenschaft* in Germany, Scandinavia, and the Netherlands, and *Sciences des Religions* in France.[9] In time, however, other 'scientific' students of religion began taking exception to maxmüllerism. They became more impressed with the *ritual* or liturgical aspects of the very same documents Müller had only considered as symbolic entities.

But instead of maxmüllerist obsessions with mythical narrative, the rite of sacrifice began to magnetize the attention of many scholars. Soon, scholars began debating the relative importance of rites versus myths to the nature of religion. These new appreciations of ritual often reflected the rich ritual religious culture of certain scholars, particularly Jews such as Sylvain Lévi or Émile Durkheim. So much indeed did the Durkheimians seek to resurrect ritual's contribution to religion that they even attributed ritual agency to myths. Hubert and Mauss remarked, for instance, that "Myth, once constituted, can react upon the ritual from which it first emerged and was actualized."[10]

Bronislaw Malinowski

In the midst of debates over the relative importance of myth and ritual, anthropologist Bronislaw Malinowski produced a *pragmatic* or *functionalist* theory of religion that effectively spanned the differences between myth and ritual. Malinowski refused to draw a sharp distinction between myths and rituals, in effect, seeing both as being actions. With this theoretical move, Malinowski's "pragmatic" or "functionalist" theory of myths established itself as an influential humanistic or socio-cultural theory of myths. This was later to change, as we will see. But, in the beginning, Malinowski, in general, saw myths not so much as representations or explanations but as agents capable of *doing* something, as *performances*. In this volume's chapter on Malinowski, I shall give a fuller account of the methodological and theoretical significance of Malinowski's journey into theory, especially as it evolved into increasing materialism. Accordingly, in his last book, aptly titled *A Scientific Theory of Culture*, Malinowski concludes that "the theory of culture must take its stand on biological fact."[11] There, he also recalls the social legitimation function of his earlier cultural theory of myths—myth as "charter" or "warrant" — only to replace it by declarations of do-or-die, pragmatic biologism. "The actions, material arrangements, and means of communication which are most directly significant and comprehensible are those connected with man's organic needs, with the emotions, and with practical methods for satisfying needs."[12] As a "means of communication," Malinowski includes myths, too, among the ways people fulfill vital organic needs.

While Malinowski's grasp of what myths *do* evolved toward a materialist pragmatism, the "performative" view of myth that I am proposing is content to remain a socio-cultural or humanistic effort. I see no need to commit to Malinowski's physicalist view of how myths "do things." The test of the validity of such an approach might preoccupy ontologists and metaphysicians. I shall leave them to it. While Malinowski's biologistic pragmatism ambitiously tries to establish its *bona fides*, I prefer to pursue the well-trodden path of appreciating the ways myths *act*, assumed by cultural or social anthropologists and other cultural sciences. Here, a common reference is often made to so-called political myths. I therefore join with theorist of "political culture" Jardar Østbø in conceiving of a performative notion of myth as denoting "more or less elaborate narratives about a political society, usually as an incitement to action."[13]

A Note on Method: "Political Culture" Matters

In this volume, thus, I embrace the idea of "political culture." Many readers will recognize political culture as a notion informing the work of historians and political scientists like Richard Hofstadter, C. Vann Woodward, Lucien Lefebvre, and others. As a student of religion and politics, I find myself with great sympathy for their efforts to show how cultural factors condition the emergence of certain political structures—to show, in effect, "how to do things with" culture—and not just "myths," either.

A recent, impressive example of how cultural factors influence political behavior comes from historian R. Dean Davenport. The political division between free and slave states that eventuated in the American Civil War, Davenport argues, was rooted in the seventeenth century's *cultural* differences between settlers. Seventeenth-century Massachusetts Bay Colony Puritans and Southern, patriarchal Anglicans constituted one such critical cultural opposition. Unlike the more democratic-tending Puritan New Englanders, Virginia's settlers habitually regarded their local aristocrats with an exaggerated deference. Sometimes rising to the level of a cultish elevation of the gentry to nearly sacred status, it was common for Virginians to assume that aristocratic entitlement contained within it powers akin to the Stuart divine right of kings. Davenport and other partisans of political culture analysis believe the resultant political and social differences between slave and abolitionist states is somehow rooted in these cultural differences about the magic of aristocracy.[14] In an analogous way, I shall argue that the myths that constitute a portion of a society's cultural resources can also be said to "do" things to shape a particular society and its resultant politics.

While the effect of culture upon politics may seem obvious to many, saying that *myths* need to be taken seriously in the formation of politics and policies may be a bridge too far. It is not. Political violence turns up in a number of these essays, as readers will note. I shall argue that a culture's mythology can influence both the level and species of violence found there. I realize, at the same time, that psycho-medical factors in social violence, such as alienation, childhood abuse, or other psychoses, commonly receive serious attention as the root causes of particularly disturbing outbursts of violence. But I am arguing that myths do as well. Myths typically introduce the notion of 'script' or 'excuse' that allow political actors to plot their actions more easily. Myths provide a narrative structure enabling actors to situate themselves in some kind of meaningful social drama. Following Østbø, myths offer "elaborate narratives" that are quite often "an incitement to action."[15] This is a plea for peacekeepers to heed the kinds of *stories* potentially violent people tell themselves, because it is often just such *myths* that have captured their imaginations, and presage action. Action follows more easily with a good myth in hand. One needs only to step into a chosen role laid out in the myth. Bringing things full circle to J. L. Austin and performatives, this collection of essays tries to show "how to do things with" myths in a number of concrete historical contexts. Let me now say a few words about the plan of this book.

Müller's Surprising Legacy in the Theories of Robert A. Segal and Jonathan Z. Smith

I would misrepresent the novelty of my approach were I not to acknowledge my intellectual forebears in theory of myth. I therefore include essays on prominent myth theorists of recent times whose work has both contributed to and provoked a performative view of myths. Müller, Robert A. Segal, and to a lesser extent, Jonathan Z. Smith, represent some notable alternatives to a performative theory. In chapter 2, "'*Sola Scriptura*': Max Müller's Theory of Myths," I try to give Müller his due—and a bit more. Müller deserves rather more rehabilitation than some of my contemporaries have given him. He should not be patronized or cavalierly dismissed as *passé*. Present-day fashions don't favor his kind of theorizing, but neither will tomorrow's tastes in theory necessarily be kind to ours today. Müller belongs at the head of any list of myth theorists for creating the first comprehensive, thoroughgoing, and data-informed theory of myths.

Theorists of myth began showing radical signs of a changing register in conceiving myths with the advent of Émile Durkheim's sociological approach to culture and society. Therefore, in chapter 3, "French Connections: Durkheimian Ritualism Replaces Müller's Hegemony of Myth," I show how Durkheim and his associates launched a broad attack against a purely textual treatment of myths. It was not enough just to consider them merely as static texts; they needed to be fully and fairly located within a social context in order to interpret them. In chapter 8, "Conceptual Problems for Robert A. Segal and Jonathan Z. Smith," I seek both to demonstrate how, to his surprise, Segal actually theorizes in much the same spirit as Müller, even though he has psychoanalytic approaches to myths available when Müller did not. Segal does interpret the story of King Saul in Freudian terms but retains Müller's literary conception of myths. Jonathan Z. Smith, too, latches onto myth theories unavailable to Müller, such as Claude Lévi-Strauss's structuralism. Yet, like Segal, Smith essentially never strays from a maxmüllerist literary conception of myths. The story of how two such prominent myth theorists as Segal and Smith remained essentially untouched by Malinowski's pragmatism or "performative" conception of myth is yet untold.

Beginning the Break with Müller: Durkheim's Mythologist, Henri Hubert

Arrayed against maxmüllerism in chapters 4 and 5 is the work of one of Émile Durkheim's closest collaborators, Henri Hubert (1872–1927). Chief myth theorist of the Durkheimian *équipe* and trained as a historian and archeologist, Henri Hubert anticipated broad outlines of a *performative* theory of myth. Indications of this movement away from maxmüllerist literary conceptions of myth emerge here and there in Hubert's oeuvre about myths having "practical value."[16] Later, fully exploited by Malinowski as he became acquainted with Durkheimian scholarship, the elements of a pragmatic conception of myth were developing in Hubert's research. Hubert was someone who indeed deserves to be called "Durkheim's mythologist," not only because Durkheim had charged him with mastering the subject but also because he set many of the theoretical terms that inform the work of three of the twentieth century's leading myth theorists. In chapter 4, "Henri Hubert: Durkheim's Mythologist,"

I provide the only thorough, English-language account of Hubert's career.

Lately, the legacy of Durkheimian thought, as evidenced by Durkheim's influence in the work of Hubert and Mauss has come into question through the claims of Claude Lévi-Strauss to that legacy. The most prominent of the three mythologists who conspicuously claimed Durkheimian lineage, Lévi-Strauss has provoked controversy over his right to claim Durkheimian provenance for his anthropological theories. In chapter 5, "What Lévi-Strauss May or May Not Owe to Henri Hubert," I argue that while Lévi-Strauss can claim *some* Durkheimian lineage, his work succeeded mostly because he *departed* from Hubert's model of myth study. Following Hubert and Mauss's theoretical views more closely, however, are two celebrated French mythologists: Georges Dumézil and Maurice Leenhardt.

Malinowski and the Pragmatist Concept and Theory of Myths

Finally, in chapter 6, "Müller's Legacy, Broken: Malinowski and the Pragmatist Concept and Theory of Myths," I declare my debt to Bronislaw Malinowski as the chief precursor of a *performative* approach to myths. Although Malinowski clearly acknowledged his debt to Durkheimian scholarship, he may have already staked out elements of a performance theory on his own. But nowhere does Malinowski credit Durkheim with the notion of "function," so critical to the idea of performance. On the other hand, Malinowski's chief rival in England, A. R. Radcliffe-Brown, made frequent reference to Durkheim's functionalism. Recent evidence has come to light that Malinowski's knowledge of Ernst Mach's philosophy of science, in addition to his familiarity with the 1898–1899 Torres Straits Expedition, nudged him toward functionalism. Yet, decisive in Malinowski's conversion to a performative theory of culture was his exposure to myths *observed* in the field. Beginning with myths as active parts of a culture he sought to understand, the concept of myth as maxmüllerist static text seemed limited indeed. For this reason, Malinowski's functionalist theory of myths fits best with the cultural concept of myths elaborated by Østbø—as "more or less elaborate narratives about a political society, usually as an incitement to action."[17]

Malinowski's approach to myth is particularly instructive as an inside view into proper theorizing about myths. Alone among theorists, Malinowski models the *constructed* nature of both the conceptualization and theorization of myths. Myths are not things with names written on them. "Myth" is not "*in re.*" Instead, given certain criteria, the theorist *decides* what particular stories *ought* to be called myths. In my case, I have *decided* that myths are what I call "important stories." Thus, in relating how the Trobrianders regard myths, Malinowski also shows them in the act of *deciding to name* certain stories as "important"—what are, in effect, their "myths," in Malinowski's translation. For the Trobrianders, they have *decided* that the *important* stories—the myths—are what the Trobrianders call "*lili'u.*" As Malinowski further reveals, these *lili'u* are regarded by the Trobrianders as important because they "do things" valued in Trobriand culture. Similarly, in theorizing myths, Bruce Lincoln *decided* that a myth would be "a narrative making powerful—and highly consequential—assertions."[18] Not only did Malinowski learn—for the most part—how to theorize myths, he also followed the Trobrianders' lead in assigning pragmatic functions to what the *lili'u* do. Accordingly, chapter 6 provides what I believe to be the most complete account available of the historical origins and nature of Malinowski's pragmatic theory of myth, including a thoroughgoing account of the deep logic of his "functionalism."

Taking Responsibility for the Concept of Myth

Having referred several times to "myths" as "important stories," impatient readers will naturally want to know more about this concept of myths for which I take responsibility. I believe that anyone trafficking theoretically in discourse about myth should be ready to elaborate a defensible concept and theory of myth. For this reason, chapter 7, "Taking Responsibility for the Concept of Myth," poses the question of conceptual "ownership." That is to say, for what concept of myths do I accept responsibility or accept "ownership"? How would I defend such a concept as viable? How would I justify the conceptual *decision* that my definition represents?

I speak in moral terms of 'responsibility' because I believe that the meaning of "myth" or "myths" is not self-evident or uncontroversial. The choice to speak about "myths" therefore presumes a decision to use the word *myth* in a certain way. I ask, why that way, rather than another? Since a researcher needs to *decide* — to make a *judgment* about — what sense of "myth" or "myths" they believe can be used fruitfully, successfully, what is the *basis* of that judgment? Should others abide by the same decision, and why?

As a short example of how ownership figures, I offer my best attempt at a sustained argument for the concept of myths that I employ in the analyses of myths mentioned: those of the Russian, French, biblical, and Christian ethno-nationalist contexts. I also show how Indian nationalists have quarreled about the use of violence, based in large part on divergent tellings of classic "important" Hindu stories — "myths."

Performing Myths in Paris and Moscow

In chapters 9 and 10, I discuss cases where myths are used to "do things" in the domain of real historical politics, religion, and society, focusing on the role of myths in modern French and Russian political cultures, respectively. Chapter 9 shows how Hubert exposed twentieth-century French fascist appeals to the same kind of ancient Indian myths to which the Aryanist Müller was also attracted. Moved by the same conceptual decision about myths as "important stories," chapter 10 argues that, starting in the 1860s, legitimations of Russian imperialism and/or Russian Orthodox theological geo-politics frequently and have conspicuously been incited by an appeal to the "Myth of Moscow, Third Rome." Modern-day, nineteenth-century Russian imperial politics drew upon the pseudo-historical narrative — "myth" — of imperial Muscovite Russia as the only legitimate successor to the world hegemony, divinely granted to the Roman Empire, most recently, in its Byzantine incarnation. In extended ways, these final two chapters show how "myths" can "do" consequential things by granting legitimacy and purpose to political entities otherwise lacking it. The seven chapters that precede these conclusory ones show how the progress of myth scholarship slowly struggled to appreciate the political potential of what might be thought of as just curious, fanciful tales, or *mere* "myths." I trust this book will reinforce that lesson to us in our own time. Myths matter!

In the Rear-View Mirror: Retrospectives on Studying Myths and Theories of Myths

A word about the experience of reviewing a lifetime's work on myths: I had not foreseen the unanticipated benefits of assembling and radically revising this collection of essays spanning thirty-odd years of thinking and writing about myths and theories of myths. The first was appreciating how decisively what can only be called "intellectual fashions" have influenced the choice of topics in academe and publishing. When I finished my PhD dissertation in 1969, I was enthralled by Lévi-Strauss. But I shall never forget the shock I felt at learning, upon joining a faculty seminar at Yale in the early 1970s, that everyone else had dumped Lévi-Strauss and moved on to "post-structuralism." What I thought was something with a healthy shelf-life—at least relatively—was already *passé* a handful of years after I had devoted so much energy to mastering Lévi-Strauss and structuralism. I continued to stay close to Lévi-Strauss for another fifteen years, despite the change of fashion. Whatever Lévi-Strauss's shortcomings, they were insignificant to what Derrida, his replacement, offered. My way out from under Lévi-Strauss's shadow started by trying to trace structural mythology back to its allegedly Durkheimian beginnings. See chapters 3 to 5.

This leads me to a second point, realized only in retrospect. I am particularly grateful—although I felt anything but at the time!—to a journal reviewer who *soundly* rejected my first efforts at understanding the genesis of Lévi-Strauss's theory of myths. Thankfully, at a crucial point in my intellectual growth, someone took the trouble to offer me sharply deflating—but constructive—criticism. In its present, suitably chastened form, that chapter here appears as chapter 5, entitled "What Lévi-Strauss May or May Not Owe to Henri Hubert." It began as what I thought was my brilliant discovery of the roots of structural mythology in what I believed to be Marcel Mauss's essay in *L'Année sociologique*, "Introduction aux mythes." Even though the article was—I am embarrassed to admit now—*unsigned*, conformity to the fashions of the time led me to assume Mauss's authorship! My mistake was that I had believed Lévi-Strauss's origin "myth" of his alleged indebtedness to Mauss and thus assumed both that Mauss was the author of this unsigned article on theory of myth and that Mauss specialized in theory of myth. Compassionately, but firmly and unmistakably, disabused of my error by my reviewer, I crestfallenly accepted my article's rejection, in fact. A good thing too. It saved me the greater embarrassment of later finding myself duped by Lévi-Strauss's own attempts to boost his status by claiming intellectual descendance from Mauss. As I learned from the gracious Lévi-Strauss during the summer of 1983 in Paris, he had never even met Mauss! In those days, one was able to look Lévi-Strauss up in the Paris phone directory, call him, and arrange an interview! The fact was that, in the context of the hothouse Parisian academic world, Lévi-Strauss had indulged a fair bit of poetic license in linking himself historically to Mauss. To be sure, Lévi-Strauss has learned much from Mauss — especially regarding gift and exchange — but *not* about myths, and *not* from personal mentoring! He allowed those connections to be rumored about and assumed, in part, to certify his place as someone who, though absent from Paris during World War II (having fled to the Americas), nevertheless owned a claim to legitimacy in the lineage of Durkheimianism. Not strictly speaking true, but understandable, nonetheless.

The third point about the benefits of being able to review one's work is that I was able to revise my youthful work and correct mistakes made there along the way. The original articles are still available for anyone to see. But for the purpose of the coherence of this book's argument, I had to revise. And I have — mainly by revisiting judgments made in light of lesser knowledge. So, this collection, while *based* largely on previously published works, does not merely trot them out again. This book represents my better-informed and reconsidered views of today over and against what I had written years ago. This volume, therefore, is not a museum piece of old, outdated works. It represents, in a way, a second chance at getting things right! Everything collected here, therefore, has been closely revisited, and as a result, much has been re-written, oftentimes radically. Everyone, as the saying goes, deserves a "second chance." I hope my readers will feel likewise that I do!

Chapter 2

"Sola Scriptura": Max Müller's Theory of Myths

Myth, Religion, and Ritual

Myths have most often been regarded as narratives, texts, or oral literature, and later, when written, classified as literature or folklore. They have not typically been conceived of or theorized as actions, as "doing things" — behaving performatively or pragmatically. At one point in the history of the study of myths, some myth theorists did, however, come to be convinced of the pragmatic nature of seemingly innocent stories. How did that transformation come about, and why? How did a scholarly consensus develop that myths ought not to be seen exclusively as static "texts," but also as "performances," as active "deeds"? Understanding this transition requires a deep dive into the history of the study of myths.

Diving deeply into that history requires some understanding of the larger cultural, political, and religious contexts that constitute it. For instance, Müller's style of conceiving and theorizing myths was sustained by passionately held cultural, political, and religious convictions rooted in the primacy of the *text* of the Biblical narrative for Protestant Christians. But how and why it began to become "good to think" — to conceive and theorize — about myths as actions, deeds, and "rituals" likewise depended on its own contextual factors. Here, Émile Durkheim and his research team of ethnographers, social scientists, historians, and philosophers associated with *L'Année sociologique*, demand our attention. In Durkheim's case, his encouragement of empirical — ethnographic, sociological, and historical — studies of religion prepared the way for seeing myths as active performatives — as "doing things" — rather than static texts.

Why, then, begin this book with a lengthy chapter on philologist Friedrich Max Müller, a thinker so unlike Durkheim and his company? Today, Müller's theories are often ridiculed as being hopelessly *passé*. As recently as 2023, Robert A. Segal, one of our leading specialists on theories of myth, decried Müller's "theory of religion and of myth" as "hopelessly out of date"[1] or "at best quaint."[2] In similarly unflattering terms, literary theorist Tomoko Masuzawa charges that Müller's "work on myth" amounts to little more than Müller's "hobby horse," "a mythologizing of his own philological discourse."[3] For Masuzawa, Müller's work on mythology, like myth itself, was at best "accidental," a mere "transformation of words."[4] In a funny, perhaps unintended way, Masuzawa reflects the even more devastating commonplace scorn for the dry, antiquated, bookish scholarship of Müller, here calling to mind George Eliot's *Middlemarch*. Therein, the pedantic Edward Casaubon putters about futilely in dusty archives, seeking the key to "all the mythical systems or erratic mythical fragments in the world" and "to condense these voluminous still-accumulating results and bring them, like the earlier vintage of Hippocratic books, to fit a little shelf."[5]

I, however, take exception to these dismissals of Müller by my otherwise esteemed colleagues. First, to judge Müller's theory of myth "quaint," as Segal does, seems needlessly "presentist." Although I intend to interpret Müller's theory of myth sympathetically, I am not recommending its retrieval for present-day use. But dismissing it as "quaint" mistakes fashion-consciousness for criticism. Judging a theory's worth in terms of its conformity to present-day fashions does not constitute intellectual criticism. Müller obviously flowered in the nineteenth century, while we toil in the twenty-first. In addition, belittling Müller's theories as "quaint" only serves to remind us that theorizing will vary as our knowledge does. Theories are only "quaint" from the retrospective viewpoint of those who fancy themselves more "advanced." Müller might reply by labeling his critic's evolutionist perspective as equally "quaint." As his generation's world-class leader in the field of philology and Indology, Müller had the best possible reasons to think he was "right" about myth, just as some of our contemporaries assume they are "right" for thinking about myth as they do. We all depend on what counts as "knowledge" in generating our theories. But that dependence says nothing about the quality of the theorizing that takes account of that knowledge. In many ways, Müller's method of theorizing remains exemplary.

Consider this thought experiment: Masuzawa and Segal are transported into Müller's mid-nineteenth-century world and equipped with the same mental acuity and data accessible then to Müller. How would they have unraveled the puzzles presented by the burgeoning field of comparative historical phonology of Indo-European languages? Can they really say that they would have reached different conclusions than Müller? Given what was considered "knowledge" at the time, I am unsure that I would—or could—have improved on Müller's theorizing about myths. It must mean something that Müller had few equal competitors at the time. Perhaps if Müller had direct—ethnographic—knowledge of ancient Indian society, balanced with ample data from field studies, he might have reached different conclusions? Tylor, for all the gentleman-traveler informality of his fieldwork, managed one of the only major rivals to Müller's theories of myths. But Tylor's challenge to Müller was hardly decisive. I would suggest that the reasons lie in the fact that neither sociology nor social anthropology yet existed in a way that could have made a difference to Müller's theorizing. Segal's favorites, Freud, Jung, Raglan, Campbell, et alia had not yet arrived on the scene. In decades long before the heyday of modernism proper, the counter-cultural thought of Masuzawa's postmodernism was inconceivable. This is not to say that we, or Segal, or Masuzawa, need to return to Müller. But I am urging that we first appreciate the high quality of Müller's mind as it was applied to myths before we dismiss him and his theories.

Four Reasons to Celebrate Müller's Theorizing Mind

To give an example of just how much of a contribution Müller made to theorizing myths, consider that he pioneered at least four features now taken-for-granted in theorizing myths. Müller approached myths cross-culturally, comparatively, and systematically. He specifically applied the latest critical-historical methods, originally developed in biblical criticism, to the study of myths across the globe. True to his humanistic orientation, he balanced his historical-critical studies with empathy. For these and other achievements, Müller deserves to be honored, not rejected for being a man of his times.

Of note, Tomoko Masuzawa's criticisms of Müller lack the historical merit I seek to bring to bear.[6] How and why could one say, for instance, as Masuzawa does, that Müller's theories of myths were either a "hobby horse'" or "accidental"? Recent scholarship from the likes of Sarah Barnette brings out the genius in Müller's intellectual projects with myth. Accordingly, Barnette links Müller's theoretical efforts as a social and cultural radical to those of one George Eliot. This greatest of English-language woman novelists in the English language thrilled at the real achievements and generosity of spirit of Müller's scholarship.[7] What Barnette exposes in the process, in effect, is the weakness of Masuzawa's post-modern reading of Müller's sophisticated—if ultimately wrongheaded—theory of myth. In a word or two, Müller is very much *not* the hopeless Edward Casaubon of *Middlemarch*, George Eliot's own characterization of the myth theorist.

Müller and George Eliot: Post-Colonial Culture Heroism in the Heyday of Colonialism

In fact, George Eliot saw Müller as the inverse of the provincial, sterile Casaubon. Both Eliot and Müller ran in tandem along similarly radical paths of cultural reform. Both were devoted promoters of radical liberal German religious authors like biblical critic D. F. Strauss. Both joined in the projects of "illumination of ties between past and present, and insistence upon recognizing such ties."[8] The cross-cultural, comparative-critical nature of Müller's "Science of Religion" challenged the hide-bound, parochial, Anglo-centric religious and academic conventions of the latter half of culturally insular nineteenth-century England. They inspired a cross-cultural empathy that made "otherness" more accessible to readers, instructing that educated awareness of difference aids self-understanding.[9] Müller accomplished these results by advancing Herder's method of vital, empathetic understanding—"*Einfühlung*"—"a method comparable with exercising sympathetic understanding."[10] A scholar must, says Müller, balance being too remote and at the same time "refrain from becoming too distant, in danger of fostering prejudice or hostility."[11]

These similarities cut short the notion that Müller could ever have been the model of Eliot's pedantic Edward Casaubon. Unlike the barren erudition of Casaubon, Eliot believed that Müller's "Science of Religion" would change the world.[12] Eliot, thus, describes Casaubon's ultimately failed comparative study of mythology as "a groping about in the woods with a pocket-compass while [the Germans, like Müller] have made good roads."[13] In Eliot's mind, Müller would be the antithesis of Casaubon. While Müller actually published his work, Casaubon never does. While Müller famously succeeds as a public lecturer, Casaubon and his work remain abstruse. As Müller pioneers a historicism "balanced" by *Einfühlung*, Casaubon is mired in maintaining establishment Christian orthodoxy. Beginning with the extension of German methods of critical-historical scholarship of sacred texts, to historical philology, to rigorous methods of cross-cultural comparison, Müller delivered an intellectual earthquake to the smug divines dominating the Church of England. For Eliot, "Müller widened his audience's awareness of the world's diversity while enumerating the elements that unite the world's inhabitants..." so that "through Müller's eyes, the English public might see 'Unity in diversity.'"[14]

Müller, Theorist of Mythical Narrative

However genuine a culture-hero Müller as theorist of myth may have been, I devote this chapter to showing how his theory confined itself to but one *dimension* of myths—their static *narrative* or textual nature. Müller's theory treated myths exclusively as linguistic, textual, literary, narrative entities. Robert A. Segal too shares this view, accordingly, describing Müller's characterization of myths as his viewing them "poetically, metaphorically, or symbolically"—in effect, *literarily*.[15] In the Hindu scriptures, the Vedas, Müller thus saw "one God hidden behind the veil of nature."[16] He saw hidden treasure in the "rubbish" of "physical religion," dominated as it was by tedious rituals.[17] Again, in Segal's acute judgment, "for Müller, 'primitives' originally took the image symbolically and only eventually came to misread it literally. For Müller, 'primitives' are like poets."[18] Indeed, I agree they are, if, however, too much so for my "performative" tastes.

As narratives, myths served Müller in presenting the best evidence available for, among other things, supporting a healthy sense of national identity. Rituals might have served the same purpose, but scholars in mid-nineteenth-century Western Europe had virtually no access to data giving them that kind of information about India. Because of Reformation theological biases, they may also have been discouraged from undertaking such field research. For this, and other reasons, Müller displayed a common interest in the narrative, literary, textual appreciation of ancient Indian religion—later to be extended comparatively and cross-culturally in his development of what became known as the "Science of Religion."

We can easily confirm the priorities Müller gave to narrative, language, literature, and such from a cursory review of the contents of a major five-volume anthology of Müller's essays, *Chips from a German Workshop*. Consider the contents to volume 3, which includes "Literature, Biography, and Antiquities." There, unsurprisingly, he devotes his lead essay to "German literature," followed by chapters on literary themes, such as old German love-songs, the early modern fable, "Ye Schyppe of Fooles," the life and works of romantic poet Friedrich Schiller, and Müller's father, the romantic poet and Schubert librettist Wilhelm Müller, then, on the language and poetry of Schleswig-Holstein, ending with an essay on Shakespeare.[19] Lending weight to Müller's literary preoccupations, even in the first volume of *Chips from a German Workshop* on the "Science of Religion," literary subjects dominate. Three-quarters of volume 1 consists of Müller's essays and addresses with an unmistakable literary bent. These are expositions of texts like the Vedas or the *Sacred Books of the East*, another on the Veda compared to the Zend-Avesta, three more on Zend scholarship, then on the Aitareya Brāhmana, Chinese translations of Sanskrit texts, the works of Confucius, and the Meso-American *Popol Vuh*.[20] Even when it came to Müller's fifth and final volume of *Chips*, "Miscellaneous Later Essays," four of the five essays there focus on narrative materials: the philosophy of mythology, "false analogies in comparative theology," spelling, and "Sanskrit texts discovered in Japan."[21]

Given the success of arguments linking European languages to remote Indo-European sources, Müller found the field wide open for the extension of his linguistic scholarship into the exotic realm of myths and stories. Both myth and language gave access to the innermost recesses of ethnic self-consciousness. Said Müller,

> …mythology is inevitable, it is an inherent necessity of language, if we recognize in language the outward form and manifestation of thought; it is in fact the dark shadow which language throws on thought, and which can never disappear till language becomes altogether commensurate with thought, and which it never will.[22]

As we will see, in thus taking up the study of myth, Müller also accomplished some serious cultural work. His myth theory rides the wave of the then-flourishing German cultural self-discovery. Given Müller's conviction about the origins of myths in minds of the folk, myths expressed the essential mentality of a culture at its most authentic levels of everydayness. This link with the soul of a people, at the same time, accounts in part for the popularity in Germany of the work of the Grimm Brothers and their collections of folktales gathered orally from all parts of the new German nation-state. So close were myth and language for Müller that myth was "only a dialect, an ancient form of language."[23] How then did myths originate out of the language spoken by ordinary folk, as Müller suggests?

Myths Originated in a "Disease of Language"

While both language and myth opened windows into the "soul of a people," they revealed different "compartments" of that soul. Hubert and Mauss took this to mean that "for Max Müller and his disciples, myth is born immediately from the need to animate the things represented in language by symbols."[24] One chamber housed the thinking mind; the other chamber was responsible for religion. This is to say that myths did not correspond to thought in the way that Müller felt that language did. Language mirrored thought directly; myth did not. Myth was symptomatic, says Müller, of a natural process of "linguistic breakdown."[25] Explaining further this natural process in his *On the Philosophy of Mythology* (1871), Müller says that,

> ...the real question which a philosophy of mythology has to answer is this [whether] mythology [was] a mere accident, or was it inevitable? Was it only a false step, or was it a step that could not have been left out in the historical progress of the human mind?[26]

For Müller, myth was no mistake, not a "bug" in the system, so to speak. It was a *feature*, made inevitable by the imperfect way humans perceive and "know" things. "Mythology is inevitable," declared Müller, "it is natural, it is an inherent necessity of language…"[27]

But, again, how? Müller answered with his little-understood theory of myth as a "disease of language."[28] By "disease of language," Müller meant a natural process in which the literal meanings of words were personified. For Müller personification counted as a "disease" because in "mythology" we meet "language going beyond its first intention" — which was just to *name* natural objects.[29] Müller felt language had exceeded its proper limits — hence, it was "diseased" — because language here had deviated from its normal function of representing thought. Instead of representing thought, language was now creating objects of its own — the personal gods and goddesses of myths.

While it deviated from right thinking, personification was a well-understood and natural human inclination. For example, the word, "fire" stands for the concept of fire. But were English speakers to begin inventing stories or myths about "fire," it would become personified as a "he" or "she." If it turned out that this personified "fire" was powerful, feared, admirable and so on, it would not be surprising if it began to be revered and hence deified as a god whose name might be rendered as a capitalized and re-named "Fire." This "Fire" would not stand for the concept of ordinary fire but for some kind of personified version of fire. It was by the same process that the Vedic deities originated. Consider the root meaning of words like "divinity," "divus," and "deva." They reveal a literal linguistic meaning consisting in naming bright natural phenomena, like stars and comets. But in telling stories or myths about fire, sun, moon and so on, they would soon be acting out their parts as personal actors do.

With this "disease of language" theory of the origins of myth in hand, Müller was led easily to see myths as integral to many religions. The Indo-European root "*Div*," once diseased and rendered mythically, became the name of a class of transcendent religious personages — "*deva*s," "gods." For Müller, myth and religion grew up in close proximity to one another.

Myth, Religion, and "Religion-as-Such"

One semantic snag kept Müller's view of the relation of myth to religion from easy acceptance. Müller used "religion" in two different senses. "Religion" named the many different historical religions studied by anthropologists, historians, philologists, and others. But "religion" also meant *Religion* in a normative sense — true religion, "religion-as-such," religion in its true essence. Making matters more confused, Müller refers to both kinds of religion as "natural religion" and "nature religion," "religion of nature," or "naturism." Müller's "religion-as-such," natural religion, is the real and essential religion: one and unchanging. Religion-as-such is the purely *spiritual* religion—a mystical "perception of the Infinite."[30] As to "naturism," the "religion of nature," or "nature religion," there may be many different forms, depending upon what aspect of nature is worshipped—sun, mountains, thunder and lightning, etc.—since the history of "religions" is a history of change. Müller's view was that many historical religions were only "sects if not corruptions" of a normative "religion-as-such," the original innate (and thus "natural") religious impulse of humanity.[31] Myths, on the other hand, belonged variously to the many religions, to the different sorts of nature religions, or religions of nature, but not to "religion-as-such," or to natural religion.

Müller argued further that the religions, like the nature religions, religion-as-such, and "natural religion" are also intimately *related to each other.* "Natural religion," said Müller, existed before the "religions of nature."[32] Müller uses "before" in both a temporal and an ontological sense. Natural religion, religion-as-such, thus both *predates* the religions of nature *in time*, but also precedes the religions of nature in being—*ontologically.* Thus, first, *before*—in time—there were sacrifices, rituals, myth, and so on in the many religions, there was only a pure, mystical, contemplative "religion-as-such": "natural religion." But some time *afterwards*—Müller's doctrine of The Fall—the many religions (of nature and so on) arose, replete with their myths, rituals, etc.[33] Müller also held that even though natural religion and the religions of nature are *temporally* separate, the essential root of the many religions of nature is religion-as-such. Lying *behind* the riotous diversity of the religions is their ultimate essential unity in religion-as-such. For Müller, an effective way to achieve a contemplative experience of natural religion was by working one's way up through the worship of nature to natural religion. The earnest devotion to "naturism," or religion of nature, eventually led the devotee to the mystical state of natural religion. A major task of Müller's Science of Religion was to show how this essential religion shone through in the many religions that come and go over the course of the ages.

> To men who lived on an island, the ocean was the...the Infinite, and became in the end their God. To men who lived in valleys, the rivers

that fed them and whose sources were unapproachable, the mountains that protected them, and whose crests were inaccessible, the sky that overshadowed them, and whose power and beauty were incomprehensible,...their infinite beings, their bright and kind beings, what some of them called their Devas, the Bright, the same word which, after passing through many changes, still breathes in our own word, Divinity.[34]

Although reluctant to declare his mystical, pantheist convictions in the midst of conservative established ecclesiastical power structure, occasionally, Müller would do so. "The mind must become immaculate and rise superior to itself; or it must close its eyes and shut its lips in the presence of the Divine."[35]

Typical of the idealism and romanticism of his generation of young German intellectuals, Müller's own religion, then, culminated in a gentle pantheism. While Müller's pantheism may have been kindled by his romantic love of nature or desire to bow down in worship, real religion was both *more* and *less*. This "more," as we have seen, was hinted at in the way some natural phenomena evoke infinity in their transcendence of our ability to comprehend them. Müller speculated that these first notions of "the transcendent" came from contemplating the enormity of the sun, ocean, mountains, earthquakes, and so on.[36] The "less" was the wordless, mythless silence enveloping Müller's existential realization of the One.

Typical of the authentic mystic, Müller refrained from *speaking* about the ultimate reality. He never wished to upset or undermine traditional established religious belief by publicly boasting of his pantheist inclinations. But he did confront Christianity's parochialism. At the very least, Christians were obliged to look upon religious "others" with Christianity charitably. Given that the British Empire was targeting these cultures and religions for both economic and religious colonial domination, imperialist charity was in short supply. But Müller showed profound respect for colonial India and the long history of its religious communities—especially monistic Hinduism and Vedanta philosophy. Müller had such immense respect for Hindu pantheistic religious sensibilities that he virtually identified them with the German romantic nature mysticism of his home country. The effect of this linkage was so great, believes historian Richard Dorson, that Müller's publication in 1856 of an essay titled "Comparative Mythology" "reoriented all previous thinking about the origin of myths."[37] Immediately after elaborating this nature worship in the Vedas, Müller had the confidence to ask rhetorically, "And are we so different from them?" In contemplating nature "do we not feel the overwhelming pressure of the Infinite...from which no one can escape who has eyes to see and ears to hear?"[38] Free of the slightest doubts, Müller answered his own question forthwith!

The complexity of Müller's practical theology often—understandably—threw critics off his scent. In his critique of Müller, Durkheim assured readers that he would have none of the sort of "philosophical and abstract" thinking about religious notions such as God that results from the dismissal of myth from the religious domain.[39] Durkheim is only partly correct, of course, since he was attacking Müller for not thinking of myth as part of religion-as-such. But insofar as the many religions are concerned, Müller sees religion and myth as integral to one another.

Thus when it came to the Greeks and their myths, Müller said, on the one hand, that he did not believe that the Iliad was the Greek "Bible."[40] So close were myth and language that myth was "only a dialect, an ancient form of language" in Müller's view.[41] Surely, this was a distinction without a difference. So close were myth and language that myth was "only a dialect, an ancient form of language" in Müller's view. He claimed that in the Vedic narrative,

> ...we get one step nearer to that distant source of religious thought and language which has fed the different national steams of Persia, Greece, Rome and Germany, and we begin to see clearly that there is no religion without God, or as St Augustine expressed it, that "there is no false religion which does not contain some elements of truth."[42]

Thus, for Müller, despite the failings of myth in capturing the high-flown abstract truth of mystical religion-as-such (Müller's personal preference), the many ancient religions were often constituted by these special narratives—by myths. Proper everyday piety, thus, presupposed a special reverence for myths, even if lofty mystic contemplation did not.

Müller Maneuvers around Anglican Orthodoxy

For a person of such sophisticated, if highly complex, religious orientation as Müller, we can only imagine the difficulties he encountered when confronted by hostile critics in Oxford's powerful Anglican establishment. Oxford's hostility toward Müller was rooted in both his Lutheranism and his suspected pantheism. On one occasion, Müller tried to explain his views about the relation of myth to religion to some of Oxford's Christian divines. Müller's pious orthodox critics suspected his affections for otherwise "pagan" religions of nature. Did his naturism not make Müller little better than the idolaters condemned by the Hebrew Bible and Reformation theologians? Perhaps to appease his theological critics, Müller classified the original nature religion as "Physical Religion"—a religion he acknowledged to be lower in nobility than the "Philosophical Religion" of his own day. Significantly, however, Müller did not *condemn* "physical religion" as heretical or pagan. Müller saw all the religions *relatively*, since they were all in the process of developing. He really condemned none. Sometimes, he even indulged a nostalgia for "Physical religion," as he had for the simplest religions of nature.

Müller confessed that, myth-laden though they were, the Vedas displayed certain "childish" features—evolutionist code for polytheism. But ever the historical-developmental *relativist*, he felt polytheism had redeeming qualities in its straining for the absolute.[43] Said Müller,

> I wish I could tell you some more of these stories which have been gathered from all parts of the world, and which, though they may be pronounced childish and tedious by some critics, seem to me to glitter with the brightest dew of nature's own poetry, and to contain those very touches that make us feel akin, not only with Homer or Shakespeare, but even with Lapps, and Finns, and Kaffirs.[44]

While the Vedas were not religion at its absolute finest, they were still a *relatively* true "revelation" in their own way. Perhaps it was Müller's Lutheran biblicism speaking when he referred to the ritual and priestly aspects of Vedic religion as "childish"? True though that may be, Müller saw Vedic polytheism more precisely as a "henotheism," a waystation on the road to monotheism or Müller's monism. A "Physical religion" like the Vedas, Müller said, exemplified something to celebrate—at least *relatively*. It marked a vital *progressive* stage in the history of the growth of religion. That perspective gave Müller's "Science of Religion" a special vocation: showing how the "real history of man is the history of religions: the wonderful ways by which the different families of the human race advanced toward a truer knowledge and a deeper love of God."⁴⁵ This theologically tolerant Müller, thus, looked behind and through appearances by reading myths *allegorically*. In 1871, Müller wrote:

> There is this common feature in all who have thought or written on mythology, that they look upon it as something which, whatever it may mean, does certainly not mean what it seems to mean; as something that requires an explanation, whether it be a system of religion, or a phase in the development of the human mind, or an inevitable catastrophe in the life of language.⁴⁶

Among many young German theological liberals of his day, Müller's tolerant, developmentalist, liberality, and mystical religious vision inspired enormous admiration. Its inclusivism promised relief from confessional exclusivism and the religious conflicts thus generated. We are reminded again of George Eliot's respect for Müller in the latter's *Introduction to the Science of Religion*, in which Müller wrote, "If we have once learned to be charitable and reasonable in the interpretation of the sacred books of other religions, we shall more easily learn to be charitable and reasonable in the interpretation of our own."⁴⁷

Beyond the "Disease of Language"

Müller's plenary theory of myth was to proceed beyond the idea of myths as "diseased" deviations from normal language. Diseased or not, they formed part of a culture's lore, its cosmology—including its religion. Myths had value; they mattered. Thus, Müller never radically separated his philological studies, e.g., the idea of the "disease" (decline) of language, from both his scholarly and personal views of religion. Unlike what some post-modernist devotees of disjunction—Tomoko Masuzawa⁴⁸—think about Müller, philology was prelude to both mythology and theology, not "disjunction." "Disease of language" merely laid out the discrete steps by which mythology developed according to natural laws uncovered by the philological sciences.

Without this step-by-step explanation of how myths developed out of ordinary speech, readers might be tempted to literalist readings of myths. But literalist readings of myths would require reducing myths to the nonsense condemned by enlightenment demythologizers, and in the process, denying value to "the other."

(Or, of course, reading myths literally may just constitute a poetic effort.) As Segal observes, Müller "did not reduce God to the sun or to any other natural entity."[49] Müller left open the other's access to the same ultimate reality that he cherished in his own mystical religious sensibilities. Thus, no disjunction severed Müller's philological reasoning from his thinking about religion. One served as a step on the way to the other, where even the most concrete and particular pointed the way to the ineffable *one*.

Religious Culture Enables Müller's Theory of Myth: Lutheran Biblicism

Müller posed many questions about myths, but one he never seriously put to himself was why he prioritized myths at all? Why, also, did this favor the study of myth as collected in scriptures and texts? As a devotee of the "Science of Religion," Müller was free to emphasize anything about religion: its doctrines, ethics, experience, religion's material dimension, or actions and deeds—loosely, "rituals." But he didn't. He focused on a special class of *stories*, accessible in scriptural and textual anthologies, but *not* on liturgies, sacraments, sacrifices, pilgrimages, Yogic *āsanas*, initiations, blessings, etc. Such data was of relatively little interest to Müller, especially when compared to the work of collecting, editing, researching, and translating *myths* as they were found in texts, scriptures, chronicles, journals.

My answer to the question of why he studied myths is threefold. The mid-nineteenth-century moment in which Müller wrote defined him *culturally*. First, his membership in a liberal brand of German Lutheranism biased him in favor of "biblicism," the study of religion by way of sacred scripture. Second and third, Müller participated in two cultural movements native to his German origins: romanticism inclined him to study the folkish and local (and thus myths rather than doctrines or ethical systems), and the quest for Germany's classical civilizational ancestors in the ancient Aryans encouraged him to specialize in India, the legendary homeland of the Aryans.

I am not saying that a scholar's confessional commitments will determine that they study myths. But a scholar's religious commitments might, nevertheless, nudge them in that direction, rather than to study ritual. Prominent among the causes of this anti-ritualism was the prestige of the written and spoken word over deed, rooted in a heightened reverence for literacy and especially the biblical word and text. This surplus of reverence for the Bible dates from the Reformation, when Martin Luther's stern slogan, "*sola scriptura*" led the way. In the realm of secular scholarship, such as in the fields of classics and philology, reverence for word and text swept myths along in their wake. As we have seen, Müller's intended his "disease of language" thesis to account for how abstract or impersonal notions became personalized in myths. Other species of religious discourse, such as creeds, law, chants, prophecies, and so on, remained impersonal and abstract. But not myths.

Müller's *oeuvre*, in effect, stood for the proposition that "myths" should be conceived of intellectually — as meaningful arrays of words, static narratives. As such, myths consisted of putatively cognitive entities, representations or symbols, but of a special kind, alongside doctrines, creeds, prophecies, chants and song, etc. Müller and those like him distinguished myth from other sorts of narrative in its being populated by personal beings of various ontological statuses. As we have seen, Müller's "disease of language" thesis was meant to explain how and why the prominence of personal actors in myths, creeds, chants, prophecies, and even other types of religious narrative need not be populated by personal beings.

German Romanticism Enables Müller's Theory of Myth

If one cultural force inclined Müller to study of myths (as opposed to high literature, philosophy, etc.), it was the German romanticism of the late nineteenth-century. A survey of essays and addresses over the years attests to Müller's interest in classic romantics and their writings. In one later collection, *Auld Lang Syne*, the great historical philologist finds time to write on the charm of music, his romantic poet-father, Wilhelm Müller, as well as Shelley, Keats, Wordsworth, Heinrich Heine, Rückert, Eichendorff, Chamisso, Schiller, Bürger, Klopstock, and many others.[50]

Although the myths Müller studied originated from sophisticated, literate ancient India, they were still "myths," and therefore not equal to philosophy, higher mathematics, etc. Myths were, in his view, the oral literature of the people, not the high literature of the literati. From his childhood in bucolic Dessau, Müller always retained a German romantic affection for the folkish and local. By contrast, in Oxford, he never warmed to the ritual formalism and institutionalization typical of the Church of England. Müller was especially interested in the elements of nature often celebrated in Vedic myths. Sanskrit names of the gods depicted in myths seemed connected to natural phenomena, the dawn, sun, moon, fire, water, and other natural phenomena.

Accordingly, in Rig Veda 46:1, 9-10, the Vedic singer praises the rising sun — the Dawn, "Ushas" — depicting her as woman in a myth or narrative where Ushas brings boons to humanity.

> 1: Dawn on us with prosperity, O Ushas, Daughter of the Sky,
> Dawn with great glory, Goddess, Lady of the Light, dawn thou with riches, Bounteous One.
> 9: Shine on us with thy radiant light, O Ushas, Daughter of the Sky,
> Bringing to us great store of high felicity, and bearing on our solemn rites.
> 10: For in thee is each living creature's breath and life, when, Excellent! thou dawnest forth.
> Borne on thy lofty car, O Lady of the Light, hear, thou of wondrous wealth, our call.

In recognizably romantic style, Müller celebrates the genius of the same Vedic tropes of nature worship. Putting himself into the mind of a Vedic Hindu, Müller speculated…

> think of the Sun awakening the eyes of man from sleep, and his mind from slumber! Was not the Sunrise to him the first wonder, the first beginning of all reflection, all thought, all philosophy? Was it not to him the first revelation, the first beginning of all trust, of all religion?[51]

Then, in his autobiography, Müller paused to note how Vedic nature mythology and contemporary — for him, romantic — poetry express similar sensibilities about the fragility of nature, even the mighty sun:

> If the people of the Veda did not turn out to be quite such savages as was hoped and expected, they nevertheless disclosed to us a layer of thought which can be explored nowhere else. The Vedic poets were not ashamed of exposing their fear that the sun might tumble down from the sky, and there are no other poets, as far as I know, who still trembled at the same not quite unnatural thought.[52]

Parochial English assaults on the liberal romantic character of his work made Müller even more loyal to German culture, although of a remarkably open kind. Protesting a series of particularly nasty chauvinist attacks on his German nurture, Müller complained straightforwardly that "National jealousies and animosities have no place in the republic of letters."[53] In his protest, Müller would conclude without lapsing into his own national chauvinism. His reply to critics concluded with a brave statement of hope in the triumph of a rousing universal humanism, which "[he trusted], always will be, the true international republic of all friends of work, of order, and of truth."[54]

German Aryanism Enables Müller's Theory of Myth

With such romantic sensibilities, the young Müller had gone off to Berlin, and later Paris, to study Asian languages and philosophy. As a well-educated German of his generation, Müller came prepared to steep himself in the "other" world of India. Already enamored of the dreamy glorification of India embodied by the works of romantic poets, such as Friedrich Schlegel's *Über die Sprache und Weisheit der Indier* (1808), Müller gained a sophisticated appreciation of myth from further studies with F. W. J. Schelling. The philosopher claimed that myths not only narrated fantastic events, but they also embodied a real philosophy. As the first real philosopher of myth, Schelling undid some of the French Enlightenment's iconoclastic demythologizing project. Instead of crass "errors," myths captured something about the identity of the folk who produced them. Myths represented, in a sense, the "soul" of a people by giving voice to a people's wishes, imaginings and aspirations. Myths thus embodied a folk wisdom, indeed, an ancient philosophy, which despite its simple bucolic origins gave articulate expression to the defining self-conception of a people. In that way, myths pointed to the universal in human culture at the same time.

For both Schelling and Müller, the study of mythical narratives was "only a means to an end, namely a philosophy of mythology," or theory of myth.[55] But, however much Müller had learned from Schelling about theory of myth, Müller knew far more than Schelling about the world's myths and scriptures—especially India's. Equipped with his vast knowledge of Vedic mythology, Müller used much better data than "Schelling had to build his earlier philosophy of mythology."[56] Soon, then, the student, Müller, would outshine his own teacher, Schelling, as Europe's leading theorist of myths.

But given what we know about culture's role in the German quest to define a national identity, Müller's theorizing about a cultural phenomenon like myth inevitably involved him in the cultural politics of national identity too. One such ideology that became a prime contender for defining Germany's cultural identity was Aryanism. Müller passionately involved himself in Aryanism's ethnonationalism, just as others of his generation of young German culture warriors did. But what precisely did Aryanism mean? Aryanism presumed the general theory that the earth had been populated via far-flung migrations of ancient peoples. Aryanism held that one branch of an ancient, migrating folk, "the Aryans," in part, peopled much of both Iran (literally meaning "Aryan") and India as well as the bulk of Europe. A first group of Aryans had wandered south and east from their original homelands (perhaps in the Caucasus), passed through and settled in Iran, and then moved on to settle in northern India. In the process, they defined many of the key features of classic Indian civilization that one knows today: Sanskrit language; a richly ramified mythology; a religion peopled by gods bearing names closely related to natural things, forces, or celestial bodies; a three-fold, hierarchical social structure; elaborate rituals, prominent among them, sacrifices of horses; and sacrifices to the sun, god of fire, among others. Along with such cultural transmissions many, if not all, Aryanists believed in a "Caucasian" ethnic and racial uniformity shared by these migrating Aryan people.

Aryanists also claimed that a second exodus of these primeval folk branched out in the opposite direction from the Caucasus Mountains and found their way into what is now Europe. They too, like their Iranian and South Asian counterparts, made an analogous set of both cultural and ethno-racial contributions to the ethnic mélange that became the peoples of Europe. Aryanized India had Sanskrit; Aryanized Europe had Greek and Latin. Aryanized India had its caste hierarchy of Brāhman-Kṣātriya-Vaiśya *varnas*; Aryanized Europe had its analogous array of king-warrior-commoner social classes. Similarly, numerous gods and goddesses populated the spiritual-mythological universe of Aryanized India's Vedas and Purānas, while an equally abundant European polytheistic world likewise filled Greek, Roman, Slavic, and—significantly—Norse and Germanic mythologies with their countless heroes, gods and goddesses.

In terms of myths, Müller and his Aryanist colleagues argued, to great effect, that a common deep grammar of Aryan or Indo-European mythology united and underlay both.[57] These analogies not only inspired awe at the connections between parts of the world once thought to be fundamentally different, but they also made possible Müller's career as a cross-cultural comparativist of myths. As Mrs. Müller said of her husband's Aryanist research into myth, its "highest object was to discover reason in all the unreason of mythology."[58] In terms of a common lore, ancient Aryan myths, such as the Vedas, would then constitute Indic traces of the common Aryan sacred root repository of the ancient wisdom. These could then be further compared with other epic literatures, such as those of the Greek, Romans, and Nordic, among others. Since all the peoples speaking the Indo-European (or "Aryan") languages shared the root meanings of so many fundamental notions, when he encountered the Vedas, Müller felt as if he also touched something of his own German ideals.

But most of all, the prospect of links to ancient India by way of a presumed common Aryan history lent the newly formed German nation-state the added dignity Müller and other young German patriots sought. England and France, Germany's major competitors on the European scene, all laid claim to illustrious histories reaching well back into Greek and Roman times. With its Frankish, "barbarian" roots, Germans lacked such classic and "noble" civilizational forebears. Discovering an ancient, classical past of their own would then help ground the fresh, young nation-statehood in a "noble" past.

The cultural stature the Vedas and other Indian repositories of myth gave the Germans the classical ancestors they sought. They also provided a direct route into a profound philosophy, the primordial wisdom of the human race, and in particular, what Müller believed to be the mother race of the West—the Aryans. In the Vedic myths, Müller felt that he had found the bible of the Aryans. As Müller's wife recorded, Müller now felt that he had been able "thus to vindicate the character of our ancestors, however distant,"[59] principally because "We [Germans] are by nature Aryan, not Semitic."[60]

Aryanism's Dark Side: Anti-Semitism

Regrettably, although Aryanism contributed to the enhancement of German ethno-national dignity, it also justified invidious comparisons with other ethnic groups, and Jewish people in particular. This can be seen in Schopenhauer's anti-Semitic radicalism. The Vedas—a new Aryan "old" testament—would replace Christianity's Semitic heritage. Müller reported Schopenhauer feeling: "'…oh how thoroughly is the mind washed clean of all early engrafted Jewish superstitions, and of all philosophy that cringes before those superstitions!'"[61] Nothing so crude and hateful is to be found explicitly in Müller's work. However, he reveals himself capable an unmistakable "garden-variety" anti-Semitism, such as his promotion of stereotypes about Jews and ostentatious wealth. In his autobiography, Müller reflected on the causes of anti-Semitism in the Germany of his own time in an unsettling manner. Müller begins innocently enough, saying, "I knew several Jewish families, and received much kindness from them as a boy. Many of these families were wealthy, but they never displayed their wealth…"[62] Then he speculates about how this affected anti-Semitic feelings among his fellow Christians, concluding that "in consequence [these Jews] excited no envy."[63] Turning to the present day, Müller observed that contemporary Jews differed from the Jews of his youth:

> All that is changed now. The children of the Jews who formerly lived in a very quiet style at Dessau, now occupy the best houses, indulge in most expensive tastes, and try in every way to outshine their non-Jewish neighbours. They buy themselves titles, and, when they can, stipulate for stars and orders as rewards for successful financial operations…[64]

As a result of this supposed change between generations, German Christian attitudes have migrated toward anti-Semitism, Müller hypothesized:

> Hence the revulsion of feeling all over Germany, or what is called Anti-Semitism, which has assumed not only a social but a political significance…The Anti-Semitic hatred is the hatred of money-making, more particularly of that kind of money-making which requires no hard work, but only a large capital to begin with, and boldness and astuteness in speculating, that is in buying and selling at the right moment.[65]

As if it were not bad enough to promote the anti-Semitic trope of Jewish greed, Müller concluded his observations about the current fashions for anti-Semitism by blaming the victim. Again, beginning on a kind note, Müller says, "One cannot blame the Jews or any other speculators for using their opportunities."[66] Immediately, however, his words turn ugly:

> ...they must not complain either if they excite envy, and if that envy assumes in the end a dangerous character. The Jews, so far from suffering from disabilities, enjoy really certain privileges over their Christian competitors in Germany. They belong to a regnum, but also to a regnum in regno. They have, so to say, our Sunday and likewise their Sabbath. Jew will always help Jew against a Christian; and again who can blame them for that? All one can say is that they should not complain of their unpopularity, but take into account the risk they are running.[67]

For this and other reasons, suspicions of anti-Semitism dogged Müller, however unfair they eventually may have turned out to be, the evidence did not weigh in his favor. For instance, in 1865, at the height of his infatuation with all things Aryan, Müller lavishly praised Jewish civilization as "one oasis in that vast desert of ancient Asiatic history."[68] After 1871, Müller seemed repulsed by the ethno-nationalist implications of Aryanism, confessing as much to none other than Ernest Renan. Léon Poliakov, a leading critical historian of anti-Semitism, is convinced of Müller's sincerity in refusing to identify race and language. Poliakov conditions this judgment by characterizing Müller's retraction of earlier Aryanism as "timid," because Müller had only argued against German nationalist Aryanists and their racialist conceptions of the Indo-European heritage. Müller denied that Indo-European philology had anything to do with race.[69] Said Müller, "let us speak no longer of Aryan skulls or Semitic blood."[70]

Later, Müller also undercut Christian triumphalism, with its attendant anti-Jewish apologetics, by resisting assigning any religion an upper hand before the truth: "we share in the same truth, and we are exposed to the same errors, whether we are Aryan or Semitic or Egyptian in language and thought."[71] For Müller, since all the holy books said approximately the same thing, accepting the Vedas and other scriptures as "revelation" alongside the Bible did not entail rejecting or replacing any other religion. Thus, Müller was, at least, consistent in relativizing the religious value of the world's scriptures. All were sacred, or none were. True to his new "Science of Religion," Müller no longer believed the Bible was an exclusive divine revelation. "A belief that these books had been verbally communicated by the Deity…was to me a standpoint long left behind."[72] In place of his Lutheran confessional and literal adherence to the words of the biblical narrative, Müller put his new "Science of Religion" to work on all the sacred texts of the world. But with the genie of suspicion out of the bottle, not even Müller could completely silence public misgivings about anti-Semitism in "maxmüllerism" which, by the late nineteenth century, had taken on a life of its own. Those earlier Aryanist ideas, for instance, went on to live in the racism of Müller's disciples, such as John Fiske, the American social Darwinist philosopher.[73]

Müller in the Rear-View Mirror

For our purposes, Müller's dominance in theory of myths shows how the hegemony of the mythical narrative developed, entangled as it was with Victorian ethnic and cultural politics. The conception of myths as narratives, representations, statements, or symbols predominated the theoretical field from the mid-nineteenth century right into the twentieth. Our contemporaries in the study of religion have long since abandoned the confessional theological prejudices against ritual embedded in Müller's approach to myth. But many scholars today still dwell on myth primarily as explanation, text, representation, statement, static symbol, etc.[74] Even in his recent treatment of that arch-pragmatist Malinowski, Segal claims that Malinowski said that the folk read "myths literally" to reconcile themselves to otherwise irreconcilable conditions of life by, for instance, referring the matter to the gods. In this way, Segal still sees Malinowski view of myths as *explaining* things by making the world "less capricious than it would otherwise be."[75] In Segal's view, today's equivalent for "myth" would be "ideology," presumably because of how it assures modern folk of the right way to act.[76]

Were Malinowski to read Segal's account of his theorizing myths, he would take rather strong exception to Segal's essentially neo-intellectualist view. In one of Malinowski's classic statements about the concept of myth, he rejects the standard narrative theory of myth we've associated with Müller, and now Robert Segal. Said Malinowski, myth "is not an idle tale, but a hardworking active *force*; it is not an intellectual explanation or an artistic imagery, but a *pragmatic charter* affirmative faith and moral wisdom."[77] That is to say that the salience of Malinowski's view of myths lies in his *departure* from narrative or intellectualist conceptions of myths, as I shall show at length in a following chapter on Malinowski. In thus departing from conventional conceptions of myths, Malinowski has not merely tinkered with a few peripheral aspects of the concept, but he has shifted registers entirely to seeing myths as *pragmatic*, and in that sense, a forebear of a *performative* theory of myth — the power of "*doing things*" in culture.[78]

Segal and others of the mythophilic persuasion have, in effect, thus tried to give renewed life to some of the narrative explanatory priorities of nineteenth-century myth theorists like Müller, rather than moving confidently in the eccentric directions taken by structuralist, performative, or other newer theories. One exception is Segal's embrace of psychoanalytic approaches to myths and their concern for the "functions" of myths, rather than their literal meaning. There, Segal states that in Freud's theory, myths "function to vent the unconscious," while in Jung's theory myths "function to encounter the unconscious."[79]

Chapter 3

French Connections: Durkheimian Ritualism Replaces Müller's Hegemony of Myth

From the Hegemony of Mythical Narrative to Myths Acting in Living Contexts

In this chapter, I shall show how a performative theory of myths took its rise, in part, from a critique of Müller's textualist theory. If one factor hastened the emergence of a performative theory of myths, it seems to have been a growing acceptance of the essential contribution of *action* or *behavior* to the constitution of religion. An early sign of this reappraisal of *action* in culture and religion was a sweeping reassessment of the relation of ritual to myth, culminating in the emergence of methodological *ritualism*. Methodological ritualists theorized religion as constituted by rituals and actions, rather than beliefs, experiences, doctrines, and moral codes. Émile Durkheim and two of his key collaborators, Henri Hubert and Marcel Mauss, were principally responsible for this methodological reorientation to ritual. Coincident with the new ritualism—and not accidently—was the rampant increase in ethnographic and other empirical studies of lived religion. In effectively promoting the methodological place of formal *observation*, fieldwork-based empirical and ethnographic studies heightened the value of *what* could be observed, viz. rituals. These "observables" even included myths, such as those recited in public performance, appeals to, or citations of myths to justify or convey legitimacy to given social practices, institutions, and so on. Myths, then, not only "said" something, but they also effectively "did things."

    A great patron of the sociological study of myths, Durkheim was not always consistent in his devotion. The luxuriant growth of perverse or false stories seemed to escape rational management. Consider the way that racist stories fed Müller's Aryanism and catalyzed the Dreyfus affair. We will see in chapter 9 how Henri Hubert exposed some of these myth-laden racist projects that masqueraded as "science." Hubert's critique was well-founded in the research of French Sanskritists Abel Bergaigne and Sylvain Lévi, the latter of whom was an intimate of both Hubert and Mauss. There, they found evidence that some Indological scholarship concealed and encoded anti-Semitism in asserting the hegemony of myth. For their part, Bergaigne and Levi wished to rehabilitate ritual, and in so doing also rehabilitate the reputation of religious traditions—Judaism, in particular—often derided for their ritualism by scholarly anti-Semitic mythophiles.[1]

The strands of my story come together when we realize how Müller's mythophilia was most congenial to the—equally Liberal Protestant—French representatives of *"sciences religieuses."* In Paris, leading the study of religion as founder and head of the Fifth Section was Albert Réville.[2] Both Müller and Réville conceived religion largely in intellectual, doctrinal, or mythical terms. The rituals found in religions were regarded as "magic," mere "externals," and thus deviations from a true spiritual religion. In their view, religion had begun with the powerful impact of natural events, causing naïve "primitive" folk to bow down in worship before physical forces.[3] Humans responded to their feelings of powerlessness before the forces of nature with religions of rituals—religions in which people believed that they could "magically" manipulate their environments by ritual means.[4] But before myths could be reassessed as performances, as actions, scholars would need to reassess religious *actions*—primarily *rituals*. In that way, the first long step toward a performance theory of myth was to overcome anti-ritualism, with its resistance to a spiritual appreciation of any physical action or performance as legitimately religious. Our first task then is to understand anti-ritualism in the "science of religion" and the theological sources sustaining it. Once scholars like the Durkheimians redeemed ritual, it seemed almost axiomatic that they should begin thinking about myths as more than texts, narrative, and the like—but as actions, as performances.

Deconstructing Protestant Anti-Ritualism

Müller's *sola scriptura* Lutheranism inclined him, as we have seen, toward a static, textualist view of myths. Albert Réville's Liberal neo-Calvinism similarly sustained a broad anti-ritualism. In the late nineteenth century, such theological positions often conformed to one's political situation. This was very much the case for the politically and theologically republican French Protestants in an increasingly autocratic Catholic France. Protestant republicans like Réville were often faced with the unenviable decision of whether to remain underground in France or flee its authoritarianism and religious bigotry in search of some democracy and religious tolerance in places like the Netherlands. Too prominent in the Huguenot community to avoid being targeted, Réville fled to Rotterdam. There, Réville assumed leadership of the exiled French Protestant Arminian community. He and other Protestant refugees simply waited for a more tolerant democratic regime to permit their return in France.[5] The advent of the Third Republic presented just such an opportunity. With the moral support of scholars like Müller, Réville founded and then subsequently led the officially non-confessional, academic study of religion in France, under the title "*Sciences Religieuses.*"[6]

Under the anti-clerical Third Republic, one way the government sought to control its unruly Catholic population was to promote *laïc* citizens or French Jews and Protestants to leadership positions in national education. In the all-important domain of higher education, the anti-clerical Third Republic government systematically elevated their ideological brethren in the Jewish, Protestant, and *laïc* communities over Catholic incumbents. Soon Liberal Protestants like Réville and Jewish professors like Durkheim commanded major influential university posts. Réville led the study of religion at the Sorbonne's École Pratique des Hautes Études, Fifth Section, while Durkheim and those like him were sponsored for key educational projects affecting mass education in France. Catholic scholars at the university were often shunted off to the peripheral and expressly parochial Instititut Catholique. There, they enjoyed the freedom to indulge as much *odium theologicum* as they chose — but not in the Fifth Section! As we will see, the liberal Protestants, in effect, shaped the Fifth Section along theological lines, as well. The only difference between the illiberal Catholic theological hegemony imagined by the Fifth Section and the real Liberal Protestant's neo-Kantian one was the relative invisibility of the liberalism shared by Protestants and Third Republic government. Appealing to the Third Republic's neo-Kantian "scientific credo," the Liberal Protestant-led Fifth Section claimed it offered value-free, ideologically neutral "scientific" studies of religion similar to Müller's "Lutheran" Science of Religion in Oxford.

The Fifth Section was originally a French version of the German Higher Criticism of the Bible in which Müller had been schooled. But by the end of the nineteenth century, under Réville's leadership, the Fifth Section had evolved into a preeminent center for the study of the world's religions. Indianists like Abel Bergaigne and Sylvain Lévi held forth there; eminent Jewish scholars Israel Lévi and James Darmesteter thrived; and eventually the Durkheimians, Henri Hubert and Marcel Mauss, won posts in the Fifth Section. Growing out of the critical, secular study of *texts* pioneered by German Higher Criticism of the Bible, study of religion in the Fifth Section accordingly focused — *sola scriptura*-like — on *textual* and *critical* research, where it became the source for rigorous philological studies, definitive "critical editions," modern translations of exotic sacred texts, and the like.

French Liberal Protestants joined the Lutheran Müller in a generic Protestant biblicism. This tendency to focus on sacred texts likewise favored studying myths. For both Müller and Réville, myth-laden religions might not be the best of religions, but those that relied on rituals were clearly "superstition" or "magic." Reinforcing this theoretical conviction was Protestant distaste for Roman Catholic ritual practice. Catholic Eucharistic transubstantiation, for instance, was, to Réville and his ilk, nothing more than ritual "magic" — not religion in a pure sense.[7] After all, Catholics believed a mere human, the priest, could mystically transform bread and wine into the body and blood of Jesus! Catholic "religion" differed little from the "magic" that ethnographers observed among "primitive" folk. For the Protestant Liberals, religion was something deeply personal and "spiritual," not ceremonial and priest-ridden like Catholic practice. Placing themselves in sharp opposition to the Catholics, the Protestants emphasized true religion as that which focused on inner experiences, ethics, and the inspiring words of scripture.

Albert Réville exemplified this Protestant anti-ritualism. For him, ritual was mere "religious materialism."[8] By contrast, he believed that a "really religious person will inform their sensibility with a religious 'spiritualism,' originating in a "more elevated moral and religious sense."[9] Rituals, by contrast, betrayed an unwholesome "need to make use of religious forms, as if they were indispensable receptacles of the divine reality,"[10] and accordingly, were "always more or less superstitious."[11]

Trying to Get Serious about Ritual: Robertson Smith and Durkheim

With the advent of the Durkheimians in the Fifth Section, the prevailing anti-ritualism would be challenged. Grounded in the conviction that their empirical studies showed how rituals exerted a *"causal"* influence in making religions what they were, the arrival of the Durkheimians in the Fifth Section promised conflict with Réville and his colleagues. Durkheimian "causal" ritualism implied a *"constitutive"* ritualism in which religions were actually made up of — *constituted* by — rituals, as well as other dimensions, such as myths, doctrines, ethics, experiences, and so on. But the Durkheimians insisted that rituals could no longer be dismissed for theological reasons such as magic or superstition.

While the origins of Durkheimian ritualism are obscure, it is improbable that it derived from the liberal Calvinist William Robertson Smith's writings on sacrificial ritual.[12] Neither Smith's Calvinism nor Durkheim's *liberal* Judaism gave them good theological reasons to entertain ritualism. Had the Durkheimians been *Orthodox* Jews, perhaps that would have pushed them toward an appreciation of ritual. But the Durkheimian Jews were scarcely even observant. While Smith was an observant believer, I have no evidence of his thinking much of the religious value of rituals — at least not outside the "primitive" societies he encountered in the Saudi Arabian desert. Let me elaborate on Smith's relation to rituals.

Despite the common view that Robertson Smith inspired our modern appreciation of rituals in religion, Smith believed that ritual had only *relative* value in religion. Religions dominated by ritual were, by definition, *lower* in Smith's Calvinist hierarchy of religions. Certainly, for him, what constituted religion were its religious experiences, morality, doctrines, and philosophy — all aspects favored by his Calvinism. It would not be surprising if Smith's critique of ritual corresponded exactly to Albert Réville's. Calvinist Christianity represented unquestioned theological *evolution* over anything Catholic. Freeing Christians for a lofty spirituality, he left it to Catholics to stay mired in physical religions of mindless conformity to rituals.[13]

Because the so-called "primitive" religions were theological like Catholicism, Smith therefore considered them "magical," "pagan," "heathen," and "superstitious." Smith instead saw that "the real living power... in Christianity is moral.... [Our] personal Christianity is not a play of subjectivities, but moral converse with God practically dominating the life."[14] So potent were Smith's biases against ritual that even Protestant liturgies were, to him, no more than devices for facilitating personal piety and moral rectitude. The church may be a "fellowship of worship," but Smith saw it as the "common worship of many *individuals*."[15] All that should matter to the Christian was what was "to be gained in converse with God, in hearkening continually to His Word."[16] Christians should even be cautious about the Bible's frequent references to sacrificial rites. In many cases, they were forms of bribery and hence irreligious acts.[17] While Durkheim did indeed lavish extravagant praise on Smith, unlike Smith, Durkheim believed rituals constituted religion at *every* stage of its evolution, and not just at the primitive level of religious evolution. So, we discount Smith's role as the source of Durkheimian ritualism.

The Durkheimians as Diffident Ritualists

Under the direction of the Liberal Protestants, the study of religion in the Fifth Section was thus decidedly bookish. No chairs devoted to the *observation*, or even scientific study, of rituals, institutions, cultures, or societies existed there. Those only appeared around the turn of the twentieth century with Durkheim and his sociology of religion's promotion of empirical studies of religion. Under Durkheim's empirical influence, the first chair in the ethnography and archeology of ancient Europe was founded, with Henri Hubert as *titulaire* in the *Religions primitives de l'Europe*. A second subsequent appointment of Durkheim's nephew, Marcel Mauss, at the Fifth to the chair of *Religions des peuples non civilisés* came soon thereafter. With these two chairs, the empirical observation of religious subjects would forever become integral to the academic study of religion in France. In consequence, since ethnography "peoples" our analyses, "we are more able to see cultural products as embedded in networks of cultural and social processes—in action—leading us toward...a more performative understanding of daily life."[18] I am suggesting that the Durkheimian promotion of ethnographic studies of religion accounts for their ritualism, which on its other side, is to depart from a strictly literary conception of myths. From this point, a *performative* theory of myths is not distant, as we will see.

From the vantages of their two new prestigious chairs, Hubert and Mauss would soon make the Fifth Section into an outpost for Durkheim's empirical sociology and anthropology. Mauss pioneered his own sociological and ethnographic studies of religion, while training generations of ethnographers. He soon came to be known as the father of French ethnology. With Hubert and Mauss, as well, came a new appreciation for the study of *rituals* in religion. Instead of the prevailing principle of *sola scriptura*, Hubert and Mauss made the study of ritual respectable in the Fifth Section, eventually producing classic works on such religious rituals as gift, sacrifice, magic, and prayer.[19] This scholarly production on rituals did not reflect any influence upon religious practice by Hubert and Mauss.

Even as they kept aloof from formal religious rituals themselves, Hubert and Mauss believed that rituals mattered greatly to all aspects of human life — religion included.[20] They pioneered appreciation of the positive value of certain everyday rituals, such as the celebration of civic rites, or indeed whatever is required to stir the community into a state of creative, high emotional effervescence. Now granted some of these modern rites may be best interpreted as vestigial forms of religious ritual life typically found in traditional society. All societies needed their moments of intense enthusiasm in order to lift themselves out of periods of emotional and moral mediocrity, as Durkheim lamented in his own day. One of Hubert's prize pupils was the lesser-known Philippe de Félice (1880–1964), author of 1936's *Poisons sacrés, ivresses divines*.[21] In that text, Félice credits Hubert with teaching him about the many ways world religions cultivated ritually induced religious raptures, often by using inebriants like beer or exotic drugs. Such religious ritual behavior, said Félice, is a "general human phenomenon" fundamental to religion.[22] Moreover, such practices as quaffing "nectars" and "ambrosias" can also be found in the writings of the Church Fathers and fervent language of the mystics. A basic "need" exists, he wrote, "to transcend the self, which imposes itself upon human beings."[23] We "desire to enter into the source of the immense river, where people, since their existence, have sought to refresh their souls…"[24] Rituals were precisely the instruments needed to achieve transcendence. Thus, Félice argued, in effect, rituals were not just appropriate for "the primitives," but for people of his own day. Unlike Smith, the Durkheimians believed that rituals had perennial value for society.

The Durkheimians were also more positive about myth, even as they held to a causal, constitutive, and methodological ritualism. On the matter of the relation between ritual and myth or belief, for instance, the Durkheimians held that they were causally interdependent, albeit in sometimes asymmetrical ways. As society made visual, rituals had a certain causal priority over myths or beliefs. In his 1887 review of Guyau's *L'Irreligion de l'avenir*, Durkheim announced what amounts to an appreciation of the causal priority of ritual.[25] Incidentally, this came more than a year or two *before* William Robertson Smith suggested something similar in print in his *Lectures on the Religion of the Semites* (1891).[26] There he says that—for primitive folk at least—"cult is religion become visible and tangible; like religion, it is based on a sociological relationship, formed as an exchange of services."[27] Making clear the same sense of *causal* priority of ritual over myth some years later than both Smith and Durkheim, Henri Hubert colorfully wrote, "Myths are social products; it is in the rituals that society is visible, present or necessarily involved. The mythological imagination dances on the threshing floor trodden by rituals, and it is there that one might grasp it."[28] This reflects the Durkheimian view that rituals—as *actions*—were closer to the bedrock of actual social reality than mere words. They were the "*sine qua non* of the maintenance of society."[29] In another place, Hubert says,

> First of all, as for a ritual, it implies, by definition, the collaboration of the entire society in which it takes place. The rite carries in itself the idea of its efficacy and reason for its observance. Secondly, every religious act puts the sacred things into action.[30]

Therefore, against the anti-ritualist position of most *laïc* or religious liberals, Hubert and Mauss adopted a causal or constitutive ritualism. Religion *is* its rituals, not just its beliefs or even morality. Ritual is the locus of the positive power of the sacred that injects effervescence, energy, and power into people, and the thing that causes people to be religious at all. Thus, sacrifice is for them what makes (things) sacred, as the root meaning of "*sacri-ficium*" testifies. It even creates the gods. Sacrifice performs a positive function of creating the religious life of people. As Durkheim noted, rituals make "religion made visible and tangible."[31]

Hubert's brilliant metaphor also spelled out the interdependence of ritual and myth that the Durkheimians were apparently otherwise unable to explain. In "Individual and Collective Representations" (1898), Durkheim clarifies what he means by "ritual causal priority." Once myths are launched, they become causally independent of any rituals previously related to them.[32] In certain contexts the Durkheimians even saw myths *acting* to shape rituals, thus rendering them worthy of study in and of themselves — or at least as sometimes causally *prior* to rituals. In *Sacrifice: Its Nature and Functions*, Hubert and Mauss begin discussing the sacrifice of the god. There, they explain that "Our main efforts will be especially directed toward determining the considerable part that mythology has played in this development."[33] Yet, the Durkheimians seem somewhat unsure of themselves. While the Durkheimians wanted to admit that myths could acquire autonomy, they always seemed to want to keep their feet on the ground by asserting that flesh-and-blood social realities (like ritual) were *the* primary realities. The guiding methodological principle here is that ritual is the way society manifests itself, thus making it available for empirical study. In the end then, although the Durkheimians wanted to have it both ways in the balance between ritual and myth, they preferred ritual.

How was it then that the Durkheimians got to the point of embracing ritualism as much as they did? Why did they not turn out more like other cultural and religious liberals like their contemporaries, Albert Réville, William Robertson Smith, and Salomon Reinach? How was it that they parted the seams of the nearly seamless anti-ritualism of their times as extensively as they did? Part of the answer is, as I shall now show, bound up in the larger, overarching cultural strategies of the Durkheimian group.

We already know how Müller's preference for myth was embedded in a whole network of cultural strategies. The same is true of the evolution of the Durkheimians' ritualist positions. Where Müller was Aryanist and quickly acquired a reputation as an anti-Semite, the Durkheimians were cosmopolitan and non-exclusive. Where Müller was enthralled by romantic individualism and mystic rapture, the Durkheimians looked to Enlightenment fellowship and co-operation. Where Müller saw society as formed by its language, myths, philosophy, and poetry, the Durkheimians saw society forming its modes of ideal expression. Where Müller saw myth and philosophy, the sociological Durkheimians saw ritual and concrete human relations.

Even though the Durkheimians seem to have come by their ritualism for the reasons thus canvassed, several peripheral colleagues also seem to have played influential roles. Prominent here is Mauss's mentor in Indic studies, the pious Jewish scholar Sylvain Lévi. His ritualism had been explicitly hammered out in opposition to Müller's mythophilic interpretation of the Vedas. Lévi's ritualism was additionally thickly nuanced by involvement in a program of cultural strategies diametrically opposed to Müller and his Aryanism.

Ritual Makes the Gods

Insofar as Müller's theory of myth owed anything to Aryanism, it presumed a picture of the Vedas as "a profound philosophy" from which Indian religion degenerated into the mindless ritualism of Hindu polytheism.[34] First to challenge this interpretive scenario were certain French scholars of Hindu texts such as the Brāhmanas, like that great friend of the Durkheimians, Sylvain Lévi. He argued that nothing indicated that the Brāhmanas, for instance, resulted from a "long and profound degeneration of religious feeling," as the Aryanists claimed — and that Robertson Smith took over from his German biblical scholar-teachers, Julius Wellhausen and the *volkisch* Paul de Lagarde.[35] Such a devolution from philosophy to ritual made little sense because it was not possible to separate the supposedly philosophic wisdom of the Vedas from practical ritualism. Lévi indicated that even the elaborate ritualism of the Brāhmanas,[36] for instance, reached its peak among an elite class of *brāhmins* — who were also philosophers. Ritual and philosophy are not mutually exclusive; they co-exist under the same conditions. Even in the brutal brāhmanical sacrificial system, ritual contains a speculative theological core that gives immediate rise to the lofty philosophical speculations of the Upanishads.

But, beginning with Bergaigne, some prominent French Indologists went further toward recognizing the role of ritual in the earliest stages of Indian religion. Beginning with Abel Bergaigne and continued by Sylvain Lévi, the leaders of French Indology taught that Hindu texts would be better read as indicators of ritual, rather than as philosophy.[37] Once the mists of philosophy cleared, other readings of the Vedas could emerge. Bergaigne, for instance, believed that the hymns of the Vedas needed to be put into the *performative* context of their settings. Müller, on the other hand, felt that the Vedic hymns had only "incidental dramatic value."[38] If they were not philosophy as Müller believed, then they were myths. But with the growing attention to the performative settings of the Vedic hymns, Bergaigne, for one, began to suspect their mythological character as well. In a testimony of intellectual conversion remarkable in the history of science, Bergaigne tells us of being "suddenly stopped on the road leading to Damascus" shortly after an article of his on Vedic mythology, done in the solarist style of Müller, went to press. "What was it," Bergaigne asks, "if not the evidence of the texts, or in any case, something which appeared to me to be such, that could have been the reason for the change?"[39] Bergaigne no longer believed:

> I ultimately came to recognize that exclusively solar interpretations, just like exclusively meteorological interpretations…when they applied to the analysis of the Rigvedic myths, almost always leave behind a liturgical residue, and that this residue…is exactly the most important portion from the point of view of the exegesis of the hymns.[40]

In the words of the eminent Paul Mus, Bergaigne had started a "heresy in traditional Indianism" by "showing that one ought above all to interpret the Vedas as explaining a ritual."[41] Thus Bergaigne's rejection of Müller's mythophilic reading of the ancient Indian texts led him directly to methodological ritualism as a key to reading Vedic texts.

Bergaigne's lead in Vedic studies was eagerly taken up by Sylvain Lévi. But to Lévi, as to Bergaigne, it was clear that the Vedas were heavily committed to ritual, a trend that continued into the Brāhmanas. Sylvain Lévi's *La Doctrine du sacrifice dans les Brāhmanas* (1898) substantially argued the position that ritual, not the idea of gods, was the key to the origins of religion.[42] In Sylvain Lévi's view, the Brāhmins also acted with considerable violence in their rituals — a view contrary to Herder's Romantic view of the *gentle Brāhmin*.[43] Sylvain Lévi, therefore, did much more than Robertson Smith: the thrust of his arguments was about the way ritual *made* religion — notably theism — not merely how to go about *studying* it. The religion revealed in the Brāhmanas is constituted by sacrificial ritual — it "is God and God par excellence."[44] Further, sacrificial ritual "is the master, the indeterminate god, the infinite, the spirit from which everything comes, dying and being born without cease."[45] So potent is the sacrificial ritual, that even if gods are relevant, those very gods are "born" from sacrificial ritual, are "products" of it. Behind the figure of Prajapati, a major Hindu creation deity, is the sacrificial ritual: "Prajapati, the sacrifice is the father of the gods... and its son."[46] Sylvain Lévi in effect argued what Renou calls the "omnipotence" of ritual, or what I have earlier termed *causal* ritualism.[47]

Sylvain Lévi and Marcel Mauss[48]

An observant Jew of complex Zionist sympathies, Lévi promoted major relief efforts to aid Jewish refugees fleeing pogroms in the Russian Empire. Developments in Tsarist Russia surely alerted him to the possibility of anti-Semitism spreading to the West, even if only in scholarly form. Lévi was both a major intellectual and moral influence on both Marcel Mauss and Henri Hubert and set an example for them of how an academic ought to act in the public world outside the university. There, scholarship about ancient India was often exploited by anti-Semites to score ideological points against Jews. It was Lévi's view that other scholars should expose and counter perverse ideological scholarship as a normal part of their role as truth-seekers. In terms of theory of myth, Lévi's appreciation of ritual, "sacrifice" in particular, freed Hubert and Mauss of whatever traces of the fashionable anti-ritualism of the *"sciences religieuses"* they may have shared. In the process, Lévi's interventions aided the Durkheimians in valuing rituals both in and for themselves and as things capable of *action* in the world—something perhaps only fully recognized by an early admirer of Durkheimian sociology of religion, Bronislaw Malinowski.

Marcel Mauss came to Sylvain Lévi at precisely the moment Bergaigne's ritualism had ripened to its fullest point. Early in his career as Sylvain Lévi's student, Mauss underwent an initiation test. He was told to assess the theoretical thrust of a text about which he, at the time, knew nothing. This book turned out to be the locus classicus of Bergaigne's ritualism, *La religion védique*.[49] After three days of intense reading, Mauss returned to Lévi, and reported that he felt that Bergaigne had made his case. Were Bergaigne correct, Mauss concluded, the major assumptions of Vedic studies would be overturned. Since he had made such a stark and uncompromising judgment on the book, Mauss awaited Lévi's reaction with some apprehension. But naturally Sylvain Lévi was pleased, and Mauss gained the confidence of his future teacher for life. It would do well to recall, however, that things might well have gone otherwise. Mauss was at that time very much an idealist philosopher and thus, in theory, more likely to be sympathetic to German idealist readings of the Vedas than to the emergent contextual and liturgical interpretations begun by Bergaigne and continued by Sylvain Lévi. As it happened, this meeting between Mauss and Lévi was pivotal in Mauss's intellectual development as a partisan of ritualism — something which Mauss recognized in his review of *La Doctrine du sacrifice dans les Brāhmanas*. There Mauss recites the lessons of Sylvain Lévi's view of the causal power of rituals, even to create the gods themselves.

Sylvain Lévi had been interested in the cause of ritualism beyond the scope of academia for some time. As an observant and politically attentive Jew, he knew that the mythophilic Aryanist program of Müller and his fellows posed potential cultural threats to Jews' fragile status in Europe. Müller's interpretation of the Vedas as a body of Aryan, archaic European philosophical wisdom and mythological lore was at its worst a piece of Aryanist (and thus anti-Semitic) ideology. Lévi reacted against the Aryanists by leveling a devastating attack on the supposed superiority of the Vedic religion. The language of the Rig Veda was notoriously "barbaric"; the very existence of something called a "Vedic society" remained unproven; claims about its archaic character had been refuted by the discovery of the pre-Aryan Indus Valley civilization of Mohenjo-Daro. In sum, the Vedas were far from anything marking a golden age with respect to which later Hindu religion — such as the Brāhmanas — could be seen to have fallen.[50]

Sylvain Lévi's criticisms also took on existential pertinence because the German Aryanists and others, including the priests of the notoriously anti-Semitic Roman Catholic Assumptionist Order,[51] symbolically identified post-Vedic, "degenerate" (sic) Hinduism with contemporary Talmudic Judaism. This follows the pattern assumed by German biblical scholars like Lagarde, Wellhausen, and through them, William Robertson Smith. They had paired their admiration for long-gone ancient Israel with an equal distaste for contemporary "Judaism" proper, Talmudic Judaism. Thus, in terms of symbolic relations, Talmudic Judaism was, for the German Aryanists, like Hinduism in decline after the glory of the Vedic period, and before the philosophical renaissance of the Upanishadic "reform."

To Sylvain Lévi, the course of Hindu and Jewish religious histories was much different from the picture painted by the Aryanists. While he agreed with them and Jewish modernists that Jewish religious history ought to be divided along various lines, there were no stages of an irreversible historical evolution. For Sylvain, what the evolutionists might call "stages" ought rather to be called aspects of Jewish religion and "aspects" in a perennial rhythm of change. He addressed these issues, oddly enough, in a tract written for the Ligue des Amis du Sionisme.[52] First, from his perspective as a republican French thinker, he recognized "prophetic" Judaism, doubtlessly echoing James Darmesteter, as enlightened, universalist, or reformed Judaism. This Judaism "holds out a fraternal hand to humanity to march in concert, anticipating the triumph of justice." Sealing the pact with the French Enlightenment, he immediately adds that,

> French genius with its passion for universal humanity which expresses itself in its classics as well as in the Revolution is the closest relative of this messianic spirit. It is its natural safeguard against sectarians who have never renounced its suppression.[53]

But, in this tract, Sylvain Lévi also speaks as someone deeply affected in his own Jewish particularity by the Dreyfus affair. Without minimizing its difficulties from the viewpoint of "prophetic Judaism," he nonetheless applauds Zionism. He likewise recognizes the value of the "Mosaic" Judaism — that aspect of Judaism contrasting with the "prophetic." Mosaic Judaism "tends to regroup the chosen people into its ethnic isolation, to multiply the barriers which separate it from the nations."[54] Sylvain Lévi felt both aspects were perennial and, in their own times, desirable for Judaism to encompass.

The Aryanists (though not, apparently, Müller) also sought to replace the very scriptural heart of Western culture, the Jewish bible, with an "Aryan bible," the Vedas.[55] Alternative Aryan foundations for the religious traditions of the West would then replace those linked with Jewish traditions and religion.[56] Although apparently not a radical Manichean Aryanist like his former professor of philosophy, Schopenhauer, Müller's work tended to decenter Judaism from its privileged relation with Christianity. Thus, the radical cultural anti-Semitism of the Aryanist interpreters of the Vedas motivated Sylvain Lévi to undo their entire project. Part and parcel of the Aryanist program was a ritual-hating mythophilia to which Sylvain Lévi reacted by asserting the power of ritual.

Bergaigne's methodological ritualism, mediated in this way by his student, Sylvain Lévi, passed on to Lévi's own student, Marcel Mauss. Thus, through the classics of Indological scholarship of Bergaigne, mediated by Sylvain Lévi, Durkheimians like Mauss began taking ritual seriously as a key to the study of religion. Thus, the real historical line followed by the movement to rehabilitate ritual in this century stems from France, and in particular, as I have shown, from the Durkheimian group.[57] This polemic line matters materially to the formation of our own sense of the value of ritual because Lévi's critique of Müller's preference for mythological interpretation of the Vedas aided the formation of the Durkheimian sociological approach to religion. In its Durkheimian incarnation, Lévi's opposition to Müller and myth amounted to an assertion that religion is primarily constituted by ritual, and thus that social life is founded on concrete human relations rather than merely upon ideas.

Chapter 4

Henri Hubert: Durkheim's Mythologist

A Division of Labor inside Durkheim's Équipe

I have argued that Durkheimian criticism of maxmüllerism contributed significantly to the development of a performative approach to myths. Leading many of these critiques was a little-known member of Durkheim's *équipe* and its chief mythologist, Henri Hubert (1872–1927). Hubert directly shaped the theories of myth of such celebrated figures in twentieth-century French myth scholarship as cultural historian Stefan Czarnowski, Indo-Europeanist Georges Dumézil, ethnographer Maurice Leenhardt, and Sinologist Marcel Granet. Claude Lévi-Strauss's absence from this story of Durkheim and myth is conspicuous, but we will explore that puzzle in chapter 5, "What Lévi-Strauss May, or May Not, Owe to Henri Hubert." How and why the Durkheimians and Lévi-Strauss should have parted ways can only be understood in terms of the role of Hubert and other leading Durkheimians like him. Down one path, we find a theory of myth that anticipates performative theory and is much indebted to the Durkheimians: Bronislaw Malinowski's pragmatic-functional theory of myth. Down the path taken by Lévi-Strauss, we find approaches to myth that revert to the intellectualism typical of maxmüllerism. Readers will then find that Henri Hubert's part of the story of the development of both Durkheimian and Malinowskian theories of myth fills in many gaps in our understanding of the development of a performance theory of myth.

As much as scholars like to believe that knowledge for its own sake, like virtue, guarantees its own reward, others may conclude that the inattention to Henri Hubert's work is well-deserved. Yet, the fact of our near total ignorance of someone who, with Mauss and Durkheim, made up the nucleus of the Durkheimian *équipe* should give one pause. Is a hidden genius to be discovered here, or just someone better relegated to the shadows cast by Durkheim and Mauss? I argue both that Hubert's real accomplishments are yet to be recognized and that the academic neglect of Hubert had its own causes unrelated to the quality of his *oeuvre*. I submit that the eccentric—to Durkheim—nature of Hubert's interests in the arts, archeology, material culture, and technology account in some—but not all—part for his neglect.

Even though Hubert's reviews on the arts and technology were relegated to an obscure corner of each annual volume of the *Année*, Durkheim had other ways to exploit Hubert's education and talents—especially in the study of religion. Hubert was both schooled and interested in religion, and he also participated—I would argue, centrally—in the *Année*'s all-important work on religion. So, Henri's role on the *équipe*, largely evident in the course taken by the *Année*, was unique. Although Hubert specialized in fields subordinate to the major components of Durkheim's research program, he worked in the closest possible collaboration with Mauss on religion. Together with Durkheim, they formed the hub around which the *équipe*'s efforts to crack the secrets of the place of religion in human flourishing revolved.

The unreliability and free spirited bohemianism typical of Mauss in his twenties gave Durkheim no end of headaches when it came to practical matters of scholarship. Luckily, Durkheim could rely upon Hubert's bourgeois reliability for assistance with critical tasks like physically producing the *Année*. Durkheim found Hubert's steadier, if predictable temperament, indispensable to the success of his publishing ambitions for the *Année*. Since Hubert died abruptly at age 55 in 1927, much of his immediate intellectual influence ceased then, putting him a decade or so beyond range of twentieth-century masters of French theory of myth like Claude Lévi-Strauss. Only the very long-lived Georges Dumézil had worked with Hubert, and then only briefly. Mauss draws more contemporary attention largely because Lévi-Strauss claimed his influence—controversially, as it happens. Yet, Hubert's writings reveal some remarkable theoretical breakthroughs in the study of myth. For that reason alone, he is worth getting to know.

Accordingly, Hubert's research strategy followed a number of steps. First, the modern secular world is an evolutionary outgrowth of Christian civilization. Thanks to Hubert's mentor, Louis Duchesne, he sought to write real history of Christianity by demolishing the *mythical* accounts produced for apologetic purposes.[1]

Once Hubert had cleared away the *myths*, one could begin to understand Christianity's contribution to the formation of contemporary Western civilization.[2] Fully embracing the Durkheimian ethnographic impulse, Hubert sought to make sense of Christian Europe in terms of the elements of its "barbarian" ancestors,[3] the ancient Celts, Germans, and Slavs. "The Christian imagination," wrote Hubert, "was constructed on the basis of ancient blueprints."[4]

In the same spirit, Hubert's work on the ancient Celts and Germans was meant to inform readers about the comparative formative values beneath French and German nation-states in his own time. Admittedly, Hubert may not have been entirely even-handed in his comparison of Celtic and German prehistories, since he betrays a certain tenderness for the Celts. Nevertheless, for Hubert the Germans are literally "*germain*" — the neighbor, not the promoter of an aggressive "Germanism."[5] Similarly, is not "France" really the home of the Franks, a "Germanic" people? Then, we ought not forget how the three-hundred-year Merovingian rule over Francia informed such consequential and complicated institutions as Salic Law. Hubert also pointed out that Germany is also a vast syncretic "Celtique-Germain" terrain encompassing Alsace, Lorraine, the Rhineland, Luxembourg, and even Switzerland.

Thus, when we comprehend the strategy behind Hubert's efforts in the prehistory and ancient history of occidental peoples, we can see how well his work complements that of Durkheim. The entire program of Durkheimian comparative history of world civilization was worked out via a radical division of labor: Mauss was assigned Africa, Australia, the Americas, India, and Oceania; Hubert took on the Celts, Greeks, and Romans, as well as their Mesopotamian and Near Eastern fellows. Mauss studied Buddhism, Hinduism, and the "primitive" religions; Hubert was in command of Druidism, Gnosticism, Judaism, Christianity, and the "mystery" religions. Within the structure of this global plan, Hubert showed how Aryans, Celts, and Germans reveal "elementary forms" that went into the formation of the peoples of Europe. If we can isolate the elementary forms of our ancestor civilizations, we can uncover some of the deep determinants of our own national character. If we can discover their "primitive" — not necessarily primordial — forms, we can understand our "developed" ones. What "they" were, "we" are. When we further try to comprehend the place of Hubert in the overall Durkheimian research project for religion, his role on the *équipe* has special meaning. Mauss studied Buddhism, Hinduism, and the "primitive" religions; Hubert studied Druidism, Gnosticism, Judaism, Christianity, and the "mystery" religions. Hubert, thus, played an essential complementary role in the coherence of Durkheim's vision for his ambitious—and totalistic—"science of society." Despite this devotion to science, Hubert sometimes was steered into polemics having to do with the political consequences of particular scientific theories, such as the various "sciences" that became the basis of "scientific" racism. He was, thus, capable of interventions into the realm of public discourse, as we will see in chapter 9. As we will see, Hubert's role in delegitimizing the myths of racist social science prevalent in his day is a noteworthy example how politics or public moral matters influenced the direction of Hubert's scholarship.

The Political Formation of Hubert's Peer Group

Like Mauss and many of the Durkheimians, Hubert was occasionally something other than disengaged scholar (or even an artist-scholar). But how did he come to be the kind of progressive republican who would launch attacks on the myths employed by Aryanist anti-Semites? From early in his life, Hubert had been nurtured in the progressive moral revival that swept through his *Normalien* generation around the time of the Dreyfus affair. Although not himself Jewish, Hubert was galvanized in both progressivism and philo-Semitism by the Dreyfus affair. Deep personal friendships with Jews like Sylvain Lévi, Israel Lévy, Durkheim, and Mauss, as well as intellectual concerns for Near Eastern studies and Jewish religious history all spoke to Hubert's philo-Semitism.[6]

Adding to the political influences of Hubert's milieu was the great socialist, Catholic-born Lucien Herr. Hubert met with the influential Herr daily while employed as his student *bibliothécaire* at the École Normale. Victor Karady claims both Hubert and Mauss contributed regularly, for example, to Jaurès's radical *L'Humanité*,[7] and Philippe Besnard lists Hubert among the original stockholders in Herr's socialist successor to Péguy's Bellais press, *La Societé Nouvelle de Librairie et l'Édition* (1899).[8] Furthermore, Hubert collaborated on writing dozens of reviews along with his *Normalien* contemporary and fellow *Année* editor, economist Francois Simiand, on the socialist *Notes critiques*.[9] Hubert's reviews tended to focus exclusively on books about religion, such as those by Paul Carus, Morris Jastrow, and Andrew Lang. One might imagine the bookish Hubert taking his moral recreation in the streets during the Zola trial in the company of other young socialists connected to *Notes critiques*. Although one does not find direct "interventions into the normative sphere"[10] like those of which Mauss spoke on subjects like bolshevism, cooperatives, or money, Hubert occupied a comfortable position, like many young Durkheimians, on the left of France's political spectrum. In sum, Hubert is to be counted among those morally awakened youths who strove to overcome what Durkheim lamented as the moral mediocrity of the age. Testifying to Hubert's depths, Mauss called him someone who found "social phenomena...more and more complex, on the one hand, and more and more spiritual on the other."[11]

In such a state of moral awakening, Hubert was well prepared for his association with Durkheim, Mauss, and the *équipe*. Marcel Drouin claims he introduced Hubert to Mauss in 1897 or so, although the two had apparently studied Hebrew together under Auguste Carrière and Israel Lévy before that date.[12] As chief recruiter, Mauss probably brought Hubert into the *Année*'s inner circle. Durkheim, thereupon, assigned Hubert to work on the first volume reviewing publications in Hubert's specialties: history of Christianity, Mesopotamian and Near Eastern religions, mythology, and folk religion. Here Hubert doubtless exploited the critical history of religions—especially Christianity—he had learned from that liberal Catholic church historian, Louis Duchesne. Drouin says that Duchesne urged Hubert to publish what would become his first major article for Monod's prestigious *Revue historique* in 1899. There, Hubert dealt with the curious relations between political matters, like the legitimacy of the Papal States and theological controversies, like the iconoclasm controversy.[13] Later that year, Hubert and Mauss published the first of their several collaborations on religion, "Essai sur la nature et la function du sacrifice." A veritable cascade of *comptes rendus* signed either jointly or individually by Hubert and Mauss followed, making their section of the *Année*—"*sociologie religieuse*"—perhaps the most prominent, if not most important, section of the *Année*'s first series.

Birth to Death

Born in 1872, the same year as his *jumeau de travail* Marcel Mauss, Henri Pierre Eugene Hubert descended from a comfortably established Parisian commercial family.[14] The second of three children, he apparently enjoyed the attentive company of his recently retired father, Francois Hippolyte Hubert, a Roman Catholic. From the family residence, within sight of the towers of the Sorbonne, Hubert's father indulged a gentleman's interest in higher education, attending public lectures at the great university. His mother, Rosalie Virginie Vitry, is described by Marcel Drouin, as of a *santé delicate*. Indeed, Salomon Reinach described Hubert as being "*valetudinaire*" himself.[15] Similarly afflicted with ill-health throughout his nonetheless productive life, Hubert died prematurely at age 55 in 1927.

On the whole a studious—even bookish—young man, Hubert showed keen interest in archeological field trips, material artifacts, ancient technologies, and the visual arts. In his professional life, he played the curator's role as *conservateur* of the Musée des Antiquités Nationales in the Paris suburb of St. Germain-en-Laye. Hubert dabbled in *aquarelles*, typically done on holiday *en plein air*. Also, among his notes and letters from later years, one finds the odd freestyle drawing or pencil sketch of plans for arranging the museum collection he commanded. Hubert showed scant, if any, interest in the revolution in the *beaux arts* then underway among artistic *avant-garde* Fauvists, Surrealists, and their ilk, instead preferring the "primitive" ethnographic arts that so enamored Georges Bataille, Michel Leiris, and Lévi-Strauss. As late as 1923, when reviewing a volume that argued for connections between Stone Age art and the latest efforts of the Parisian *avant-garde*, all Hubert could manage was a meek acceptance of the author's thesis.[16] Earlier, in 1913, while reviewing a work on aboriginal African art, Hubert pays no attention to the new esthetics on display there but rather observes that a rich mythology must surely inform such imagery.[17] Remaining rigorously sociologistic, Hubert argued that artistic production must be seen within the larger, overarching system of collective *social* representations.[18] As an esthetic soul, Hubert remained firmly within the sociological camp that saw art reflecting social structures.

Prepared at Lycée Louis-le-Grand, Sorbonne, École Normale Supèrieure, and École Pratique des Hautes Études (IVième and

Vième Sections) in geography, history, as well as Near Eastern, Mesopotamian, Greco-Roman, Celtic, and German studies, Hubert's range and erudition were remarkable. Of Hubert, it was also said that, like Mauss, "il lisait tout, savait tout."[19] Indeed, their thirty-year collaboration can only be explained by their success at combining an abiding friendship with an almost perfect, though complementary, equality of professional mastery.

Did Religion Matter?

As the most prominent Catholic on the *équipe*, the question of Hubert's personal relationship to religion naturally arises. What was his relation to the agitations of the contemporary religious scene in France? While there is no evidence of personal Catholic piety, Hubert kept abreast of struggles within the Church, as did many French intellectuals, whether religious or *laïc*. They did so in part because struggles between the liberals and intransigent Catholics had repercussions for the whole nation. Hubert did too, but he also brought his sociological sensibility to the subject of the Church, mostly for its relevance in making France what she was over many centuries of history. But two issues of the day attracted all informed citizens. These were a movement that promised to bring the Church into the modern world of science and liberalism — the Modernist movement — and an issue that aimed to bring the severe principles of *laïcité* — strict separation of religion from public life — the Separation issue (1905).

Of greatest intellectual import for Hubert as student of myth was the Modernist movement and the epistemological issues it entailed about how to study and write sacred history. The Durkheimians supported the principles of *laïcité*, although perhaps with less rigidity than those on the far left. For Hubert, the intellectual issues raised by Modernism spoke directly to profound issues of truth. Would church history be written as an edifying story, designed to cultivate piety, typically through the vehicle of *myth*? What should the historian do when encountering data that might cause embarrassment or skepticism among the faithful? What place did the *mythical* have in relation to the historical? Although Hubert never explicitly identified with the Modernist liberal Catholics who promoted "history" proper over mythologized histories, his demythologizing publications already answered any doubts about Hubert's loyalties.

Hubert did however have influential colleagues among those Catholic historians we might call Modernist, or at least "pre-Modernist." One was the Modernist Alfred Loisy, with whom Hubert had something of a professional relationship. But standing out above all others was church historian and mentor to Hubert, Louis Duchesne. A man of immense influence and distinction in his own time, Monseigneur Louis Duchesne pioneered the publication of classic studies of the early Christian church and liturgy.[20] Duchesne continued the skeptical history-writing of Ernest Renan and became for Hubert a principal conduit of Gabriel Monod's *histoire historisant* in the study of religion.[21]

Having cultivated a skeptical eye, Duchesne taught believing Catholic historians to look beyond the accretions that had accumulated on the surface of legendary or mythological narratives. Instead of being credulous believers—even of pious, edifying myths—the new Catholic historian should bravely seek what lay beneath appearances. In terms of the official Modernist movement, the cautious Duchesne was, at most, a *précurseur*, but certainly not a member.[22] Duchesne brutally demythologized many immensely popular tales (myths?) of the lives of the saints.[23] Likewise, he prepared the way for the reforms of the Second Vatican Council with his critical history of all manner of Church traditions and practices.[24] While some may call him a historical positivist, Duchesne would have preferred being identified as a historian obsessed with facts.[25]

Although Duchesne never explicitly identified as a member of the Modernist movement, either Duchesne enters our story because he had mentored Hubert, and thus had encouraged him to practice the new scientific history. Through Duchesne, Hubert was apparently also introduced to other leaders of French liberal Roman Catholicism, such as Albert Houtin, Alfred Loisy's biographer and an intimate of Lucien Herr's—Hubert's Catholic socialist head librarian at the École Normale.

Hubert, Religion, and Mythical Politics

From 1898 until the end of the Great War, Mauss and Hubert—certainly not Durkheim alone—spearheaded and sharpened the thrust of Durkheimian religious studies. In 1904, Hubert's "Introduction" to the French translation (which he directed) of Chantepie de la Saussaye's *Manuel d'histoire des religions* attracted the attention of no less a figure than the public intellectual Henri Berr. Reviewing Hubert's introduction, Berr, the founder and editor of the *Revue de Synthèse historique*, identified the radical purpose of Hubert's introduction. Berr saw immediately that it was a true manifesto of then-current Durkheimian theoretical thinking on religion.[26] Mauss confirms this in his review for *Notes critiques*:

> Monsieur Hubert has enriched this otherwise simple manual, of which the method is completely classic kind, but of which the "Introduction to the French Translation," is brimming with knowledge and originality. Now, that introduction was needed because the author failed to maintain for students the rights of the science of religions, the rights of history. He failed to show that the chronological and geographical way of classification of facts was the only possible one, the only true and instructive way. He also failed to demonstrate how important it was to discover the logical order of religious phenomena, using the comparative method. I shall, therefore, be content to say that Hubert exposes the reasons that one has to consider religious facts as social—religions, or religious systems, rituals, myths, organizations as the fruits of pressure exerted from outside by the simultaneous action of co-religionists—that is, the central notion of religion, that of the sacred.[27]

In its scope and articulation of a theoretical viewpoint on religious studies, Hubert's "Introduction à la traduction française de P. D. Chantepie de la Saussaye, *Manual de l'histoire des religions*" has no equal in the Durkheimian literature. Primarily, Hubert uses Chantepie's *Manual* as a prop to pronounce his own emerging (Durkheimian) theory of religion. It follows Durkheim's "De la définition des phènomènes religieux" (1897–98) by five years and seems to supply a missing link in the evolution of Durkheimian thinking up to *Les Formes élémentaires* (1912). Hubert accordingly sketches out a vision of religion and its study—not religion, really, but religion*s* in the plural. All religious facts should be the preoccupation of the study of religion. Philosophical and theological work waits upon the results of the positive scientific study of religion as a human phenomenon. For Hubert, this means understanding religion as a social phenomenon first—the beliefs, myths, representations, rituals, and such that make up the concrete reality of religion. It also briefly forecasts some of Hubert's developing thoughts about myths. In contrast to Durkheim's apparent ritualism, Hubert asserts the importance of beliefs and myths.

In 1905, Hubert published his "Étude sommaire sur la représentation du temps." In 1919, Hubert wrote the "Preface" to his student Stefan Czarnowski's *Les Cultes des Héros et ses conditions sociales. St Patrick, héros national de l'Irlande*. In 1901, Hubert succeeded to the chair he had originally proposed at the École Pratique des Hautes Études, Vième Section: *"Les Religions Primitives de l'Europe."* By 1911, Hubert had risen to *conservateur* at the Musée des Antiquités Nationales in St. Germain-en-Laye, where he had been *attaché libre* since 1898. There, he reorganized the exhibits according to a theoretically informed comparative scheme that introduced the "revolutionary" guiding principle of technological development that offended conventional notions of civilizational development. These institutional affiliations precisely reflected the character of the sections of the *Année* that Hubert personally commanded: "Anthropologie et Sociologie" (Volume IV); "Civilization en Générale et Types de Civilization" (Volumes V, VI, VIII, VII, and XI); "Le Milieu Social et la Race" (Volume V); "Races et Societés" (Volume IX); and "La Question de la Race" (Volume X). Likewise, the particular teaching Hubert did during this period covered the same ground. From 1901 until his death in 1927, Hubert taught courses on the German civilization and society in ancient Gaul and the prehistory of European sculpture. He also lectured on concepts related to time, such as the calendrical systems of ancient civilizations and their seasonal feasts. These courses may have become venues where he rehearsed the ideas informing his various studies in these areas, such as the frequently referenced study, *Étude sommaire de la représentation du temps dans la religion et la magie*.[28] Hubert, of course, also lectured on his better-known specialities: religion, mythology, and material culture, such as the ancient monuments of the Celtic and Gallo-Roman civilizations.

Stefan Czarnowski, *Les Cultes des Héros et ses conditions sociales*

But for a taste of Hubert's view of myth, his "Préface" to Stefan Czarnowski's 1919 *Les Cultes des Héros et ses conditions sociales. St Patrick, héros national de l'Irlande* serves us well. The author of the work, a Polish nationalist student rebel and political refugee, Czarnowski found his way into the Durkheimian circle in about 1902. Interpreting Durkheim's own attention to the "primitive" and elementary in his own way, Czarnowski took up the study of European "popular" or folk religion just as Hubert had. Czarnowski found Hubert a congenial guide to his studies in part because Hubert was profoundly interested in the mythic identification of modern European peoples with their prehistoric and ancient ancestors. Czarnowski shared this interest of Hubert's, especially for the potential political uses of this identification.

Hubert was keenly aware of how the Germans were already making nationalist, even racist, ideology and propaganda from the mythic materials of ancient folk history. With Germany a perennial threat to both France and Poland, neither Hubert nor Czarnowski could ignore the nationalist uses of myth. In his posthumously published books on the Celts and Germans, as well as his critical reviews of German racist mythologizing, Hubert shows himself well aware of political mythmaking. By devoting his attention to the St. Patrick myth, Czarnowski combined his interest in archaic folk religion with modern Irish nationalist struggles.

In the course of Hubert's preface, he also gives us valuable insight into Durkheimian theoretical views on sociological understanding of religion in general, the myth/ritual relationship, the sociological institution of heroes and saints, and the promotion of the study of the "elementary" in society and culture that the Durkheimians believed could be accessed in the study of folk societies and peoples without writing. Czarnowski aimed to understand the power of the Saint Patrick myth, both in terms of myths as vehicles by which heroes were created, and also, sociologically, in terms of the saint's political alliance with a key division of ancient Irish history in particular, the "*filid*," or old Irish intellectual class. As a vehicle, Hubert claims that it is not an actual heroic death that makes the hero, but the *myth* that makes the hero! It is the social renown of the "hero," created as it was by the telling of the saint's myth, that makes the hero, not the other way around.[29] Second, as to politics and society, Saint Patrick was able to attain hero status across the whole nation, not only because of his renown, but also because of his association with the "*filid*," who were themselves a national rather than tribal or clan social entity.

World War One

Yet, as we know, the constructive enterprises led by Durkheim and ably assisted by Hubert and Mauss were shattered by the outbreak of the First World War. For Hubert and many of this generation just coming into their own, a decade of heightened professional activity broke off sharply with the outbreak of the war that would remake the cultural face of Europe. Patriotic calls to defend the nation would mute some of the anti-establishment stirrings of the Dreyfus period. Unlike some of his *dreyfusard* comrades, however, Hubert seems to have always kept a kind of faith in the army. It may be true, however, that Hubert was keeping faith with Jaurès's ideal of *la nouvelle armée* as a corps of model citizen-soldier. Hubert performed his required military service from 1895 to 1896 without apparent incident; he served with distinction from 1914 to 1919 in the Great War. Hubert first served in the infantry, attached to the Ministry of Armaments and dealing with the design and manufacture of auto-transport. Then, he drew special duty under leading socialist diplomat-intellectual Albert Thomas, working abroad as an archivist in Tsarist Russia, Italy, and the United Kingdom. In the end, Hubert accumulated a brilliant military record. He was involved in the successful negotiations to keep Russia in the war; he originated the concept of the military application of "caterpillar" tractor tracks for battle tanks—apparently inspired by seeing farm tractors in in the American Midwest. Hubert ended his military service supervising the protection and repair of historic monuments in the recently restored territories of France. For this and all his patriotic labors, Hubert won the Croix de Legion d'Honneur in 1920, the only Durkheimian apparently to be so honored.

The Post-War Years

After the war, Hubert readily picked up his research where he had left off. He produced a general survey of European prehistory from the end of the Neolithic period to La Tène, followed by specific investigations into each of the great civilizations making up Europe: the Celts, Germans, Greeks, Romans, and Slavs. Hubert never assembled his works on the Celts and Germans into finished books. They had to be completed for posthumous publication by Mauss and other editors. Indeed, Hubert left much unfinished business when he died. In an interview I conducted with Dumézil a year or so before his death in 1986, he offhandedly remarked that, with only two posthumous books to his name and none published during his lifetime, Hubert was a bad model for a professional academic. Dumézil knew Hubert well in an official capacity; he was Hubert's *élève titulaire* in a course on Celtic mythology and the Arthurian cycle at the EPHE in 1924–25. Recognizing Dumézil's erudition, Hubert invited him to offer a *leçon* on the Vedic *soma* sacrifice in one of his courses in 1924.[30] But the prolific Dumézil—who published more than fifty books—never felt Hubert lived up to his potential.

In the years since that conversation with Dumézil, I had not given this incident much thought. However, thanks to Bruce Lincoln's suggestion, I read Arnaldo Momigliano's tribute to Dumézil's work on the trifunctional paradigm in Roman civilization and put it together with bits of information from Marcel Fournier's masterful biography of Mauss.[31] There, both scholars bring out a fundamental ideological rift between the philo-Semitic socialist Durkheimians and Dumézil's (non-Nazi) Far Right proto-fascist (Charles Mauras's *Action Française* and Italian *fascisti*) sentiments. So tense was the mood set by these differences that it was inevitable that politics should color scholarship and collegial relations in the academy. Momigliano, for instance, notes that Dumézil's work in his *Le Festin d'immortalité* celebrated the Indo-European (Aryan) warrior values beloved by the Far Right and then honed to perfection by the Nazis. To play down these unsavory affinities, Dumézil softened passages of the book that might have raised suspicions about Nazi sympathies in anticipation of the book's American edition.[32] No one on the left, including Hubert or Mauss, could have been oblivious to the rightist flavor of Dumézil's early scholarship. Indeed, they seemed to have acted to stifle Dumézil's career in France because of it. Dumézil spent nearly a decade whiling away in obscurity, first teaching history of religions at the University of Istanbul from 1925 to 1931 and then as a lowly French instructor at Uppsala from 1931 to 1933. And although Dumézil had drawn closer to the Durkheimians in later years, when he criticized Hubert's professional underachievement to me in 1985, he still may have been feeling the sting of his exile from French academe, allegedly on the initiative of none other than Hubert![33]

Still, all in all, Hubert did leave his mark on a generation of students of myth, as we will see in the next chapter. One could say that his work on Celtic and ancient Germanic civilizations presages the flowering of Durkheimian civilizational studies exemplified in Granet's works on China or Dumézil's own comparative mythological studies. Dumézil, for instance, generously credits the Durkheimians for what they had taught him in his first book, *Mythes et dieux des Germains* (1939).[34] But Hubert did not live to see either the completion of his own projects or their flowering in the work of his students. His health gradually failed, and he died on 25 May 1927, still working on his volumes on the Celts and Germans for Henri Berr's series.

Chapter 5

What Lévi-Strauss May or May Not Owe to Henri Hubert

Lévi-Strauss's Structural Study of Myth as a Historical Problem

At crucial junctures in his career, Claude Lévi-Strauss sought to appropriate Durkheimian traditions in the French *sciences humaines* for his structural anthropology. But his assumption of a Durkheimian legacy mired Lévi-Strauss in some nasty academic politics when he insinuated structuralism's descent from the work of Marcel Mauss. At the time, Lévi-Strauss's celebrity owed much to his newly launched structural theory of myths. Murmuring skeptics wondered if Lévi-Strauss was really suggesting that structural mythology derived from Mauss? And if so, on what basis? An immediate problem with Lévi-Strauss's evocation of Mauss, particularly with respect to myth, was that Hubert, not Mauss, was Durkheim's mythologist. Worse yet for structuralism's supposedly Durkheimian provenance, Hubert's theoretical approach to myth was not remotely structural. If anything, Hubert's approach tended toward the religious phenomenology of Maurice Leenhardt and the historical studies of Georges Dumézil, both of which were quite at odds with structuralism. Thus, despite attempts to drape himself in a Durkheimian mantle, Lévi-Strauss's structural mythology sought to displace Durkheimian mythology rather than elaborate on it. But this only raises further questions about the nature of Durkheimian conceptions and theories of myth.

For historians, discovering the elements of the original Durkheimian research project has been both stimulating and surprising. We've come to realize both how little and how much we understand about what Durkheim and his *équipe* thought they were doing. Details of a decades-long research project start to come into focus. Beginning in the 1970s with Steven Lukes's massive intellectual biography of Durkheim, followed by Philippe Besnard's organizing and publishing efforts in Paris on the *équipe*, the early 1980s saw James Clifford's biography of Maurice Leenhardt and studies of Marcel Griaule and Michel Leiris. Victor Karady's editions of the collected works of Maurice Halbwachs and Marcel Mauss appeared in the early 2000s. In Britain, Oxford's Durkheim Centre and the periodical *Durkheim Studies/Études Durkheimiennes*, overseen by Bill Pickering and Willie Watts-Miller, provided an intellectual home for scholars worldwide. These pioneering efforts spurred decades of publications, including Laurent Olivier's *Dossier Henri Hubert* and writings on Hubert by Jean-François Bert, Robert Parkin, and others.[1] Without such colleagues working in the Durkheimian soil, the subsequent flowering of so much scholarship cannot be imagined.

Simply by most well-known, however, Lévi-Strauss has attracted the keenest curiosity about the provenance of the structural theory of myths. His massive *oeuvre* on myth, rendered in stylish prose, and his regular forays into high-brow media culture, often display a visionary perspective extending to issues of public concern like ecology, human destiny, racism, and the plight of colonized peoples. The autobiographical *Tristes Tropiques* has been read as something of a Lévi-Straussian *moraliste* travel diary. But it is Lévi-Strauss's celebrity that has invited special probing into the genesis of his visionary theorizing. By his own account, structuralism represents a great, if eclectic, intellectual synthesis. Lévi-Strauss names not only Franz Boas, Émile Durkheim, Marcel Granet, Roman Jakobson, Robert Lowie, Marcel Mauss, and Ferdinand de Saussure as influences but also Henri Bergson, Sigmund Freud, Karl Marx, Norbert Wiener, Charles Peirce, Jean-Jacques Rousseau, Richard Wagner, Buddhism, geology, Gestalt psychology, serialism, surrealism, and more! Lévi-Strauss even hints occasionally that any number of these intellectual influences foreshadowed specific elements of structuralism. All of this is laid before the dazzled reader in an extravagant intellectual buffet. However, it is not easy to track specific intellectual sources of inspiration.

If Lévi-Strauss's grand manner incites readers to ask questions about structuralism's origins, that is well and good. At the same time, the grandeur with which Lévi-Strauss articulated his often mythical origin story invites caution about writing a *history* of the genesis of his main ideas. I shall begin by narrowing my focus to the possibility of Lévi-Strauss's substantial intellectual debt to the Durkheimians as his French intellectual ancestors in the human sciences. Can Lévi-Strauss's structural theory of myth be said to be Durkheimian in any meaningful sense?

Durkheim, the Durkheimians, and Lévi-Strauss

The full story of Lévi-Strauss's relationship to Durkheim's thought deserves a full-length study itself. It contains, at once, minefields of misinformation and conceptual tangles. Some unpleasant academic politics also rear their ugly head. Georges Gurvitch's veto of Lévi-Strauss's participation in Durkheim's centenary celebration was but one case in point.[2] Gurvitch aside, Durkheim must be disengaged from the way he and Durkheimianism have recently come to be known through the success of Lévi-Strauss and the fashion for structuralism. So thoroughly have many readers assumed Durkheimian provenance to structuralism that it is common to hear of the "well-known structural nature [sic] of Durkheimian sociology."[3]

Were this the case and we were able to read back from Lévi-Strauss's words and works to Durkheim, the historical inquiry into the sources of structuralism would be a straightforward matter. But it is not. When we look at how Durkheim appears through Lévi-Strauss's eyes, we do not get such a clear picture. Even though Lévi-Strauss is sometimes assumed to be Durkheim's greatest intellectual representative, he has described himself, instead, as Durkheim's "inconstant disciple."[4] On his arrival in Brazil in 1934, Lévi-Strauss made known his sharp feeling of estrangement from Durkheim's thought, describing himself as being "in a state of open revolt against Durkheim."[5] Later, however, Lévi-Strauss piques the historian's curiosity, when he expressed that "at this moment [1955] I am probably more faithful than anyone else to the Durkheimian tradition," adding for the sake of his French audience that "abroad everyone is aware of this."[6]

What Lévi-Strauss means by this may perhaps be deduced from what he says in his two most complete surveys of Durkheim's thought. There we see references to Durkheim's views, gathered, it seems, from the viewpoint of how they do or do not fit with nascent structuralism. Lévi-Strauss interprets Durkheim as saying that sociology is a kind of "psychology…irreducible to individual psychology,"[7] that synchronic styles of explanation are superior to historical ones,[8] that symbolic analysis is central to social analysis, etc.[9] Yet, Lévi-Strauss assigns scarcely two out of thirty-five pages to Durkheim's (and Mauss's) view of the central place of historical inquiry or the study of religion in their respective research, even when Mauss clearly insisted upon referring to his work as "the comparative history of societies and of religions especially."[10] Thus, without failing to be grateful for Lévi-Strauss's brilliant new reading of this great master, the critical reader will exercise care about presuming structuralist continuities with Durkheimian theory. In the end, we will need to examine the specific positions of Durkheim and Lévi-Strauss, as well as how the latter represents those positions. This is particularly true of the subject of myth.

Here, I must question other commentators like Miriam Glucksmann who claim that Lévi-Strauss's structural mythology follows some of the lines of the Durkheimian problematic as outlined in *Primitive Classification* (1903) and developed in *The Elementary Forms of the Religious Life* (1912).[11] Affinities may be there, but how superficial are they? In *Primitive Classification*, Durkheim and Mauss wrote, "Every mythology is fundamentally a classification, but one which borrows its principles from religious beliefs, not from scientific ideas."[12] How does this emphasis on religion square with Lévi-Strauss's remoteness from it? Yet, nine years later, where one might have expected Durkheim's detailed discussion of myth—*The Elementary Forms*—Durkheim notes that myth is not the "subject of our studies."[13] Myth presents, Durkheim says, "a very difficult problem which must be treated by itself, for itself, and with a method peculiar to itself,"[14] something he does not propose to do. Could the grand edifice of Lévi-Strauss's structural mythology rest on such a shaky foundation?

Working diligently with the Durkheimian corpus, the scattered fragments of a theoretical position on myth can be collected. Dating from 1912, a Durkheimian view of myths includes the following tenets: myths are essentially religious and connected with rituals,[15] typically as interpretations of rituals.[16] Myth is, therefore, not a mere "idea" or "work of art."[17] Myth is a collective representation, and thus expresses "the way in which society represents man and the world; [it]...is a moral system, and a cosmology as well as a history."[18] Myths are contradictory and confused;[19] they veil reality, rather than reveal it.[20] Given such a list, it will surprise no one that Lévi-Strauss never cites Durkheim's conception of myth.

Durkheim's concept of myth neither contradicts conclusions Lévi-Strauss has reached, nor does it represent anything that has made structural mythology distinctive and original.

Mauss to Lévi-Strauss?

When we turn to Lévi-Strauss's relation to members of the Durkheimian *équipe,* one may be tempted by Lévi-Strauss's enthusiasm for Marcel Mauss. Moreover, when we consider Mauss's record as teacher, author, and reviewer of works on myth for *L'Année sociologique,* Mauss would seem to become the prime candidate to supply a Durkheimian basis for structural mythology. Yet, the issue of Lévi-Strauss's intellectual debt to Mauss has sparked even more controversy than his intellectual debt to Durkheim.

Lévi-Strauss seems responsible for the confusion about his relation to Mauss. Consider Maurice Merleau-Ponty's *De Mauss à Lévi-Strauss,* Jean Piaget's *Structuralism,* or Lévi-Strauss's many citations of Mauss. Both Merleau-Ponty and Piaget presume a story of close, even personal, connection between Lévi-Strauss and Mauss. From there, it is but a short step to believing that Mauss taught a germinal, if disorganized, version of what today, in Lévi-Strauss's skilled hands, has become structural anthropology.[21] However seductive this myth, history says otherwise. Unlike every other major French ethnologist of his generation, Lévi-Strauss never trained under Mauss. One can understand why commentators presume that Lévi-Strauss did so, given his ethnographer's calling. To his credit, Lévi-Strauss never explicitly claimed to have been trained by Mauss, even as he let that impression circulate. In an interview with Lévi-Strauss in 1983, he told me he'd met Mauss a few times in the 1930s, and then only briefly. Contrary, again, to prevailing impressions, Lévi-Strauss also "knew" the Durkheimian *équipe* only from their published works. The single exception to this rule remains Celestin Bouglé, who alerted Lévi-Strauss to a teaching post in Brazil in 1934.[22]

This lack of living, historical contact with the Durkheimians seemed, however, to inspire Lévi-Strauss to educate himself about their work. So successful were these efforts that even on minor points, Lévi-Strauss ably represented the *équipe*'s views when needed. Case in point is Lévi-Strauss's brilliant, if selective, recovery of the work of Marcel Granet for the *Elementary Structures of Kinship.* A glance at the bibliography of *Elementary Structures* further confirms Lévi-Strauss's diligent mastery of the Durkheimian *oeuvre*.[23] In the same 1983 interview with Lévi-Strauss, he confirmed how he immersed himself in the writings of the Durkheimians while exiled in New York City, all the better preparation to assume Maurice Leenhardt's chair in the Fifth Section.

As for Mauss, Lévi-Strauss still insisted that Mauss anticipated many features of the structuralist program. After all, Mauss promoted linguistics, psychology, the unconscious, the total social fact, as well as gift and exchange, all of which are *core* structuralist themes.[24] The *locus classicus* here is Lévi-Strauss's "Introduction à l'oeuvre de Marcel Mauss," published first in 1950 for his anthology of Mauss's writings titled *Sociologie et anthropologie*. There is something modern about Mauss's thought, Lévi-Strauss insists in that volume—something proto-structural.[25] Lévi-Strauss wished Mauss had pressed beyond the "borders of these immense possibilities" but instead, Mauss stopped at the gates of (structuralism's) "promised land."[26]

But controversy still swirls about Lévi-Strauss's view that Mauss—at a minimum—anticipated principal features of structuralism. Tellingly, in the "Introduction," Lévi-Strauss makes the strongest case for Mauss as proto-structuralist. But it was one of the last major essays by Lévi-Strauss to be anthologized, republished, or translated (at least into English). Most of the "Introduction" consists of original expositions of central structuralist ideas, while the remainder of the content is devoted to Mauss. Indeed, a close reading of the "Introduction" reveals Lévi-Strauss budgeting more space to an outline of structuralism than to expounding on Mauss. Thus, although Lévi-Strauss seems ambivalent about Durkheim and distant from the other Durkheimians (except Granet), he conspicuously celebrates Mauss and, in the process, shows passionate familiarity with Mauss's *oeuvre*.[27]

Mauss to Lévi-Strauss on Myth?

Strangely, however, once Lévi-Strauss positions himself to cite Mauss as precursor of structural mythology, he neglects to mention him! Thus, despite Mauss's work on myth and his comfort with citing Mauss as a precursor of structuralism, Lévi-Strauss never truly presents a case for Mauss as forerunner of structural mythology. Why? Part of the reason is that Mauss does not really anticipate structuralism *of any application*. Another reason is that, as the reader will recall, Henri Hubert, not Mauss, was Durkheim's myth theorist! I thus conclude, first, that had Lévi-Strauss mastered the *équipe*'s theory of myth, he would have mastered Hubert, not Mauss. Second, Hubert's theory of myth was at odds with structuralism's and therefore not its precursor. Hubert prepared the way for Marcel Granet, Maurice Leenhardt, and Georges Dumézil's approaches to myth, not Lévi-Strauss's structuralism.

Lévi-Strauss's decision to minimize the work of Leenhardt, his immediate predecessor in Mauss's chair, can now be read in light of the sociology of institutional knowledge. Public association with Leenhardt's religious phenomenologist approach to myth would have confused Lévi-Strauss's narrative about his own structuralism's genesis[28] — especially since Lévi-Strauss's first teaching duties at the EPHE were on myth![29] Slighting Leenhardt's work as he did helped Lévi-Strauss displace Leenhardt's theory of myth in favor of his own. In an address made to his new colleagues in the EPHE, Lévi-Strauss, in effect, denounced, Leenhardt's phenomenology:

> Ethnographers tend to believe too readily that they have succeeded in grasping beyond their own preconceptions, the ideas of the indigenous people. Their descriptions are too often reduced to a phenomenology. We hope to introduce an additional exigency into our discipline: to discover, beyond men's ideas of their society, the hinges of the "true" system. We hope to carry the investigation beyond the limits of consciousness.[30]

Thus, Lévi-Strauss could not claim a strong Durkheimian precedent for his theory of myth because doing so would have either diluted his special infusion of Mauss with a strong dose of Hubert or confused his new mythology with Leenhardt's. It is small wonder that Lévi-Strauss cannot cite the Durkheimians who shaped Leenhardt's phenomenology — especially Hubert — as precursor of his structural mythology. He was not!

The *Année Sociologique* Introduces Myth

If Durkheim had wanted to announce some consensus theory of myth, he would have done so in the *Année sociologique*. The *Année* served many purposes, and one of them was to be a venue for the publication of theoretical statements on key subjects — here, myth.

The volumes of the *Année* followed a standard pattern, beginning with a survey of the state of theoretical debate on a subject, followed by reviews of the year's major relevant publications, and concluding with an official Durkheimian theoretical verdict. For "myths," the *Année sociologique* 6 produced a short discussion, entitled "Introduction aux mythes," (1903),[31] and a "Conclusion" to complete the discussion.[32] No less a contemporary than Henri Berr vouched for the first-order theoretical importance of such document in a general assessment of the Durkheimian program, the expanded details of which he published later as a foreword to Hubert's *Les Celts*.[33] How plausible is it that the theoretical views mooted here served Lévi-Strauss's purposes as an acceptable Durkheimian — not to mention Maussian — anticipation of a structuralist theory of myth?

Two considerable obstacles prevent us from seeing the "Introduction aux mythes" as the precursor to Lévi-Strauss's theoretical program. There is little if anything "structural" included therein; nor is it clear that Mauss even was the author. First, the "Introduction" articulates what Durkheim said more completely in the *Elementary Forms of the Religious Life* years later. And when we compare Mauss's individually signed works on myth, they seem even less structuralist, even in anticipation. Consider Mauss's only individually signed paper on myth, "L'Art et le mythe d'après M. Wundt" (1908). There, Mauss calls myth, above all, a religious and social entity, not something structural in the sense of being defined by a schema of oppositions nor by being anchored in the unconscious mind. Mauss declares elsewhere that "the sacred character of myth is well noted."[34] But, unlike Mauss, Lévi-Strauss never promoted religious studies. Instead, he preferred to insist upon making Mauss a model for integrating psychology into the human sciences.[35] A second obstacle concerns the authorship of the "Introduction" and, more importantly, the "Conclusion." Notably, while the "Introduction" stands unsigned, the "Conclusion" carries the initials "HH."[36] The "Introduction" conforms to standard Durkheimian views, but HH's "Conclusion" fairly sparkles with new details and vigor. Distinct echoes of the ideas mooted in the "Conclusion" turn up in Hubert's later writings on myth up to the time of his death in 1927.

Hubert and Mauss equally shared the intervening reviews between them. From a simple arithmetic viewpoint, the entire treatment of myth here seems a fine example of the remarkable collaboration between Hubert and Mauss, something Mauss caught nicely in his reference to Hubert as his *jumeau de travail*.[37] Thus, had Lévi-Strauss considered using these texts to support his proto-structural reading of Mauss, he would have seen that they were probably chiefly Hubert's, even if the two worked on them together.

Henri Hubert, Mythologist

Concentrating on Hubert's role as chief author of this text on myth, let's look at Hubert's career, with an eye for his place in the *équipe*'s division of intellectual labor. There, Hubert clearly emerges as the pivotal thinker on myth in the original *équipe*—a view confirmed by Francois Isambert's reference to the "sociology of myths" undertaken by Hubert.[38] Hubert wrote his doctoral thesis on a Syrian goddess, a "polymorphous divinity, linking different mythologies."[39] Hubert's *Divinités gauloises* (1925) included two essays analyzing various Gallo-Roman religious sculptures in terms of the *myths* associated with the deities depicted therein.[40] In these and other works on "old Europe," sometimes Hubert hid a deeper political or ethical purpose. Chapter 9 of the present volume, "Henri Hubert Undoes Aryanist Political Myths," shows how Hubert was also a critic of certain uses of political myths. His books on the Celts and the Germans show him as a mythmaker-historian in the tradition of Michelet, elaborating the liberal French myth of *celtisme* against its autocratic opponents.[41]

Yet, Hubert's theoretical views were neither extensively developed nor widely appreciated by scholars, even potential ethnographers. We can understand why this would have been so when we consider the generational and institutional burdens that weighed on Hubert's scholarly productivity. A man of frail constitution, Hubert died young, having produced no books on myths. Throughout his life, he committed himself to a heavy teaching load at Hautes Études and the École du Louvre, all while maintaining his curatorship of the Museum of National Antiquities in St. Germain-en-Laye. We should also not forget the costs of Hubert's five-year period of military service in World War I. Still, he seems to have left something of an intellectual legacy among his students in Celtic and primitive European studies. George Dumézil carried on some of Hubert's interests in Aryan origins.[42]

For the sake of balance, we ought to note the extent to which Durkheim, Hubert, and Mauss collaborated far beyond what is implied in their joint publications. Mauss may have provoked nothing less than Durkheim's official conversion to the study of religion; Mauss recounted specially designing the first course on religion that Durkheim taught at Bordeaux.[43] From that period, Mauss "worked on everything he [Durkheim] wrote as he also did with me; often he even rewrote entire passages of my work."[44] Of Hubert, Mauss says the same: "I took part in everything which he did which was not strictly criticism or archaeology. He always read over everything I wrote."[45] Unlike the hierarchic relations that prevailed between Durkheim and Mauss, Hubert and Mauss were peers. They were born in the same year (1872) and matched each other in erudition, education, and moral orientation. Mauss reports that when they met,

> H.H. and I identified with each other and shared a period of intellectual exhilaration. Together we discovered the world of the prehistoric and primitive and exotic.... Having established a division of labour in our studies and specialised in order to know these worlds better, we felt somewhat mad. By sheer good sense and hard work, however, I believe we have accomplished our objective. Only with the death of Hubert did the project lapse.[46]

Together, as we know, they also formed part of a socialist circle centered around Lucian Herr at the École Normale Supérieur. (See "Hubert, Religion, and Mythical Politics" in chapter 4 of this volume.) Hubert may well have joined with comrades in all manner of socialist agitation, from street battles during the Dreyfus affair to managing Herr's socialist bookshop across the street from the august Sorbonne. Even today, Hubert and Mauss are conceived as so inseparable that a good-natured caricature circulates in the EPHE of the bicephalous "Monsieur Hubert-et-Mauss"! In the rare cases, however, where this collaboration is recognized, Hubert generally assumes the lesser position. Since the mid- to late 1960s, his works have been republished and various essays anthologized.[47] In addition to the works cited above, chapter 4 of the present volume, "Henri Hubert: Durkheim's Mythologist" tries to fill this gap in our knowledge of Hubert's life and career.

Persistent Themes in the *Équipe*'s Theory of Myth

Taken together, standard Durkheimian fare about the myths found in the "Introduction" and "Conclusion" include six points: (1) Myths are essentially religious, and thus always related to a belief; (2) myth and ritual are paired together, although inconsistently; (3) myth is a "collective representation" and, therefore, always connected to a particular society; (4) myth functions in certain specified ways within a given collectivity; (5) myth possesses a logic of its own and conveys meanings, although not as ordinarily language does; (6) myth can be autonomous, even, at times, from its social foundations. I propose to explore five of these themes (excluding "function") and to add three others that occur in only one part of the *Année*'s statement under consideration but which nonetheless appear prominently in other major theoretical statements about myth issued by Hubert. These additional themes are (1) myth and time; (2) myth and the creative imagination; and (3) myth and thought.

Society, the Sacred, and Myth

In listing the major aims of the "Introduction," Hubert (and, presumably, Mauss) thrice mentions the importance of the religious nature and function of myth. In the course of the "Introduction," they say that they will inquire into the relation of myth to ritual. But, at least the "Conclusion" says much more. There, myth is an "object of belief" and it depicts a "divine world" or the "sacred forces which manifest themselves in the world."[48] Mauss even attacks the great Wilhelm Wundt's theory of myth for "letting one of the essential elements of every myth escape his ken — belief!"[49] In fact, Mauss insists that myths should be defined by their "religious function" — as a "part of religion," as Hubert puts it.[50]

By associating myth with belief, the Durkheimians wed myth to the collectivity. Unlike a dream or nightmare, myth is fixed by social forces.[51] The legends of the saints, wrote Hubert, become myths when they become an object of collective belief.[52] In this connection, Hubert applauds the Roman Catholic modernist Alfred Loisy for interpreting the gospels as mythological. By seeing the gospel stories as myths, Hubert believes that Loisy has made the gospels "more true than history, because it is society which creates it and which needs to believe it."[53] From an overall theoretical viewpoint, then, in defining myths as collectively actualized, Hubert and Mauss situated myth at the center of Durkheim's sociological vision. As Durkheimians, the "study of the sacred" is, they affirm, the "ultimate end of our joint researches."[54] Since the sacred was for the Durkheimians the very key to understanding social reality, and since myths made the sacred explicit, myths gave us access to the nature of a particular society.

Like religion, Hubert also sees myth as indicating "practice" or "performance," not idle fantasies.[55] Thus, in placing myth in the social and religious world, Hubert removes it from the realm of the merely esthetic, literary, or fanciful—from the world of "pure form" and the "play of images," as he says.[56] Religion grounds myth, religious life, and the performance of it.

Society, Myth, Ritual

Put otherwise, by connecting myth to society and religion in this way, Hubert and Mauss *ipso facto* associated myth with ritual. But this association tended to be fraught with controversy as to the relative priority (whether ontological, methodological, or both) of each element. Even the Durkheimians wavered about such priority. We already know how much the Durkheimians felt that ritual made religion. This, however, did not stop them from saying the contrary. In "Individual and Collective Representations" (1898), Durkheim wrote, "once a basic number of representations has been created, they become…partially autonomous realities with their own way of life.…Thus, the luxuriant growth of myths…is not directly related to the particular features of social morphology."[57] Again, the Durkheimians liked to keep their feet on the ground by asserting that flesh-and-blood social realities (like ritual) were primary.[58] Yet, as we have just noted, they also seem to say that myth could be relatively autonomous.[59] To assert, in turn, that myth is autonomous is *ipso facto* to empower myth, to see it as pragmatic. Thus, on several occasions, Hubert declares that myth "has, in itself, a force"; a myth can change the festivals[60]—it accomplishes a "thing in itself, as substantial as that which it is."[61] Thus, despite the Durkheimian reputation for stolid sociologism, for Hubert, at least, myth seems able to cut free from its social substratum.[62]

Perhaps to disguise their difficulties, or perhaps simply out of confusion, Durkheim, Hubert, and Mauss tried to resolve this conflict by converting the question of the priority of myth or ritual from an *a priori* matter, a principle, to an empirical issue. The "Introduction" says "the question [of priority] does not seem to us to admit a general response."[63] Even ten years later, Hubert reiterated this view by declining to "pose the question of the priority of rituals to myths or myths to rituals."[64] Yet at the same time, Hubert also appeared to say the opposite: "Myths are social products; it is in the rituals that society is visible, present or necessarily involved. The mythological imagination dances on the threshing floor trodden by rituals, and it is there that one might grasp it."[65] Perhaps recognizing this conflict within the same passage, Hubert says, "The making of heroes is a mythological process where mythology seems to do without the ritual background. This is not to say, however, that religious practice has not brought something forth."[66] In a way, Hubert's brilliant metaphor serves as a way to explain a relationship the Durkheimians were apparently unable to describe or otherwise clarify: myth "danced" on the floor provided by ritual. One might say the Durkheimians wanted to keep their feet *on* the ground, but not *in* it.

As a result of this ambivalence, at least two traditions have developed from the protean Durkheimian teaching about myth and ritual. Those emphasizing the autonomy of myth tend to treat it by itself, thus generating the subspecialties of cognitive or symbolic anthropologies.[67] This sort of view may also be responsible for the authority some writers in the Durkheimian tradition, like Georges Dumézil, a student of both Mauss and Hubert, assume for speaking of an Indo-European ideology in certain contexts—even when no corresponding social organization existed at the time to supply the reputedly requisite Durkheimian social foundation for it.[68] Ideology has a life of its own. Similarly, Louis Dumont writes of liberating ideology from social morphology, at least tentatively, for the express purpose of giving it the full focus of anthropological attention. In this case, "collective representations" are virtually taken as sufficient objects of study.[69]

Representing the other tradition, that of the ritualist, is the student of Chinese civilization Marcel Granet. Arguing from the specific empirical case of China, Granet said that "the majority of [myths]…are attached to the local cults."[70] They are given "support in the system of worship."⁷¹ Indeed, the colorful Granet relates a historical lesson about the impossibility of detaching myth from its ritualistic basis; when plucked from its source in the life of the people, myth dies.

> The first propagators of Christianity in China, in their apostolic kindliness towards the natives, thought they could see in their legend of the Hou Chi the sign of a pre-revelation favoring the Chinese. Later it was thought that that legend could be brought to the service of the Christian preaching. It was finally appreciated that it was dead and evoked no sentiment of faith. Such was to be the fate of a myth completely saturated with apologetic intent. The ladies and the fairies of popular belief, such as the Weaving Maiden, remain young.⁷²

Thus, Granet seems considerably less convinced than Hubert that myth can "dance" fancy-free above the "floor" of social reality. Yet Hubert would generally find Granet's views quite sympathetic on other grounds, since both men were committed to an essentially *emotional* appreciation of myth. Like Granet, Hubert disdains the rationalist reduction of myth to dogma: "As soon as one wants to give [myth] a rational explanation, it dies out or metamorphoses."⁷³ For Hubert the "unity" of myth is "emotional."⁷⁴ For Granet the links with ritual are more explicit: "religious festivals aroused so much poetic feeling, a powerful effort of mythological creation was carried out."⁷⁵

> Indeed, the only myths from the earliest times whose memory has been preserved are those in which feelings characteristic of the ancient festivals were directly recorded…their conservation is due to the fact that those emotions answering to everlasting ideals…survived.⁷⁶

Here both Granet and Hubert draw upon the Durkheimian appreciation of ritual's power in binding human beings to one another with strong affective ties. One might even speculate on an anticipation of Leenhardt's phenomenology, with its strong emphasis on the concrete data of experience. It too, perhaps, derived from the affection of Mauss for concrete data. Granet draws these strands of myth, ritual, experience, and emotion together:

> How many sacred legends must have emerged from the many and stirring practices of those festivals, the gathering of flowers, the climbing of hills, encounters with springs, stones or divine trees? Sometimes the mythological datum has served as matter for dogmatic speculation, which has reduced its elements to scholastic entities: that is what

happened to *yin* and *yang*, to the rainbow, and to the Yellow Springs. Sometimes the theologians of feudal religion collected the mythic elements... incorporated into a body of official dogmas, quickly stripped of their charm and their emotive power, they fell into oblivion that comes sooner or later to all dogmas.[77]

At the risk of tipping off my conclusion prematurely, one can hardly resist contrasting the views of myths of Granet and Lévi-Strauss, respectively. For Granet, myths die because they lose their emotion punch; for Lévi-Strauss, myths die because they lose distinctive formal configuration as their structure weakens.[78]

Logic, Coherence, and Meaning

But Hubert and Mauss were not much better about deciding matters regarding the meaning, coherence, and logic of myths. Whether this confusion resides in the eye of the beholder or in Hubert and Mauss remains to be seen. Yet, like the myth-ritual relation, their position seemed to oscillate between two opposing poles — one emotional and the other logical. On the side of emotion, myths showed an "apparent illogic."[79] But this did not mean myth formed "an incoherent and absurd world where fancy is mistress."[80] An order exists there, as well, but an "order far from being the one we might expect."[81] Since expectations about order typically involve logic, Hubert dismisses this possibility straightaway: "the unity of the parts of the myth is not logical and might not adequately express itself in rational terms."[82] Without a word of explanation, Hubert says this "unity" is "emotional" or expressive."[83] Maddeningly, Hubert told what sometimes seems an opposing story: "That apparent illogic reveals its own special logic,"[84] a "collective logic and collective psychology."[85] Hubert tells us that myth "has its laws which necessarily rule the succession of causes and effects" — something seemingly at odds with the emotional functions.[86]

Likewise, an equally ambivalent tale is told about the meanings of myths. The "meaning" of myth is "wavering" and "indistinct,"[87] or "vague,"[88] when viewed from one perspective. Yet, considered charitably, this may indicate a rather subtle alternative way of communicating, since myth "suggests meaning and form, rather than designating them";[89] "it is not exactly symbolic, it suggests things, rather than designating them."[90]

Myth is accordingly elusive and protean, something that may account for its being for Hubert and Mauss a precursor to rational thought, rather than a model thereof: "collective representations are developed in myths, just as general ideas, for the individual, are not thought in the absence of concrete images."[91] Image-rich mythology has the power to "replenish" and "nourish thought."[92] Going on, Hubert puts it this way: "the fundamental laws of thought (psychological or logical) are conditioned in the fabrication of myths."[93] But its meanings are "diverse,"[94] even "subconscious."[95] Myth contains more meaning than thought "knows."

Now these apparent contradictions might be explained in one of two ways: either Hubert and Mauss were confused about the cognitive and logical nature of myth, or they were trying to articulate a novel—"mythical"—mode of knowing, however haltingly. If we accept the first alternative, we effectively agree with Lévi-Strauss to denounce talk of affectivity as mystical and obscurantist. Of Lucien Lévy-Bruhl, a philosopher often identified with "mythical" or "mystical" knowledge, he said that,

> French sociology must keep away from an opposite danger [to Malinowski's behaviorism] i.e., to save the rights of rational thinking at the price of accumulating an external mysticism, which shall turn back against rational thought itself.[96]

In this vein, we would join Lévi-Strauss in lamenting how conceptually ill-equipped the Durkheimians seemed in grasping the unique cognitive status of myth. Lévi-Strauss's Freudian-Marxian "super-rationalism"[97] might then be touted as the meta-language that Hubert and Mauss lacked. While they tried to understand the "order" in myths, they could only talk about affectivity. Lacking the sophisticated symbolic analysis afforded by psychoanalysis, with its ideas of unconscious functioning, they could not take the route Lévi-Strauss took. Hubert and Mauss thus had no access to the idea of a fully rational meta-language or unconscious code, nor thus to the peculiar cognitive status of myth that Lévi-Strauss purports to have discovered in Freud.

We can, however, take a radically different route. Hubert and Mauss, and after them Granet and Leenhardt, were trying to articulate a conception of mythical knowledge distinct even from the knowledge described by Lévi-Strauss's "super-rationalism." In Granet, one might imagine this to be qualitative knowledge of things alive and in living connection with our affectivity. In Leenhardt's self-conscious formulations, this emotional-cum-logical quality of myth, this "pensée obscure et confuse" was explicitly called "mythical knowledge."[98] In James Clifford's account of Leenhardt's mythical knowledge, we then would see a plausible version of Hubert's cryptic "emotional unity" more clearly and in updated form.

> Mythic consciousness, according to Leenhardt, grasps complex emotional states through juxtaposed images. Leenhardt has, in effect, "denarrated" the story....He has translated it into an emotional "event" that is a cluster of participations. The ambivalences and ecstasies of passionate love are a bundle of feelings experienced as mythic times. Such ensembles form a language of emotions.[99]

Myth and Time

The final theme of myth and time is almost surely the original work of Hubert. Themes of the duplication of myth and its relation to the eternal occur not only in the "Conclusion" but also in Hubert's "Étude sommaire de la representation du temps dans la religion et la magie" (1905).[100] We should also remember that Durkheim assigned Hubert responsibility for the study of sacred time—a task Hubert faithfully carried out in his publications, subsequent lecture courses on seasonal festivals, and the comparative study of culturally diverse calendrical systems. These include "L'Année germanique" (1904-1905), "Les Grandes fêtes étés saisonnières des nations germaniques" (1905-1906), and "Les Fêtes saisonnières de l'Europe: fêtes d'été" (1909-1910). What, then, was Hubert's view of myth and time?

From one viewpoint, Hubert's assignment to "time" may only reflect this doctoral training in history noted in the previous chapter. Aside from Albert Milhaud, Hubert was the only member of the original *équipe* trained as a historian in the spirit of being a *historien historisant*.[101] As such, he seemed to fulfill Durkheim's expressed wish for a "sociological historian," namely, one who would approach traditional historical questions in light of the new sociology provided by the master.[102] Although Hubert says little in the *Année* about what such a study, when applied to myth, might be, there are clues enough to show what he had in mind. Hubert's works on the Celts, for example, amply show a historian's conservatism in keeping within the cultural limits of the diffusion of myths.¹⁰³ Mauss reinforces this neatly by saying that myth must be seen within "its historical context, in its nature as a social phenomenon, as the product of the life of a people."¹⁰⁴ Together with Mauss, therefore, Hubert exemplified the rather conservative Durkheimian attitude that the cultural and historical—sociological—integrity of myths should be maintained. They preferred not to mix motifs from myths of different historical periods.¹⁰⁵ But, if one were to exceed such limits, then one ought at least do so within the limits established by the comparison of "families" of peoples, like the Indo-Europeans (e.g., Dumézil's Celts). In effect, this review certifies the Durkheimian legitimacy of Dumézil's work, as Mauss makes clear. Dumézil's "general conclusion," Mauss wrote, "is exact and in accord with all that we teach—M. Hubert and I—on this [myth] subject."¹⁰⁶

At a theoretically more venturesome level, Hubert wanted to know how myth could relate extratemporal events through an essentially temporal medium.¹⁰⁷ Myths differ from legends, for instance, because myths concretely convey events and realities which, in principle, are neither fixed in time nor concrete. Myths also create a sense of timelessness and eternity by being what Hubert calls "ceaseless" or "repeatable."¹⁰⁸ They convey a sense of eternity by their incessant rhythm or repetition and say, in effect, that deeds recounted can happen ever anew and again, and that time can be cheated. The ascension of Jesus in the Sicilian festival mentioned by Hubert in the "Conclusion" exemplifies repetition by means of the retelling of those events. The original power of Jesus's ascension thus flows on.

Conclusion: How Durkheimian is Structural Mythology?

This essay offers trifling support for those, like Jean Piaget, Maurice Merleau-Ponty, or Lévi-Strauss himself, who seek substantial links between structuralism and Durkheimian theory. The balance of the evidence fails to support an asserted connection. There are too many fundamental differences between the consensual Durkheimian statement about myth and Lévi-Strauss's brilliant theoretical achievement in creating structural mythology. In fact, the more one compares them, the more Lévi-Strauss shows us how he deviated from key elements of Durkheimian theory of myth. Lévi-Strauss does not give religion or concrete historical societies the prominence they enjoyed in the original Durkheimian circle. Indeed, as Lévi-Strauss tells us, he seeks the "true" structures of things like myths rather than that enshrined in a people's historical and cultural consciousness. Since both religion and the Durkheimian "sacred" were, for Lévi-Strauss, part of consciousness, he tended to discount them. To Lévi-Struss, Mauss made a crucial mistake in *The Gift* by introducing the supernatural notion of the "hau" into his analysis.[109] Likewise, "mana" was not of " l'ordre du réel, mais de l'ordre de la pensée qui...ne pense jamais qu'un objet."[110] What is more, unlike Hubert, Lévi-Strauss seems completely averse to the notion that affectivity has anything to do with myth, perhaps also reflecting his unhappiness with Leenhardt as well?[111] "Mythic knowledge" is for Leenhardt something that combines thought and affectivity. It makes a certain *practical* engagement with the world.[112] It reaches its highest form in the idea of the "*mythe vecu*." Clifford sums this up by saying that

> Leenhardt refused to reduce emotion to physiological impulse, nor would he assimilate its conscious expressive modes to rationality. The heart had its reasons or, perhaps, its rhythms. Its structure of articulation was not, properly speaking, a classification or logic, a metaphysic or theology, but a given experiential landscape.[113]

Was Leenhardt mistaken in maintaining the religious, collective, and affective parts of the Durkheimian approach to myth? My preference for a *performative* theory of myths, one that assumes an active role in political society suggests that Leenhardt will prove to be the more important figure, despite the chic Lévi-Strauss enjoyed until rebellious post-structuralists and post-modernists took over the field. If so, this would urge a reconsideration of the theoretical work of Hubert, Mauss, *and* Durkheim—something already well underway as I write in 2023.

In looking back at the rather irregular, and sometimes conflicted, theoretical consensus of the original Durkheimian *équipe*, we can see how it became the source for many different types of theories of myths: Dumézil's attention to the mythologies of whole families of people, related in movements of historical and cultural diffusion; Leenhardt's religious and emotional appreciation of myth, kept lovingly close to the conscious minds of his people; and finally, Lévi-Strauss's structuralism. Although Lévi-Strauss might have legitimately claimed significant descent from Hubert and Mauss on myth, it would have been hotly disputed and counterproductive. Others had far better claims to that tradition. Indeed, the price of Lévi-Strauss's making structuralism distinctive was severing structural mythology from its Durkheimian antecedents.

Chapter 6

Müller's Legacy, Broken: Malinowski and the Pragmatist Concept and Theory of Myths

Before Theory of Myth, a Concept of Myth

Although we have seen how the Durkheimians developed the notion of myths *acting* by *functioning*, scholars more commonly associate "function" with Bronislaw Malinowski and his pragmatist-functionalist anthropology. More methodologically impressive is Malinowski's method of arriving at a *concept* or *definition* of myth. Unlike Segal, who shies away from *defining* or *conceptualizing* myth, Malinowski does so boldly and deliberately. A functionalist *theory* of myth tells us what a myth *does*, what it *explains*: "Myth fulfills in primitive culture an indispensable function: it expresses, enhances, and codifies belief; it safeguards and enforces morality…"[1] A *concept* or *definition* of myth tells us what a myth *is*, such as Malinowski saying that "we can define myth as a narrative of events which are to the native supernatural…"[2] But Malinowski has far more to say about the identity of the *concept* of a myth. I shall argue that understanding the identity of Malinowski's *concept* of myth requires us to probe more deeply into how he decided what myths are. That, in turn, will show how his *functionalist* theory of myth constitutes an early form of a "performative" concept and theory of myths.

In agreement with Bryan Rennie, I argue that it is logically prior to conceive the word "myth" than to promote a theory of myth. Here, and in chapter 8, we part ways with Robert A. Segal's approach.[3] We simply cannot know what a myth *does*—how myths *explain*—in the absence of declaring what a myth *is*—in the absence of a durable *concept* or *definition* of myth. Without a defensible *concept* of "atom"—at least to begin with—what would "atomic" *theory* explain? Yes, atomic theory *selects for* the concept of "atom," thus affirming the internal relation of concept to theory. But there is much more to atomic theory than merely the identity of the atom. Atomic theory goes further and shows how employing the concept of "atom" can help explain things. In the same way, students of myth need to decide what it is they are looking for when they talk about myths. The move to a *theory of myths* requires additional thinking to show how employing a given concept of "myth" *explains* things. That, in turn, means investigators will need, first to begin by *taking responsibility* for their concept of "myth" before they use that concept of myth in explanations. Robert A. Segal, I think, has confused chronology with logic of explanation.[4] Chronologically, concept and theory coincide. Newtonian physics arrived whole and entire, with both physical theory and critical concepts like mass and energy, in *Principia Mathematica*. But in logic, conceptualization precedes theorization because there can be no explanation without understanding first *what* it is one explains.

Conceptual problems in the study of myth arise, in part, because "myth" is not an English word. Our word, "myth," derives from the Greek "*muthos*" meaning "word" or "story." But in Western scholarly usage, "myth" seldom simply means either of these. Calling something a "myth" has thus marked various *kinds* of referents: beliefs, stories, the sacred, the exotic, points of view, attitudes, dreams, falsehoods, ideologies, etc. "Myth" is also sometimes seen as something *good*. Malinowski implies as much in saying that myth is "a statement of primeval reality which still lives in present-day life,"[5] or "a story moving in the realm of the supernatural, or better, super-normal."[6] Alternately, "myth" is often conceived of as something *bad* — as "false," "irrational," "primitive," etc. But no consensus exists as to which of these valuations is preferable. But even if we limit "myth" to mean "story," what *kind* of story is, or should, a "myth" be? As I shall argue in reference to Segal's attempts to deal with the definition of myth, we need to specify what makes (or *should make*) "myth" the same or different from a "fairy tale," "legend," "fable," or "parable"? As we will see, Segal does this by realizing that it is not enough to define myth as "story," since that term hardly excludes anything. Segal then concludes that myths are "significant" or "weighty" stories.[7] (See "Segal, Saved by Equivocation" in chapter 8.)

With myth viewed affirmatively, for instance, Malinowski's functional *theory* naturally tells us that myth *does* "good." From *Argonauts of the Western Pacific*: "the influence of myth upon this vast landscape, as it colours it, gives it meaning, and transforms it into something live and familiar. What was a mere rock, now becomes a personality; what was a speck on the horizon becomes a beacon...."[8] In a more familiar *functionalist* vein, Malinowski celebrates the fact that "the function of myth, briefly, is to strengthen tradition and endow it with a greater value and prestige."[9]

The first full articulations of Malinowski's concept of myth came early—notably in *Argonauts of the Western Pacific*.[10] Further conceptual statements came later in several minor and major writings: "Ethnology and the Study of Society," "Psychoanalysis and Anthropology," "Obscenity and Myth," *Myth in Primitive Psychology*, "Myth as a Dramatic Development of Dogma," and *The Foundations of Faith and Morals*.[11] These elaborated Malinowski's "functionalist" theory of how "myths" interact with other dimensions of cultural and social life, and in doing so, how they help us explain social life. What exactly, then, does it mean for Malinowski's theory of myth to be "functionalist"?

"Generically Pragmatic" Functional Theory

Malinowski's theory of myth, and indeed his entire anthropology, is "functionalist" in two senses: it is "generically pragmatic" and "behaviorist." In the "*generic* pragmatic" sense, Malinowski's theory of myth is "functionalist" because it considers myths as causal agents within integrated cultural wholes. Ritual, kinship, beliefs, religion, magic, politics, economics, art, music, customs, and so on are some of the other cultural elements *functioning* "generically pragmatically" within integrated socio-cultural wholes. But once Malinowski focuses on human *necessities*, his functionalism turns "pragmatic." It further becomes "behaviorist" once Malinowski singles out observable bodily actions and reactions. Note how in the behaviorist *A Scientific Theory of Culture*, the generically pragmatic language of social *legitimacy* such as "charter" or "warrant" drops out in favor of obsession with needs. As Malinowski says,

> The actions, material arrangements, and means of which are most directly significant and comprehensible are those connected communication with man's organic needs, with the emotions, and with practical methods for satisfying needs.[12]

Malinowski's first statement of what would become his classic "generically pragmatic" functionalist theory of myth came in 1922's *Argonauts of the Western Pacific*, which was rejected by thirty-seven publishers before being accepted for publication![13] Better known, however, is Malinowski's 1926 dedicated statement of a generically pragmatic functionalist theory of myth in *Myth in Primitive Psychology*. In terms of a budding "performative" theory of myths, William Bascom, for one, recognizes how Malinowski's functionalism assigned "myth" sweeping and significant powers to *do* things in culture.[14] This, would not change significantly during Malinowski's lifetime.

> Myth fulfills in primitive culture an indispensable function: it expresses, enhances, and codifies belief; it safeguards and enforces morality; it vouches for the efficiency of ritual and contains practical rules for the guidance of man. Myth is thus a vital ingredient of human civilization; it is not an idle tale, but a hardworking active force; it is not an intellectual explanation or an artistic imagery, but a pragmatic charter affirmative faith and moral wisdom.[15]

A British (Durkheimian) Anthropological Genealogy of Malinowski's Functionalism?

The question of Malinowski's concept of myth becomes the perfect vehicle for sorting through the claims about the provenance of Malinowski's functionalist thinking. The quest for the intellectual sources of Malinowski's "generically pragmatic" functionalism has given rise to considerable speculation. Malinowski's father was a notable folklorist; Malinowski devoted himself to reading Darwin, Durkheim, Hubert, Mauss, Wundt, Nietzsche, Avenarius, Mach, Dilthey, Frazer, Freud, and others. Who, if anyone, holds the key to Malinowski's intellectual formation?

French Anthropologist Alfred Métraux claims that Malinowski's "theoretical work owes a lot to Durkheim" since it "relies on a concept of culture as an ensemble of interlinked institutions of which each plays a necessary role in functioning of the whole."[16] Malinowski had indeed reviewed Durkheim's *Elementary Forms* in a Polish journal in 1913.[17] We also know that Thornton and Skalnik took note of Malinowski's admiration for the work of Durkheim's *Année sociologique* as early as the 1910s.[18] But while Malinowski surveys Durkheim's societist theory of the origins of religion there, he never mentions function or functionalism.[19] Willie Watts Miller, nonetheless, inadvertently makes an indirect case for Durkheim's impact on Malinowski by linking him with two British anthropologists who had been influenced by Durkheim, A. C. Haddon and C. G. Seligman.[20] In his 1908 chapter on "Folk-Tales" in Volume VI of the *Reports of the Cambridge Anthropological Expedition to Torres Straits*, for instance, Haddon echoes Durkheim's notion of the "effervescent" quality of religious life.[21] But British reviewers of Durkheim's *Elementary Forms*, like Haddon, focused their attention on its theory of religion and totemism, not its functionalist theory and method.[22] Nor did Malinowski's mentor, C.G. Seligman, show interest in the integral character of culture characteristic of both Malinowski's (and Durkheim's) *functionalisms*. Raymond Firth explains that Seligman failed to grasp "the complex fabric of ritual and status interrelationships," for instance, in exchange institutions like *kula*.[23] Malinowski too lamented how Seligman could have said much "more about the Kula" and its cultural inter-relations, rather than fixating on its simple "commercial" and "utilitarian" features.[24] Supporting Miller's thesis, in 1922, Malinowski's *Argonauts* often mentions "functions" or "sociological differentiation of functions" but does so without ever citing Durkheim.[25] Nonetheless, in line with Miller's suggestion, "one of [the *Elementary Forms*'] first and most eager English readers" was Malinowski's contemporary, the self-identified Durkheimian "structure-*functionalist*" A. R. Radcliffe-Brown.[26] Unlike Malinowski, Radcliffe-Brown explicitly "seized on É. Durkheim's synchronic, functionalist concerns with integrated social religious systems," often citing Durkheim.[27] We are left, then, with the puzzle of why Malinowski never explicitly linked Durkheim to "function" when, like Radcliffe-Brown, he easily could have done so.

Fertile Ground for Functionalism in England

However dubious the British Durkheimian provenance of Malinowski's functionalism might be, the anthropological scene in Britain in the early 1900s nevertheless provided fertile ground from which Malinowski's functionalism could emerge. Lessons learned from the landmark (1898–1899) Torres Straits Expedition suggest theoretical changes were in the offing. Malinowski notes, for instance, how "ethnographic field work—the research done by trained men of science—inaugurated by the memorable Cambridge Expedition to the South Seas, by Haddon, Ray, Rivers, Seligman and others—has, or ought to have, put once and for all an end to" at least one theoretical school of anthropology, the so-called pursuit of "curio-hunting in ethnology."[28]

In Malinowski's view, "a complete change in method, aim, and scope is demanded by a number of writers because anthropology "is at present going through an acute crisis."[29] Malinowski's methodological remedy for this "crisis"—ethnography—found him well-placed in London, since he rated the "English Ethnographers"—the "Cambridge school with Haddon, Rivers, and Seligman"—as the "best ethnographical writers."[30] The lessons learned by the Torres Straits Expedition seem to have encouraged that complete change in method Malinowski represented. Indeed, the analogous functionalist reorientation of W. J. Perry's Cultural Diffusionism suggests that a broad *functionalist* theoretical revolution was already in the London air by the time Malinowski began writing in the same vein.

All was not sweetness and light among these budding functionalists. Cultural Diffusionists G. Elliot Smith and W. J. Perry regularly competed with Malinowski for available research funding. Essentially devoted to tracing cultural traits' historical paths of transmission, Diffusionism had stirred lively controversies about the origins of civilization across the globe. In the early 1900s, W. J. Perry's *Children of the Sun*, for example, argued for Egypt to be recognized as the single source of transmission of civilization worldwide. In one of Malinowski's earlier publications in English, he reviewed Perry's book, criticizing it for "inaccuracies which, if space would allow, could be easily multiplied from almost every chapter containing anthropological evidence."[31] Malinowski took the opportunity of his review to promote the fieldwork methods and practices that he felt would have saved Perry from error. Malinowski concludes the review, accordingly, by urging "Mr. Perry" to engage more fully in "a deeper sociological analysis and in a closer scrutiny of the evidence."[32]

Interestingly, Perry was already beginning to do precisely as Malinowski had advised. In fact, he had already joined forces with Torres Straits veteran W. H. R. Rivers.[33] Their cooperation resulted in Perry modifying what had once been a solely "historical" endeavor with "psychological interpretations and sociological analysis."[34] To

Malinowski, Perry's gradual theoretical evolution seemed nothing short of an independent anticipation of his own (generically pragmatic) functionalism that came about solely from Perry's collaborations with Rivers. Malinowski was pleased to see that Perry's cooperation with Rivers had induced him, first, to discard the notion of "culture" as "a loose agglomeration of cultural items."[35] Then, most gratifying of all to Malinowski, Perry adopted the principle of "civilisation as an organic whole [and] the necessity of studying every item and aspect of culture in its *functional dependence upon the others*" (emphasis mine).[36] Independently of Malinowski's interventions, then, Perry had moved toward a "generically pragmatic" functionalism of his own under the tutelage of Rivers. Even though Malinowski was not necessarily in the picture at this point, a kind of "generically pragmatic" functionalism thus seemed to be emerging in England on its own. An incidental benefit of Perry's theoretical reorientations for Malinowski seems to have been making British anthropology more hospitable to the brand of functionalism he was about to launch.

Like Perry, Malinowski's functionalism emerged *gradually*. Admitting that his new theoretical orientation had not yet fully formed, Malinowski says in *Argonauts* (1922):

> …it seems to me that a deeper analysis and comparison of the manner in which two aspects of culture *functionally* depend on one another *might afford some interesting material for theoretical reflection*. Indeed, it *seems to me* that there is room for *a new type of theory*.[37]

Phrases like "*might* afford some interesting material for theoretical reflection" and "it *seems to me* that there is room for a new type of theory" do not read like the words of someone in possession of a well-formed theory. Yes, Malinowski hints at functionalism in saying that a "new type of theory" *would* chart "the influence on one another of the various aspects of an institution" — how "two aspects of culture *functionally* depend on one another." His "new type of theory" *would* focus on the interaction of constituent parts of the cultural whole. Further, it *would* resist historical explanation — as Perry had begun to do — and become "the study of the social and psychological mechanism on which the institution is based." But at this stage in the 1920s, Malinowski's functionalism was, as he says, "a type of theoretical studies which has been practised up till now in a tentative way only."[38]

In the absence of robust theoretical options dictated by the Torres Straits Expedition, along with Malinowski's reluctance to embrace Durkheim's functionalism, I suggest that "functionalism" — Perry's, Malinowski's and Radcliffe-Brown's — came gradually to fill the vacuum left by theory-shy, fact-obsessed senior mentors among the Torres Straits veterans. In *Argonauts*'s concluding chapter, Malinowski predicted a future where his theoretical innovations "will come into their own sooner or later."[39] That kind of theory, Malinowski wrote, will be one in which "two aspects of culture functionally depend on one another."[40] In effect, Malinowski was articulating the perspective of what would be his "generically pragmatic" functionalism![41]

In eschewing Durkheimian pedigree, Malinowski, unlike Radcliffe-Brown in his 1922 *The Andaman Islanders*, affirmed his commitment to Durkheim's functionalism.[42] Was Radcliffe-Brown answering an implied plea — by Marcel Mauss in this case — for British anthropologists to fulfill the theoretical potential made probable by the empirical work of the Torres Straits Expedition? In his review of Volume V of the *Reports*, Mauss practically begged the British to seize the theoretical opening called forth by the Torres Straits Expedition. There, Mauss regrettably found Haddon's subsequent attempt at theorizing — at explanation (*"explication"*) — *"un peu simpliste."*[43] Unsurprising for a Durkheimian functionalist, Mauss complained that Haddon failed to show how certain ethnographic facts — *les rites agraires et les rites d'initiation*," for example — might be *related* to one another as functional analyses were meant to do.[44] As one knows, Radcliffe-Brown eagerly took up Durkheimian functionalist theory and used it to provide explanatory coherence in *The Andaman Islanders*. In often-mirrored Durkheimian functionalist passages such as these, Radcliffe-Brown declared in *The Andaman Islanders* that in using

> the term "*social function*" to denote the effects of an institution (custom or belief) in so far as they concern the *society and its solidarity or cohesion*, the hypothesis of this chapter may be more briefly resumed in the statement that the *social function* of the ceremonial customs of the Andaman Islanders is to maintain and to transmit from one generation to another the emotional dispositions o*n which the society (as it is constituted) depends for its existence.*[45]

In his own way, Malinowski's "generically pragmatic" functionalism, too, spoke precisely to the same question of how disparate "facts" cohered together into a whole. But Malinowski did not seem to want to acknowledge a Durkheimian functionalist provenance for that purpose. I have suggested that, as Perry faced the challenge of explaining the mountains of data from the Torres Straits Expedition, Malinowski too may have drawn on other sources of his functionalist theory, even perhaps devising it *de novo*.

The Origins of Malinowski's Functionalism: The Mach Thesis

Someone who knew Malinowski from his Cracow days—Feliks Gross—offers a fresh opinion about the origins of Malinowski's functionalism. It "originates with philosophy, not with Spencer or Durkheim."[46] Andrzej Paluch has also argued that Malinowski's 1908 doctoral dissertation on Ernst Mach and/or Richard Avenarius, the Empiro-Critical positivist philosopher, already evinces "an emphasis on functional explanations."[47] Backing up Gross and Paluch, Robert J. Thornton and Peter Skalnik believe that Malinowski arrived in London already something of a functionalist in his own right.[48]

The precise textual basis for Thornton and Skalnik's argument that Mach informed Malinowski's functionalism is Malinowski's doctoral dissertation, "On the Principle of the Economy of Thought." Thornton believes that Malinowski's functionalism not only reflected Avenarius and Mach but also Malinowski's desire for a "cure for Nietzsche's nausea."[49] The dissertation was then for Thornton and Skalnik a reconciliation of Ernst Mach's "early positivist epistemology" with a Nietzschean "going 'beyond'—beyond the 'data', the given." This Nietzschean determination to transgress the limits of data, Thornton and Skalnik believe, "drove the 'whole system' of Malinowski's early functionalism."[50] But does the dissertation really do as Thornton and Skalnik say?

Malinowski's dissertation assessed the viability of the notion of "economy of thought" specific to Avenarius and Mach.[51] A rigorous exercise in "thought thinking itself," Malinowski explores the assumption that thinking should be "economical" or subject to "good management."[52] According to Mach (and Avenarius, as well), the best kind of thinking uses "the least effort" to reach its conclusions—the "minimum outlay with the same gain, or a maximum gain achieved with the same means."⁵³ What gives this refined excursus into logic interest for anthropology is Malinowski's application of such a principle of logic to understanding "social groups."⁵⁴ In its incarnation as Malinowski's "generically pragmatic" functionalism, the "principle of economy" affected "the relation between things and their mutual interdependence."⁵⁵ In the idiom of such a Machean "generically pragmatic" functional social theory, Malinowski would seek to identify the *minimum functions* "indispensable to the preservation of the individual"⁵⁶ — those, and no more.

Already inspired by Darwin, Malinowski himself had earlier extended the logical principle of "economy" into the biological domain. In what should be familiar to readers of his posthumous 1944 *A Scientific Theory of Culture*, Malinowski continued to appeal to "economy" of thought, declaring,

> Function means, therefore, always the satisfaction of a need, from the simplest act of eating to the sacramental performance in which the taking of the communion is related to a whole system of beliefs determined by a cultural necessity to be at one with the living God.⁵⁷

Darwin's notion of "struggle for survival" — his concern for the *minimum* requirements for survival of a species — fits congenially with Malinowski's possibly Machean principle of the *minimum* requirements for successful thinking laid out in his PhD.

In this way, Malinowski might have already articulated his own version of functionalism *before* both exposure to Durkheim and *before* coming to London. But did he? Being "home-gown" would explain why his fully functionalist perspective on culture and society emerges *gradually*, as Perry's had. The Machean legacy also might explain Malinowski's failure to credit Durkheim for the functionalism appearing in early works like *Argonauts*. Malinowski didn't need to behave like Radcliffe-Brown, the vocal Durkheimian enthusiast. Their very different intellectual formations meant they could not (or would not) declare common origins for their respective functionalisms. What nascent Durkheimian functionalism percolated among the veterans of the Torres Straits Expedition would only have *confirmed* for Malinowski the "new type of theory," spelled out during his early London years.⁵⁸ Both the Torres Straits veterans and Perry had moved toward conceiving "civilisation as an organic whole…[and] studying every item and aspect of culture in its *functional dependence upon the others.*"⁵⁹ One could hardly imagine a more hospitable environment in which Malinowski's originally Polish functionalism might mature. Therefore, Thornton and Skalnik's account of the Machean-Darwinian basis of Malinowski's functionalism seems to tell a significant portion of the story of the origins of Malinowski's functionalism. I shall return to of Malinowski's engagement in Mach's philosophy shortly but want to note the way Mach may have *specifically* influenced Malinowski's theory of myth.

Are Malinowski's Concept and Theory of Myth Nietzschean?

A Machean reading of Malinowski's functionalist theory would suggest that myths provide society something "vital" and "indispensable" — what a society *needs*.⁶⁰ Myth thus functions as a "hardworked active force," covering the "whole pragmatic reaction of man towards disease and death" and expressing "his emotions, his forebodings."⁶¹ As suggested by Mach and seconded by Darwin, Malinowski regarded myth as serving our basic *biological* needs.⁶² Malinowski's theory of myth, in effect, plausibly realizes an application of his dissertation's Machean concern for the *minimum* requirements for survival of our species.

Thornton, however, wants to say more — that Malinowski's theory of myth owes critical debts to Nietzsche. Thornton and Skalnik have not, however, made a persuasive case. Indeed, to say that Malinowski's theory of myth derives from Nietzsche's *The Birth of Tragedy Out of the Spirit of Music* seems rather baffling. Neither Nietzsche's *Birth of Tragedy* nor Malinowski's 1911 essay on it square very well with Malinowski's functional *theory* of myth. Ironically, this is so even when their *concepts* of myth roughly agree.⁶³ Here, again, is Malinowski's account of what myth *does*:

> Myth fulfills in primitive culture an *indispensable* function: it expresses, enhances, and codifies belief; it *safeguards and enforces* morality; it *vouches* for the efficiency of ritual and contains *practical* rules for the guidance of man. Myth is thus a *vital ingredient* of human civilization; it is not an idle tale, but a *hardworking active force*; it is not an intellectual explanation or an artistic imagery, but a *pragmatic charter affirmative faith and moral wisdom.*⁶⁴

Given its aphoristic character, *Birth of Tragedy* at times hints at general functionalist notions, but it does little more.

Part of the problem of determining precisely what Thornton and Skalnik argue is their confusion of what Nietzsche announces as the identity of his *concept* of myth with a *theory* of myth—what he thinks that myth *does*. As far as Nietzsche offering a *theory* of myth, some of Nietzsche's words do admittedly recall Malinowski's functionalist theory, such as the following phrases from *The Birth of Tragedy* that address what myth *does* (my emphases throughout):

> "The satyr...lives in a reality...*sanctioned* by myth and culture."[65]
> "Without myth, ...culture *forfeits its healthy creative natural power*: only a horizon reorganized through myth *completes the unity* of an entire cultural movement."[66]
> "And does the myth show us this life in order *to transfigure it* for us?"[67]
> "Myth, first of all *immerses* [us]...in a mystical atmosphere..."[68]
> "...Myth is the *shaping* of the past..."[69]

Whatever these enigmatic utterances meant to Malinowski, Nietzsche apparently saw myth as active—"performative"—just as Malinowski does. Myths "do" some sanctioning, founding, rescuing, transfiguring, and unifying of social formations—all views Malinowski might well have imported into his functionalist theory.

Yet, stunningly, Malinowski omits mentioning those or similar passages to support his functionalist *theory* of myth in his essay on *Birth of Tragedy*! Instead, without a single reference to Nietzsche's work or, for that matter, to functionalism, Malinowski labors over specifying the details of Nietzsche's *concept* of myth.

> "For myth must be vividly felt as *a single instance of universality and truth staring into the infinite*."[70]
> "a *symbolic picture*."[71]
> Something "*inherently mysterious*."[72]

Malinowski's essay on *Birth of Tragedy* leaves one puzzled about how much Nietzsche's views really contributed to "functionalist" theory of myth. Michael Young seems likewise unimpressed but thinks that both Malinowski and Nietzsche did share some part of what I call a *concept* of what myth *is*: "'a form of apprehension' and 'a concept of reality'" and, at the same time some scattered elements of a *theory* of myth—what it *does*. This "'consists in seeing a justification for the moral order of the world in the past,'" says Young.[73] However, Young also concludes—as do I—that key notions of

Malinowski's functional theory of myth—"myth as charter"—have yet to take form.[74] Nor do we find those elements of Machean philosophy there either.

While Malinowski shows himself to be the picture of a "generic" Nietzschean, it is less clear that Nietzsche specifically informed Malinowski's theory of myth. In his *Diary*, Malinowski makes just two mentions of Nietzsche, which hardly indicates serious intellectual indebtedness.[75] There, Malinowski quotes one of Nietzsche's aphorisms, then playfully likens himself to Nietzsche over against Stanisłas "Staś" Witkiewicz as Wagner. Leach notes how, as just this kind of "generic" Nietzschean, Malinowski fashioned for himself "a cult of the outrageous...by challenging English sexual morality."[76] Feliks Gross affirms Malinowski's association with "bad-boy" elements of his Cracow-based Young Poland generation. Gross mentions "Boy Zelenski, a kind of Polish Voltaire, popular among liberals for opposing the influence of the Church..." Gross also writes of Malinowski "mountain climbing in the Tatra Mountains" and such—all the stuff of a generic *avant-garde* Nietzscheism.[77] We are then left with the unremarkable claim that Nietzsche was "in the air" in the modernist Habsburgian Cracow of Malinowski's Young Poland. Therefore, Malinowski's essay on *Birth of Tragedy* establishes little about the Nietzschean provenance of Malinowski's functionalist theory of myth. At most, says Michael Young, Malinowski's essay on *Birth of Tragedy* reveals a young man's "unfinished prose-poem rather than a polished philosophical treatise."[78]

Marcel Mauss and Anti-Utilitarianism

Eventually, Malinowski's "generically pragmatic" functionalism became emphatically *biologistic*, *behaviorist*, and *utilitarian*, as if abiding by what Leach calls the maxim that "all behaviour must have a practical end."[79] Whether Nietzschean or not, Malinowski's early distaste for such crude utilitarianism famously emerged in his study of Trobriand economic life, especially the *kula*—a major Trobriand system of gift exchange. Whether this should recall "Nietzsche's scattered, caustic remarks on utilitarianism" that "pervade his philosophical corpus and tend to be sweepingly critical" or perhaps Wilhelm Wundt's cannot be determined from available sources.[80]

It should be noted that Wundt's *Die Ethik* (1886) and its successor, *Die Nationen und ihre Philosophie* (1915) do introduce critiques of utilitarianism. Among other things, Wundt kept *Die Ethik*'s polemic against utilitarianism alive for the next thirty years through the publication of *Die Nationen*. There, Wundt unleashed an attack on the "shallowness" of British ethical theories, especially their "egoistical utilitarianism," "materialism," and "pragmatism," strikingly reminiscent of Malinowski's views in *Argonauts*.[81] There, Malinowski embraced Marcel Mauss's analysis of the *kula*.[82] Whatever the source, Malinowski made much of how the Trobrianders alternated between being normally instrumental or utilitarian but in the *kula*, they are quite contrary to utilitarian values.

Utilitarian values became so repugnant to the early Malinowski that he excludes them even from straightforward *economic* exchanges. The Trobriander, Malinowski affirms, "works toward aims which are certainly not directed towards the satisfaction of present wants, or to the direct achievement of utilitarian purposes."[83] *Kula* may lay a foundation of comity and trust that facilitates successful, hard-nosed, practical economic wheeling and dealing. But *kula* is not typical utilitarian bartering. But, in itself, Malinowski notes that *kula* is "pragmatically useless."[84] Such an observation seemed so critical to the Malinowski of *Argonauts* that he devoted no fewer than three chapters—2, 3, and 6—to discussing *kula*. Malinowski seems delighted to declare that utility is simply not sovereign in the *kula* nor in many other performances of Trobriand life:

> I hope that whatever the meaning of the Kula might be for Ethnology the meaning of the *Kula* will be instrumental to dispel the crude, rationalistic conceptions of primitive mankind ... Indeed, the *Kula* shows us that the whole conception of primitive value has to be revised in the light of our institution.[85]

Some of the more important ethnological thinkers of Malinowski's day, including Mauss, were so impressed by these insights that they informed their own works of lasting significance. Mauss's *The Gift* cites Malinowski's discussion of *kula* nearly forty times despite being less than 200 pages long.[86] Says Mauss, "We... add our own repeated observations to those of Malinowski, who has devoted an entire study to "exploding" current doctrines concerning "primitive" economy."[87] Mauss might just as well have said the same about Malinowski's early conception of functionalism and his theory of myth.

Radcliffe-Brown, Malinowski, and a Pragmatic Functionalist Theory of Myth

If "generically pragmatic" functionalism conceived myth as part of an integrated culture, Malinowski's "behaviorist" functionalism elevated cultural integration to crisis levels of raw utility and biological "needs."[88] Otherwise, Malinowski's functionalism hardly differed from that of Alfred Radcliffe-Brown (1881–1955).[89] While Malinowski wanted to claim a common theoretical orientation, Radcliffe-Brown vehemently rejected this notion:

> This Functional School does not really exist; it is a myth invented by Professor Malinowski. He has explained how, to quote his own words, "the magnificent title of the Functional School of Anthropology has been bestowed by myself, in a way on myself, and to a large extent out my own sense of irresponsibility." Professor Malinowski's irresponsibility has had unfortunate results since it has spread over anthropology a dense fog of discussion about "functionalism."[90]

Radcliffe-Brown went on to conclude dogmatically, "I do not think that there is any sense, other than the purely chronological one, in which I can be said to be…the predecessor of Professor Malinowski. The statement that I am a 'functionalist' would seem to me to convey no definite meaning."[91]

The two functionalisms do not always agree.[92] Malinowski subordinated *sociological* functionalism to psychology, psychoanalysis, and biology; Radcliffe-Brown maintained loyalty to Durkheim's generically pragmatic sociological functionalism. Malinowski felt that Radcliffe-Brown ignored the "individual" — what Malinowski called a regrettable "legacy of Durkheimism."[93] Influenced as Malinowski was by the psychological and biological sciences, he believed that Durkheimian thought "was marred by certain metaphysical preconceptions and, above all, by the complete rejection not merely of introspective psychological speculations, but also of any reference to the biological basis of human behavior."[94] Polish historian Mariola Flis describes this divergence as one in which Malinowski believed that "the function of culture as a whole was 'the preservation of species'"; Radcliffe-Brown instead saw culture's purpose as "to unite individual human beings into more or less stable social structures."[95] Although appeals to biology fluctuate throughout Malinowski's career, his 1922 essay "Ethnology and the Study of Society" still waxes romantically of the "zest for life."[96] Yet, in the same work, a materialist Malinowski assures us that "every item of culture" has a "positive, biological significance."[97] I prefer to describe this divergence in simpler terms as one between the two kinds of functionalism I have already described—the "generic" functionalism of Durkheim, early Malinowski and Radcliffe-Brown over against the focused "pragmatic" functionalism of the mature Malinowski.

In the end, Malinowski's behaviorism and biologism determine the final iteration of his conception of functionalism, animating the arguments of his final book, *A Scientific Theory of Culture*.[98] A work of "crude reductionism," in the view of Robert Thornton, there Malinowski drops the "participant" half of his earlier method of "participant observation."[99] Empathy is dismissed as a method of investigation "always dangerous to use" since it usually amounts to guessing as to what the other person might have thought or felt."[100] Having thus dismissed empathy and understanding, Malinowski fixes on what is now his "fundamental principle of" field-work—the same as that of "experimental psychology" and "the behaviorist"—"observations of overt behavior."[101] Having begun his intellectual journey as a kind of rationalist and something of a romantic, Malinowski ends as a materialist and a positivist.

Malinowski's "pragmatic" functionalism inevitably shapes his theory of myth—a *practical* tool functioning to enhance real flesh-and-blood human survival. Even "the use of symbolism is an instrumental enhancement of human anatomy and refers directly or indirectly to the satisfaction of a bodily need."[102] Tracking how a myth works, says Malinowski, "allows us to determine the pragmatic context of a symbol and to prove that in cultural reality a verbal or other symbolic act becomes real only *through the effect which it produces*."[103] Chief among those "effects" is myth's role in "the satisfaction of *needs*," especially as these are specified as 'the *biological* or *basic needs*' of people and their cultures."[104]

Malinowski's later pragmatic theory of myth contrasts with the viewpoint of a "generically pragmatic" functionalism, where "a proper understanding of myths can only be obtained by studying them in relation to the practice, belief and ritual of the people among whom they are current."[105] Under the new "pragmatic" regime, myth becomes "indispensable" and "vital"—something a society *needs*—without which people cannot materially persist.[106] Myth, therefore, covers the "whole pragmatic reaction of man towards disease and death"; it expresses "his emotions, his forebodings." As such, Malinowski links myth practically to our basic biological needs.[107] Myth fulfilled functions that are absolutely indispensable for cultural survival.[108] Acting through myths, our innate biological will to survival impels us to deny the reality of death. Myths of immortality emerge, exploiting this biologically driven instinct. They generate — by biological reflex alone — both the *belief* in immortality and the concomitant religious *experiences* that confirm this belief.[109]

In this new mood of existential crisis, a form of intellectual terror seizes Malinowski. Cultures are vulnerable to sudden disintegration if so much as a single constituent element should fail. Every institution in culture serves a vital, "instrumental," and thus useful or pragmatic purpose. After years of dodging frank admissions of his personal beliefs, in his 1931 Riddell Lectures, Malinowski bears his (rather condescending) materialist soul, confessing that, as a "rationalist and agnostic," he "must admit that even if he himself cannot accept these truths [of religion], he must at least admit them as indispensable pragmatic figments without which civilization cannot exist."[110] Myth, religion, ritual and such are for the little people. They constitute "the embodiment of the *sublime folly* of hope, which has yet the best school of man's character!"[111] The enlightened elites — among whom Malinowski numbered himself — alone have the courage and honesty to face the abyss of existential nullity.

The Puzzle of Frazer as Malinowski's "Second Father"

Tracking down all the intellectual influences behind the thoughts of such a catholic thinker as Malinowski would be a hopeless task. Let me comment briefly upon some of the more important ones. I begin with James George Frazer, since Malinowski confessed that he decided upon a career in anthropology because of Frazer's *Golden Bough*. I question how much truth there is in this claim. I start with Malinowski's recalling a pivotal moment in his youth, around the time he was doing his PhD in philosophy. "Imagine," he says,

> a student leaving the medieval college buildings, obviously in some distress of mind, hugging, however, under his arm, as the only solace of his troubles three green volumes with the well-known golden imprint,

> a beautiful, conventionalized design of mistletoe—the symbol of *The Golden Bough*...
>
> For no sooner had I begun to read this great work, than I became immersed in it and enslaved by it. I realized then that anthropology, as presented by Sir James Frazer, is a great science, worthy of as much devotion as any of her elder and more exact sister studies, and I became bound to the service of Frazerian anthropology...[112]

But how do we know that Malinowski launched his anthropological avocation then, there, and because of Frazer? Thanks to Robert J. Thornton and Peter Skalnik, some of these questions can be answered. They have identified five of Malinowski's earliest writings, composed between 1910 and 1914, where he does engage Frazer.[113] These deal with such subjects as *The Golden Bough*, magic, religion, kinship, totemism, and social organization. Some celebrate Frazer's contributions to anthropology while others take issue with them; likewise, Malinowski was no sycophantic devotee of Frazer. Later, in 1922, Frazer wrote the Preface for *Argonauts*, which would cast Malinowski as both controversial and original. A few years later, in 1925, Malinowski followed up by dedicating his classic theoretical functionalist statement on myth to Frazer in "Myth in Primitive Psychology."[114] So, it seems we should take Malinowski's endearing tale of appreciation for Frazer at face value—up to a point, at least.

The early writings show that Malinowski picked up Frazerian themes, but also that he played his own variations upon them. Frazer would discourse on magic, science or religion, and Malinowski would, in general, systematically dismantle him. In the most extensive of these writings, Malinowski authored a three-part series of articles, "Totemism and Exogamy." Originally published in 1910 in the Polish journal *Lud* (*People*), Malinowski had apparently written the essays abroad but submitted them while visiting Cracow from the London School of Economics (LSE).[115] Occasioned by the publication of Frazer's four-volume work, *Totemism and Exogamy*, Malinowski's articles engaged Frazer's book on a vast variety of topics: magic, religion, science, the "primitive thought," social organization, exogamy, totemism, theory, and method. These essays give the impression of an apprentice Malinowski honing the analytical tools of the craft he sought to master on the sharpening stone of Frazer's penchant for repeated overreach and flat-out error. Thus, Malinowski declares firmly "the theories set forth by Professor

Frazer in the present work cannot stand up to serious criticism."[116] This judgment was informed by Malinowski's year in London with his teacher, C. G. Seligman.

Much the same distance separates the theories of Frazer from what Malinowski learned doing fieldwork in the Trobriand Islands of New Guinea from 1914 to 1918. Edmund Leach noted the discrepancy between Frazer and Malinowski's discussions of how tribal folk regarded the dead, for example. "Savages are afraid of the dead," wrote Frazer, because "savages have childlike imaginations."[117] By contrast, Malinowski's account of the *baloma* ritual for the dead contradicts Frazer. "Malinowski showed that 'In the Trobriands, in Melanesia, every village holds a month-long harvest festival (*milamala*) during which the spirits of deceased ancestors (*baloma*) are supposed to return to their erstwhile homes.'"[118] But, Malinowski added, "The *baloma*, during their stay never frighten the natives, and there is not the slightest uneasiness felt about them."[119]

Malinowski also charged Frazer with other errors, such as in classifying "totemism."[120] Contrary to Frazer, totemism is not "primitive," nor can social organization related to it be derived from totemic beliefs.[121] Malinowski effects nothing short of a damnation of Frazer's scientific pretentions:

> the author in fact has done nothing to facilitate our orientation with a clear and concise look at the facts...If we view the task of science to be the close and succinct description and comprehension of the facts...Frazer's work, which does none of this, is not, in the proper sense of the word, a scientific work.[122]

In sum, Malinowski and Frazer were generations apart in body and mind. By Malinowski's time, as Edmund Leach observed, Frazer's "capacities were reduced to those of a voraciously diligent library mole."[123] Until Frazer himself died in 1944,

> he simply went on repeating himself over and over again on an ever-larger scale, adding nothing of significance in the process. Serious social anthropologists can still read [Smith's] *Religion of the Semites* with great advantage. Frazer's works may be examined for their bibliographies; otherwise, they accumulate dust.[124]

Frazer apparently did not even understand Malinowski's "generically pragmatically pragmatic" functional theory of myth, even though Malinowski lavishly credited him for it. In a letter written to Malinowski in 1926, Frazer thanked Malinowski for two pieces on myth that Malinowski would publish. Imagine the horror when Malinowski read in Frazer's letter that "I confess that I have been in the habit of regarding myths as explanations and am not sure that I follow your reasons for rejecting this view…"[125] So much then for the "myth" of the Frazerian roots of Malinowski's theory of myth.

Leach also argues that Malinowski's appreciation of the interrelation of, say, myth and ritual, was far more complex and demanding than Frazer imagined. For one thing, Malinowski insisted upon first-hand participant observation and fieldwork as the *default* method of discovering the real workings of a culture or society. Historical data were useful if one could rely on the veracity of the sources. But imaginative historical *constructions* made it all too easy for "armchair" or "museum" anthropologists like Frazer to speculate without accountability. These historical constructions were, in effect, mere conjectures, however stimulating they may be as literary inventions. In *The Golden Bough*, notably, Frazer assumed that because a myth *described* the annual ritual murder of the king at Nemi, such a ritual must have been performed as described in the myth. But to Malinowski, Frazer was simply resorting to short cuts by inferring a rite from myth or myth from rite. Frazer simply lacked direct or indirect observational evidence for the existence of this rite. Direct observation of this ritual murder in present times was, of course, impossible, since Frazer's myth of the ritual murder dated from Roman times. But Frazer did not even supply contemporary historical reports of such a ritual. For him, it was axiomatic that one could read the existence of the rite from the myth—an assumption in which, Leach flatly concludes that Frazer "was quite fundamentally in error."[126] Perhaps best characterizing Malinowski's true feelings about Frazerian anthropology is the judgment of Thornton and Skalnik that "what Malinowski learned from Frazer was *how not to do anthropology.*"[127]

Malinowski and Freud

When we press further for the sources of Malinowski's intellectual formation we also run directly into the troubled relationship with a prominent student of myths living under the same roof: his folklorist father. Why did Malinowski strain to claim Frazer as an intellectual father, when his father already supplied a fine model of an ethnographer collecting and studying narratives "among the natives," so to speak? One reason may have been Malinowski's estrangement from the man, who he saw as "pompous, wooden, tactless."[128] Exacerbating matters, Malinowski took his mother's side in parental disputes. Their emotional bond was so strong that Malinowski and his mother would even vacation together well into his thirties.[129]

The aggravated tensions between father and son suggest a nearly classic case ready-made for the application of Freudian analysis.[130] The Oedipal-like difficulties with his father may help us understand why Malinowski found the Viennese culture rebel a source of insight into his own psyche. What matters here are the Freudian ideas that may have found their way into Malinowski's general view of human nature and his theory of myth.[131] As Malinowski explains in "Psychoanalysis and Anthropology" (1923), he admired Freud for trafficking in anthropological literature in order to support the cross-cultural validity of his theories. Some of these conclusions, Malinowski praises, such as

> the first concrete theory about the relation between instinctive life and social institutions. His doctrine of repression due to social influence allows us to explain certain types of latent wishes or "complexes" found in folklore, by reference to the organization of a given society. Inversely it allows us also to trace the patterns on instinctive and emotional tendencies in the texture of the social fabric.[132]

Besides the therapeutic implications for someone struggling with parental issues, Freud's engagement in anthropological literature posed problems for Malinowski as a budding anthropologist. Freud's idea of a cultural universal, implied in his Oedipal theory, challenged Malinowski to consider problems in the sociology of the family.

> The sociological implications of this theory indicate that throughout the development of humanity there must have existed the institution of individual family and marriage, with the father as a severe, nay, ferocious patriarch, and with the mother representing the principles of affection and kindness.[133]

Malinowski argued that his empirical field studies afforded him advantages over the "hypothetical" thinking of Freud about the sociology of the family. The ethnographer theorizes from the superior position of "actual observation among present-day savages."[134] Oedipal theory, for instance, affirmed a universal patriarchal family structure in which a male child's fear of his own father, and subsequent desire to possess his own mother, caused the young male to desire the father's demise. But Malinowski countered Freud by arguing that patriarchy was not a human universal. Matriarchal families also existed in many places. In them, the mother's brother — not the biological father — assumes the role of principal male authority. Malinowski shows that the mother's brother enforces matriarchal family rules for the matriarch. With the birth father's family authority lost, he takes the side, instead, of his own children in disputes with their maternal uncle.

Freud's imaginative interpretations of myths also left indelible marks on Malinowski. In the Trobriand myths, for instance, indigenous stories often related "conflicts and aggressions that occur between members of the matrilineage — between brothers, between sisters, between grandmother and granddaughter, and between nephew and maternal uncle."[135] But once the Freudian worm of doubt made its way into Malinowski's mind, stories could no longer pass at face value. Were the myths *actual* accounts of events that occurred in reality, or did they perhaps *function* as expressions of *wishes* or fears, whether conscious or unconscious? Freud may then have offered Malinowski a model for interpreting myths *functionally*, rather than as literal explanations. Folklorist William Bascom believes that Freudian interpretation of myths may have induced Malinowski to see expressions of the "conflicts and aggressions [that] appear in myths" as "letting off steam" and thus *functioning* "to maintain the unity of the matrilineage."[136] In Malinowski's hands, myths, then, *function* in an expectedly Freudian way of reflecting the internal, but suppressed, conflicts plaguing any social order. They function as a "psychological escape from the repressions imposed by society, and not just from repressed sexual desires."[137] In providing a conduit for expressing these conflicts out of public sight, they effectively function to tamp down aggressions that might erupt in society and threaten social order.[138]

"Geisteswissenschaften" and Malinowski's Break with Mach

In following the arc of Malinowski's thought, we know he esteemed functionalism from the time of his PhD on Mach. But in what kind of "*science*" of anthropology did this eventuate? Was it a neo-positivist or radical empiricist science, such as that concocted by Ernst Mach's "second positivism" or Richard Avenarius's "empiro-criticism," both of which were mediated through the Polish philosophers Straszewski and Pawlicki?[139] Was it, perhaps, a more modest garden-variety "empiricist" science informed by a naïve belief in neutral fact-gathering and inductive methods of reasoning, like today's mainline quantitative political science or sociology? Or was it, as I shall argue, some kind of uneasy attempt to accommodate both empiricist and rationalist notions of *concept-formation* in science, as Malinowski's Freudianism might hint at? Determining the identity of Malinowski's *concept* of science bears directly on how his notion of "concept-formation." In particular, how did he decide to *conceive* myth? Did the identity of myth come "with its name written on it," so to speak? Or did the subjectivity of the scientist determine how myth was to be *conceived*, and if so, how did that element of subjectivity square with the putative objectivity of science?

Let us begin with Mach and his positivism. First, we already know how Mach's theoretical notions informed Malinowski's doctoral dissertation. Second, it also seems that Malinowski's functionalism owes a great deal to Mach, as well. Despite Malinowski's high regard for Mach, *as evident in his PhD thesis, "On the Principle of the Economy of Thought,"* I shall, nevertheless, argue that Malinowski gradually moves away from Machean positivism as his career matures.[140] On the one side, Malinowski at first celebrated Mach's "emphasis on the biological aspect in examining mental life and its manifestations."[141] Malinowski agreed with Mach that, "Physiology...will reveal to us the true real elements of the world."[142] Thornton adds that as early as the "Entries in Malinowski's diary," Malinowski embraced the "biologization of the philosophical terms that come, surprisingly, from his readings of both Nietzsche and Mach."[143]

On the other hand, however, Malinowski's loyalty to Machean ideas does not endure. For one, Malinowski objects to Mach's materialist monism because it "does not explain the purpose and the phenomena of science by means of laws of psychological processes, but rather by means of purely biological data."[144] Machean monism, thus, gives way to an ambiguous mind/body dualism. Malinowski had understood that Mach's monism owed much to "Darwin's influence," perhaps especially its *functionalist* character. In Mach's view, Darwin, conceived of the human species as an organism struggling with nature and with other individuals. All of the functions of this organism can be conceived teleologically as the tools best suited to this struggle. The next step leads us to coordinate our thought imagination, and memory with these other functions.[145]

But Malinowski finally rebelled against Mach's dependence on Darwin, leading Malinowski to set out on his own course. In particular, Malinowski came "across a flaw somewhat offensive to us."[146] This flaw Malinowski identified as the "simple inference from the domain of biology to psychology, *Gedanken sind die Äusserungen des organischen Lebens* ['thoughts are the externalizations of organic life']."[147] Giving voice to his dualism, Malinowski explains "that... we may not transfer Darwin's principles" to the psychological or mental domain "in any other way but figuratively."[148] That is to say that while Mach's materialist monism may look good in the abstract, it did not in real life: "The most we can do here is to make an analogy capable of stimulating us and leading us onto new discoveries."[149] The reason Malinowski permits only "a figurative metaphor" rather "than a strict empirical designation" is because he believes that our "thoughts are not made of plastic and reality is not a form which can be stamped onto them."[150] Psychology apparently stands on its own in Malinowski's dualist view of human nature. Therefore, Machean monism fails because "Mach does not give the psychological definition of the process of adaptation."[151] In effect, Malinowski rejects Mach's "monism" because it betrays itself as an "absolutism," a "dogmatism," and thus fails as *science*.[152]

What lies behind this judgment on Machean monism (and positivism)? Perhaps a testimony to Freud's enduring impact on Malinowski, he seems to reject Mach's positivist conception of science because it leaves little or no room for interpretation by the knowing subject. Paluch, as well, confirms that "Malinowski diverges from the positivist programme," and eventually "represents a standpoint opposed to" positivism.[153] From the positivist and monist pole, Malinowski thus bounces to the humanism and dualism of the so-called *Geisteswissenschaften*. As indicated in *Argonauts*, interpretation or hermeneutics have moved to the center of Malinowski's concept of science.[154] That, in turn, invites contemplating the mark left on Malinowski by Wilhelm Dilthey's *neuromantik* humanistic sciences — *Geisteswissenschaften* — perhaps dating from Malinowski's studies with Wilhelm Wundt in Leipzig in 1908 to 1909.[155] Malinowski's methods of participant observation as touted in *Argonauts* are too close to Dilthey's method of empathetic understanding (*Verstehen*) and lived experience (*Erlebnis*) to be accidental.[156] Put positively, Malinowski, at least early in his career, showed what I would call "new romantic" tendencies.

Malinowski: Conflicted Empiricist and Reluctant Rationalist

But, if Malinowski is no longer a positivist, what of the commonplace view of his scientific orientation as classically *empiricist* — especially in terms of *concept-formation* in the study of myth? Taking an empiricist approach to concept-formation in the study of myth would mean a number of things. For one, Malinowski's emphasis on studying anthropological subjects *in situ* with rigorous fieldwork methods of data collection becomes salient. An empiricist in the field collects as many data — myths, in this case — as possible. Thus, Malinowski charges ethnographers with the task of providing an exhaustive objective report of the facts of a culture — "giving a complete survey of the phenomena and not of picking out the sensational, the singular, still less the funny and quaint."[157] Once this collection is assembled, the empiricist *inductively* sorts through and determines what the myths have in common. *Empirically* speaking, certain "themes" may occur most often — e.g., stories of gods or heroes. The preponderance of the data then speaks for itself. If most of the stories that one gathers, say, turn out to be stories of the gods, that feature *ipso facto* becomes the defining criterion of the *concept* of myth — what a myth *is*. Neutral facts first, then concepts, or so the empiricist story goes. To do otherwise would be to commit the cardinal sin against empiricist method — to be subject to "preconceived ideas," making the ethnographer's work "worthless."[158]

In reading contemporaneous reviews of Malinowski's early work, however, it is interesting to note that Malinowski's reputation as a consistent empiricist raised suspicions from the start. These misgivings arose as early as 1927, even though few were willing to challenge Malinowski's empiricist self-promotion directly. One exception came in a review of *Myth in Primitive Psychology* by British anthropologist Jack H. Driberg. He remained decidedly unconvinced of Malinowski's empiricist credentials, writing,

> Dr. Malinowski states that he serves up no theories of his own but deals only in plain facts: whereas in the essay itself we find such sentences

as: "This is perhaps the most important point of the thesis which I am urging"; or again... "I have now completed the survey of facts and range of conclusions. I have tried to show..."[159]

Driberg spotted a telling inconsistency in Malinowski's rendition and execution of his allegedly empiricist methods of inquiry. In truth, he felt that Malinowski was less consistent an empiricist than he made out.[160] Like a proper empiricist, Malinowski would indeed tout the *scientific* nature of his efforts in *Argonauts* by affirming the need for the "completeness and minuteness" of ethnographic surveys.[161] Yet, after having done so, he contradicted empiricist principles by affirming the role of active subjectivity—*selecting which data* are "relevant" and which data dictate the "course" of inquiry. Says Malinowski,

> ...the scientifically-trained mind will push the inquiry along really relevant lines, and toward aims possessing real importance. Indeed, the object of scientific training is to provide the empirical investigator with a *mental chart* in accordance with which he can take his bearings in lay his course.[162]

But by affirming the role of the active, knowing subject, Malinowski strayed from empiricist method. He, in effect, admits that the data themselves do not announce their own relevance and direction. The investigator must take responsibility for their concepts. Leach, among others, alludes to Malinowski as putting concept before facts in this way.[163] On this view, only the theoretical consciousness of the mindful investigator can direct the data to be "relevant." Oddly enough, Malinowski held the same conflicted views from the time of one of his first publications, a 1911 Polish article on totemism. Says Malinowski,

> The fewer hypothetical assumptions and postulates included in a given description of facts, the greater the value of this description, but because every precise description of facts requires precise concepts, and these can be taken only from a theory, every description and classification therefore has necessarily to be based on a theoretical foundation.[164]

Polish scholar Marian Kempny agrees. Malinowski's "programme of intensive fieldwork, based above all on participant observation, was heterogenous in itself."[165] By noting Malinowski's intellectual heterogeneity, Kempny affirms what I have been articulating about Malinowski's sometimes wanting to embrace both the passivity of empiricism/positivism and at other times the conceptual willfulness to legislate usage. Kempny claims that Malinowski remained confused: he "combined elements of positivist methodology (observation of "facts" in order to comprehend their function in a given culture system) and subjectivism (reaching the senses of cultural facts through grasping the native's point of view."[166]

Malinowski was then no *consistent* empiricist. He would advocate and practise what seems impossibly complete fact-gathering with a behaviorist twist.[167] Yet both *Argonauts* and *The Diary* of the same period reveal that Malinowski did *not* believe in "objectively existing facts."[168] Rather, he believed that "theory creates facts."[169] Data had to be subordinated to the "final synthesis."[170] Fact-mongering always remained an object of Malinowski's explicit disdain.[171] What matters, essentially, to the present inquiry is that Malinowski's epistemological inconsistency — his departure from naïve empiricism — has immediate consequences for his conceptualization of myth, as we will now see.

Looking for "Myth" in the Trobriands

What then is the upshot for the study of myth of Malinowski's wavering between whether facts or theory go first? At its most basic level, breaking with naïve empiricism means challenging the empiricist process before it takes its first step. The naïve empiricist Malinowski, however, commits the fallacy of *petitio principii* — begging the *conceptual* question of what story is a myth by simply assuming what a myth is in advance.

Instead, Malinowski departs from naïve empiricism and opts for a hermeneutic method by submitting to the *natives' point of view*. In order to collect things that count as "myths," the ethnographer must answer the fundamental *conceptual* question *why* — according to *what criteria* — does one pick out myths from other stories, say. In *Argonauts*, Malinowski already employs just such a method, as he tells us.

> Indeed, I have found very often that when they told me some story of the past, for me obviously mythological, they would deem it necessary to emphasize that this did not happen in their fathers' time or in their grand-fathers' time, but long ago, and that it is a *lili'u*.[172]

Two pages later, Malinowski then draws a conclusion celebrating the clarity and seriousness of Trobriand category-making.

> To sum up, the distinction between the *lili'u* and actual or historical reality is drawn firmly, and there is a definite cleavage between the two. *Prima facie,* this distinction is based on the fact that all myth is labelled as such and known to be such to all natives.[173]

After sorting through two other options—"legend" and "fairy tale" (or "folk-tale")—Malinowski concludes that this "special class of stories" constitutes "the third and most important class of tales, the sacred tales or myths, and contrast them with the legends, that the nature of all three classes comes into relief. This third class is called by the natives, *liliu*…"[174]

Fine. Malinowski has come clean. Instead of hiding behind the empiricist pretense of being passively informed about what myths are by a barrage of facts, he assumes responsibility for his own mind's active role in *concept-formation*—in *selecting* what *should* be called a "myth." Readers are then free to decide whether they agree. We all know where we stand and can now proceed in full awareness of what we are doing. This marks a tremendous advance in a critical approach to myths. Significantly, it breaks the stranglehold of naïve empiricism. We are naïve no longer, because now we know what lies behind Malinowski's use of the word, "myth"—even if Malinowski wasn't always able to overcome naïve empiricism.

I have argued, elsewhere, that we should identify the methodological option dividing Malinowski's epistemological loyalties as one poised between a combination of generic naïve empiricism plus Mach's "second positivism," as Paluch explains. "Positivism in Mach's version was only a starting point in Malinowski's vision of modern social anthropology. Undoubtedly, the empiricism characteristic of Malinowski rises from the positivist trend in science and philosophy."[175] Over against this complex of positivisms and empiricism, what I have termed a "second romanticism" nurtured Malinowski's mind.[176] The source of Malinowski's "second romantic" thinking can be located, rather, in the "hermeneutics" theory of German philosopher, Wilhelm Dilthey.

Wilhelm Dilthey and the "Ding-an-Sich" of Myth

In singling out a "special class of stories,"[177] as he does, Malinowski makes a move with considerable methodological and theoretical implications. Unlike Mach's positivist skepticism about the accessibility of objective reality—the *Ding-an-sich*—Malinowski believed he knew what the Trobrianders themselves thought about the relative value of their stories. As Malinowski declares with confidence, "I want to emphasize that I am reproducing *prima facie* the natives' own classification and nomenclature and limiting myself to a few comments on its accuracy."[178] This is why Malinowski confidently feels that the *liliu* are *objectively* a certain kind of story according to the way the Trobrianders imagine the world. Had Malinowski, instead, applied Mach's *positivist* principles of inquiry, he could not have had access to these objective facts of the Trobriander's *Weltanschauung* as he did so emphatically in *Argonauts*.[179] This is so because Mach "does not consider the objective world or an entity that lies beyond perception."[180] That is to say, Mach denies us knowledge of things as they are — the *Dinge-an-sich* — here the Trobriander worldview.[181] Mach, thus, "confined the ground of theoretical validity to immediate experience.[182] He denied "the existence of the world of *Ding-an-sich* because cognition does not necessarily coincide with immediate knowledge.[183]

But Malinowski has no such doubts about his ability to understand the way the Trobrianders objectively think about their stories. Malinowski is full of confidence that he can penetrate to the *Ding-an-sich* of the natives' point of view — to the objective way they see the world. In *Argonauts*, Malinowski declares his trust in being able to understand the subjectivity of people objectively: "it is the possibility of seeing life and the world from the various angles, peculiar to each culture, that has always charmed me most, and inspired me with real desire to penetrate other cultures to understand other types of life."[184]

As for myths, Malinowski assures us that "the third class of stories stands very much apart."[185] The legend and fairy tales have their uses. But the *liliu* — the third kinds of stories — "are regarded, not merely as true, but as venerable and sacred, and they play a highly important cultural part."[186] Part of Malinowski's self-assurance that his field methods won him access to the Trobriand mind plausibly derived from personal experience; it is if he is saying, "I was there. You must believe me!"

Let me suggest, along with Paluch, however, that Malinowski also shored up his direct experiential confidence with his first intellectual love — philosophy — and, in particular, Wilhelm Dilthey's hermeneutics. Diltheyan "understanding" makes possible the confidence Malinowski displays in abundance about knowing the "native" mind. His affirmation, for instance, that "what interests me really in the study of the native is his outlook on things, his *Weltanschauung*" betrays just such a methodological debt to Wilhelm Dilthey.[187] Applied directly to the study of myths, Malinowski's essentially Diltheyan method finds him declaring in *Argonauts* the

> ...question which presents itself first, in trying to grasp the native outlook on the subject is: what is myth to the natives? How do they conceive and define it? Have they any line of demarcation between the mythical and the actual reality, and if so, how do they draw this line?[188]

That Malinowski thinks he can have scientific—objective—knowledge of what myths really are for the Trobrianders tells us that, in this regard at least, he has set Mach's positivism aside and embraced a Diltheyan hermeneutics.

Malinowski's Real Concept of Myth

The impact of anti-positivists like Dilthey and Wundt is all well and good. If they freed Malinowski—at least for a while—from naïve empiricism and positivism, does that solve all the difficulties with Malinowski's theory of myth? How, in particular, does Malinowski know what to look for in seeking "myth" among the Trobriands, since their language does not include the word? Without telling us his reasons, Malinowski simply *equates liliu* and what *he* calls "myth." After relating what characterizes the "folk-tale" and "legend," Malinowski just slips in that "myth" means the same as *liliu*. Myth "comes into play when rite, ceremony, or a social or moral rule demands justification, warrant of antiquity, reality, and sanctity."[189] "These stories live not by idle interest, not as fictitious or even as true narratives; but are to the natives a statement of a primeval, greater, and more relevant reality, by which the present life, fates, and activities of mankind are determined."[190]

Once the Trobrianders have shown they know how to make category decisions about their stories, what then does Malinowski feel *he* should do in response? As the primary investigator must not he too make a *judgment* about what he is willing to declare should to be called "myth" and be prepared to defend it? To evade falling to the fallacy of *petitio principii*, Malinowski needs to declare the *criteria* by which he *selects* what counts as a "myth" before he even *looks for* myths, much less *theorizes* about them. Then, he would need to defend why his *criteria of selection* are good ones because we are in contested territory — a place where people have different criteria for saying what a "myth" is.

To his credit, Malinowski, at first, seems to avoid a *petitio principii*. He responds to this commonplace logical dilemma by stepping back and proposing a way to pick out what a myth is. Empiricism is helpless before the task of selection because the mind is essentially passive in face of the world of facts which, theoretically, should impress themselves upon it. But Malinowski has decided to be active mind. He understands that he needs to select the things he can call "myths" according to certain criteria. So, Malinowski dares to make a judgment, and readies himself to defend it. In *Myth in Primitive Psychology*, aware of the need to take responsibility for his concept of "myth," Malinowski confesses that "This is perhaps the most important point of the *thesis* which I am *urging*."[191] Malinowski realizes he is making a deliberate judgment in *urging* readers to follow his lead and not merely to be overwhelmed by factual evidence heaped before them. Malinowski argues a *thesis*: "*I maintain that there exists a special class of stories*," he claims.[192] Nothing is obvious here, to his mind. Nothing is, literally, a matter of *fact*. Once Malinowski establishes this forward-leaning posture, he commits his judgment of the relevant content to his readers.

Malinowski, then, just assumes that "myth" translates to *liliu* without a word of explanation. Should readers feel tricked or confused? Perhaps. That, however, does not concern me as much as what Malinowski concludes about the definition of *liliu* as myth: a "true...venerable...sacred, and...highly important" story.[193] But whence comes his confidence that this is a *concept* of "myth"? Has Malinowski *invented* a meaning for the word "myth," or does he inherit it? And, if inherited, from whom and whence?

Actually, the answer is rather transparent. We have seen the lengths to which Robert Thornton and Peter Skalnik argue that Nietzsche was the source of the functionalist notion of myth that Malinowski took into the field.[194] But anyone familiar with a history of conceptions of myth in the West will recognize Malinowski's conception of myth as the garden-variety nineteenth-century European Romantic view (which would include Nietzsche). As articulated by Herder, Friedrich Schlegel, Novalis, F. W. J. Schelling, and others, myth has value as the basis of "antiquity, reality, and sanctity."[195] Thus, when Malinowski goes out to seek "myths" in Trobriander culture, he is equipped with a concept of "myth" originating in the middle European cultural world in which he was nurtured. He is supremely confident that he knows how to identify his target because his home culture has already taught him that a "myth" is a "true... venerable...sacred, and...highly important" story. Interestingly enough, the Trobrianders identify stories of this kind as well—the *liliu*. But is that the end of the story?

I do not think so. Among the many challenges one might make to Malinowski's conclusions here, one stands out. We may, indeed, agree with Malinowski that the Trobrianders and the Middle-European Romantics *both* marked certain stories for their being "true...venerable... sacred, and...highly important," or for their being statements "of a primeval, greater, and more relevant reality, by which the present life, fates, and activities of mankind are determined."[196] Maybe the Trobrianders and European Romantics did share all the aspects of a common "romantic" sensibility, as Malinowski confidently believes they did. If so, that would be a very interesting case of cultural comparability. But *because* he was looking for myth in the Romantic sense, perhaps Malinowski missed the occurrence of myth in the Enlightenment sense? It is always easier to *find* something if one knows for what one is looking. And, unless one is quite lucky, one seldom finds things for which one is not looking. Did the Trobrianders, then, *also* perhaps have "myths" in the skeptical Enlightenment sense of "false stories"? We don't know and perhaps will never know—because Malinowski was apparently *not looking* for such stories. He seems only to have been looking for stories that were "true...venerable...sacred, and... highly important," or, statements "of a primeval, greater, and more relevant reality, by which the present life, fates, and activities of mankind are determined"—"myths" in the Romantic sense!

Chapter 7

Taking Responsibility for the Concept and Theory of Myth

Myth Trouble

Why do we need to define "myth"? In the abstract, nothing compels us necessarily to have a concept of myth. We can always talk about "myth" like we talk loosely about "them," "thing," or "stuff" — to mean everything and anything we choose. In the abstract, nothing necessarily compels anyone to specify what "myth" means. But if we do want to designate *some specific referent* for the term "myths," we will need to decide *what* criteria apply to that designation. And we will need to say what distinguishes a "myth" within this class of referents. That is what is fundamentally entailed in *defining* "myth," in committing to a *concept* of "myth."

I want to begin the process of *defining* "myth" by designating a special class of referents to which I see "myth" belonging. This is the class of referents we call "stories." There is nothing radical about locating myths within the class "stories." But beginning to define "myth" by marking myth's membership in the class of "stories" is. Robert A. Segal, for instance, prefers to situate "myths" in the class, "beliefs."[1] Why select "stories," when so many other options are available?

Several considerations recommend defining "myths" as special kinds of "stories." First, it keeps my theorizing close to common sense. In terms of a broad understanding of myths, doing so has some virtues. Little persuasion is required for people to agree that ordinary usage imagines at least one sense of "myth" as stories. Second, *tradition*. Myths enjoy a long history of being identified as stories. The word "myth" is also the Anglicized version of the original Greek, *mythos*. Similarly, all modern European languages do the same as English. Third, in modern times, much of the literature on myths originates from ethnography. These constitute studies of pre-literate cultures in which the oral performance of storytelling plays a significant role. Fourth, as a kind of discourse, speech act, or utterance, "stories" have interesting discursive properties, many of which are not shared with other kinds of speech acts. Fifth, I avoid complications by resisting *valuation* of myths in terms of their truth-value as either *false* stories or *profoundly true* stories. It may or may not turn out that myths are generally false or, alternatively, deeply true. Such matters can be decided *after* we have come to the basic definition of "myths." They need not detain us here. These five features, taken together, offer my reasons for preferring to begin defining "myths" as "stories."

One further step needs to be taken. What is so *special* about some stories that they *should* be called "myths"? Several reasons apply. First, for ages, storytelling has been esteemed as an "art"—a *skilled* kind of cultural performance. Good storytellers seem to be revered universally. Second, one reason storytellers are revered is their mastery of a recognizably special class of utterances. Only *some* utterances make good "stories," while others do not. Not everything that tumbles out of one's mouth is a *story*, much less a "good" one. Only some arrays of words that people utter have beginnings, middles and ends. Only some utterances stand out from the everyday exchange of words as having some sort of *composed unity* the way stories do. Third, only some utterances "go somewhere"—are vectored—even if implicitly. Fourth, only some utterances aim toward certain destinations—have *points*. The vectored quality of stories becomes obvious because—since they work by implication or indirection—people commonly wonder about the *meaning* or *point* of a story. Fifth, only some utterances are "bounded" like stories are. Only some stories, in effect, *bracket* the time and/or space of their telling; think of the phrase "once upon a time…." In doing so, only some stories *pause* the flow of everyday mundane time and space to announce themselves. I want, therefore, to call "myths" the kind of stories that say, "Pay attention!" To conclude, I therefore, propose that we conceive of "myths" as *important stories or derivatives thereof*—notably without committing myself to any sort of "importance." Other people will have different criteria of "importance" for naming something a "myth." So be it. That is as it is, and as it should be. In any case, these are the reasons I have decided to define a myth as an "important story."

As special kinds of stories, myths might be compared with jokes—*funny* stories. People laugh and enjoy making others laugh. But not everything makes people laugh. Slipping on a banana peel and taking a tumble may make some folks laugh. Making a funny face may do likewise. Mispronouncing somebody's name may make people laugh. Speaking in a strange voice may do the same. But telling a funny story—what we call a "joke"—is a special way of making people laugh by speaking.

Many things people say are funny. But not everything that makes someone laugh is a "joke." Only some things that make people laugh are "jokes." The same goes for "myths." Therefore, the question of what makes a joke a "joke" is like the question of *what* makes a myth a "myth." I answer by defining myths as stories that people relate to mark something they take to be "important"—whether because it is true or false, right or wrong, constructive or perverse, immediate or remote, and so on.

I devote this chapter, then, to exploring some of the issues that arise in defining myths and the *processes* involved therein. I want to use this chapter to explain how and why I *conceive* some stories to be "myths," *define* some stories as "myths"—especially as "performative," as "doing things." But perhaps even more important than the *process* of conceptualization is the epistemological and/or methodological morality of *taking responsibility*, *assuming ownership* for one's conceptual and theoretical acts. In this chapter, I argue that using the term "myth" requires committing oneself *morally* to the need to "own" one's concepts. We need to be *responsible* for concepts critical to what we say.

We can learn a lot about how the process of conceptualization by paying heed to what famous myth theorists have done to decide what they wish to call a "myth." Malinowski's dubious but instructive practice of reading the Trobriand "*lili'u*" as our Occidental "myths" indicates that conceptual difficulties with the word "myth" start early. Indeed, they begin with the problems attendant in translation from one natural language to another. *Mythos* is not our word, but "theirs." In *Theorizing Myth*, Bruce Lincoln proposes a concept of myth for our use by basing it in the genealogy of *mythos* and its original meaning for the Greeks. This endeavor finds Lincoln slipping gracefully into discourse analysis. Explaining himself, he tells us he conceives of "myth" in order to "elucidate some of the ways" the "word, concept, and category have been used to identify the most dramatic shifts that occurred in their status and usage."[2] This is all well, good, and illuminating. But Lincoln's genealogical work leaves to one side both inquiry into how concepts of "myth" articulate within a *theory* of myth and whether or not we might come to a consensus about a serviceable concept of myth for religious studies, and if so by what criteria.

Despite the chaotic uses of "myth," Lincoln wants to retain the term "myth," and so do I. Unlike "phlogiston" or "the humors," Lincoln bets the success of his conceptualization of myth on the premise that "myth" retains its usefulness. Lincoln and I agree on such a program of concept formation and therefore do not wish to make a cottage industry of constant critiques of the way "myth" is used. Criticism of conceptualization has its uses, but it should not become an excuse for eliminating the term entirely, as some of our colleagues have sought to do with the term "religion." While good arguments can always be made for eliminating the term "myth," it has had a vigorous recent past of consequential usage, as well as the promise of more in the future. Especially in the political domain, "political myths" and talk of the same flourish. In this paper, I shall propose a concept of "myth" as performative—as "doing things." I do so largely because somethings called "myths" are today being widely used in our ideologized politics.

But at the same time, I am prepared to concede that a performative theory of myth might not play as well at other times. In the early days of the discovery of the Hindu sacred texts, for instance, no one would have imagined that the myths of the Rig Veda might ever have played some role in modern European politics. Yet, as we know from Müller's involvement with cultural and political *Aryanism* and the fascist exploitation of Aryanist ideology, Vedic myths did so, even though they seemed at first to be exotic, static narratives. In time and under the special conditions of the rise of German nationalism, Hindu myths informed Aryanist political ideology. We have already seen how Müller's scholarship was queried for its relation to Aryanism. (See "German Aryanism Enables Müller's Theory of Myth" in chapter 2.) In chapter 9, we will see how Aryanism spread beyond Germany into republican France and how the Durkheimians found it necessary to recognize how the *performative* use of ancient Hindu myths informed their politics. Therefore, in a time when some things meaningfully identified as "myths" are "*doing*" similar things in our political world, I propose scrutinizing how myths are managing to "do things" such as winning hearts and minds in our public discourse. That is, indeed, what it means to conceive myths "performatively."

Using "Myth" in the Uppercase

In terms of the most basic conceptual issues, *conceptual* troubles with "myth" frequently need clarification and may as well begin as soon as we say that first loaded word, "myth." Do we mean to say "myth," for example, as "Myth"—in uppercase—or "myth," in lower case? And is the word best used in the singular or the plural? What, furthermore, do these differences in case mean? Much hangs on the answers we give to these elementary questions. Take the matter of uppercase use first.

Those who speak of (or speak with) some*thing* called *myth*, in the uppercase—"Myth"—seem to have several purposes in mind. First, they intend to indicate some sort of unique, autonomous, *universal* (and uncontroversial) category, principle, or phenomenon. Here, "Myth" is like "Reason," "Science," "Religion," "the Mind," "Democracy," etc. It is typically abstracted from more concrete media, such as actual stories. Insofar as Hitler was regarded as an extraordinary, charismatic, savior-like figure, it might make sense to say that Hitler exploited the awesome, *innate* power of *Myth*. Moreover, in being capable of wielding such extraordinary powers over ordinary citizens, one suggests that Hitler had access to equally supernormal sources of that power—the "power of Myth"! The late Joseph Campbell (1904–1987), author of the popular *Hero with a Thousand Faces*, talked this way. While the details of Campbell's thinking are far too complex to unravel here, we can note Campbell's embrace of "myth" as "Myth" as some kind of general category or principle fundamental to all human societies. For him, "Myth" suggests the existence of a so-called "monomyth"—a singular unifying structure, embracing the notion of the Heroic Journey. In Campbell's view, all myths essentially resolve into this "monomyth." That's why it merits being written in uppercase. Not long before he died, Campbell was the focus of a PBS series of six one-hour interviews with Bill Moyers, entitled appropriately, *The Power of Myth*.

By seeing myth as categorial, universal, and profound, Campbell sets himself up in opposition to a tradition of thinkers who saw myths—in the plural—as indicating prelogical mental capacities. The distinguished French anthropologist Lucien Lévy-Bruhl (1857–1939) wanted to know how the thinking of traditional folk—those he called "natives"—compared with that of "modern" Europeans.[3] He supposed that "the *primitive* (sic) natives" had very different ways of thinking about the world than so-called "*modern*" people.[4] The "primitives" seemed to inhabit a mental world where palpable distinctions between things did not strictly or generally apply. Lévy-Bruhl thought the "natives" believed, for instance, that individuals felt intimately identified with others, rather like sports fans who so identify with their respective teams that they speak of their team in the first-person plural: "*We* won!" Like our sports fans, the "natives" were capable of making distinctions between things, but their "myths" record those mystical moments when they chose not so to see the world as riven with differences—when they "participated" in the identity of others, when they *shared* the being of others with themselves.

To Lévy-Bruhl, these data either meant that the "natives" must be systematically wrong or that they must *think* differently when they spoke of those heightened moments of "participation." One possibility was that since traditional folk had survived in often harsh environments, their different ways of thinking must have been adaptive. So, Lévy-Bruhl argued that we should respect the existence of "mythical" or "mytho-poetic" prelogical ways of thinking about the world. The "myths" collected in print just recorded this naturally "pre-logical" way of experiencing the world. "We," in the *modern*, more highly "evolved" West, on the other hand, think logically, and as a result, produce history, literature, philosophy, and science, instead of "myth." We have left "myth" and the world of mystical participation behind for a world of differences and "logic" as human minds evolved.

Alternatively, those speaking of *Myth* mean some class of *value* abstractions or qualities having either an *elevating* or *diminishing* character—such as the way people believe that art, magic, power, style, are *elevating*. About a particular film, some critics might say that instead of being a *dull* and *prosaic* documentary, the film works because it is infused with the wonderful quality of *myth* or *Myth*. Then, on the other—*diminishing*—hand, the word "myth" could also signal something false, confusing, illogical, crude, "primitive," etc. For instance, a critic might say of a documentary about President

Reagan, for example, that instead of helping us to understand Ronald Reagan, it was fatally flawed by being shot through with *myth*. In appealing to "myth" or "Myth," then, a certain *contrast* is presumed — by definition — with other similarly hypostasized entities: Myth, thus, variously contrasts with Magic, History, Religion, Science, Revelation, Ritual, Literature, Philosophy, Truth, and so on. Again, all these hypostasized entities, are suitably written in uppercase and regarded as fundamentally *simple, primary, objective* and *uncontestable*.

Why I Won't Miss (Uppercase) "Myth"

But I would argue that speaking of such hypostasized categories or principles, as Myth (singular and uppercase) results in unsatisfying discourse.[5] What of consequence can be engaged, for example, by posing questions at the level of such sweeping generalities? Is not thinking about a hypostasized "Science" or "Reason," as opposed, for instance, to an equally reified "Religion" or "Superstition," simply too sweeping and general? Which "science" or *Wissenschaft* — chemistry, physics, psychology, political or social science, *Geisteswissenschaften* or *Naturswissenschaften*, etc. — does one have in mind? Which "religion" — orthodox, heterodox, revealed, pagan, Natural, "New", personal, established, etc.? Relying upon such hypostasized entities is what gives the polemic of a Richard Dawkins and other self-appointed Village Atheists their quaint antique flavor. We just know too much about the variety of possible references underlying such uppercased labels as Myth, Religion, Superstition, Magic, Science, etc. to be content to carry on with such generalities. These uppercased terms are, at best, *rubrics, headlines,* or *useful shorthand* for a host of conflicts fruitfully sorted out in terms of the specific referents for which these sweeping generalizations are alleged supposed to stand. So, that's why I won't miss speaking of uppercase Myth. It's not where the action is. Rather, in terms of where things happen, where myths "do things," at least, we need to get down to details — down to actual *myths*.

What to Do about "myth" and "myths"?

Once we put aside speaking of uppercase "Myth," where does this leave speaking about lower case "myth" in the singular versus the plural? It leaves us, I would submit, precisely where every knowledge worker in history has been left—facing choices of how to fashion our language so that we can make consequential claims about the world. Creating such a language means getting down to specifics—for us, to myths, less than to some abstraction, like "myth."

Let me appeal to the example of such a choice to overcome sweeping generalities that was deliberately made in one of the greatest works in the study of religion, Max Weber's *Protestant Ethic and the Spirit of Capitalism*. Weber sought to argue for a certain relation between religion and the economic system. Could it be said that "religion" informed the economic system? Loose-talking, opinionated thinkers were always ready, for instance, to blame economic inequity upon what they broadly branded as "capitalism." But what was it this "capitalism" that generated inequality? In what sense of "capitalism," for instance, would a system of winner and losers *necessarily* be favored? Was social inequality the result of "capitalist" *greed*, or was "capitalism" essentially just a disguised form of *robbery*?

Alternatively, social critics might also charge that "religion" bore responsibility for producing a social system fraught with inequality. But *which* religion, of the many active at the time, bore particular responsibility for economic inequality? Primitive Christianity taught that all believers should share their wealth with each other, rather than encourage disparities of wealth. Medieval Roman Catholicism forbade usury and other economic activities that might create inequality. So, which religion was to blame (or be *credited*) for a world of economic winners and losers? Did Catholic countries show greater tendencies toward inequality? Or should we point to Lutheranism, for instance? From this, it can be seen how answering questions about religion, the capitalist economy and social inequality all required serious attention to *details*—to specifics, not sweeping abstractions in the study of myths like "Myth" or even "myth."

Weber's greatness consisted in getting beyond gross categorial generalizations to the actual causes of events like social inequality. He devised a plan of inquiry that enabled him to translate what had been fruitless clashes of abstractions like those between Religion and/or Capitalism into understanding *what specific* religion, or religions, led to an economy of winners and losers. He was unwilling to surrender responsibility for his concept of capitalism to ordinary, everyday, possibly confused usage. Instead, he delimited his conception sharply and specifically, distinguished it from a host of meanings circulating in everyday speech. He was unwilling, for instance, to speak of capitalists in the same breath as one would speak of brigands and pirates, or those inheriting or simply enjoying great wealth. Weber committed to a set of defining properties to mark what he felt was *consequential* and distinctive about this thing he wanted to call "capitalism." And with that identification of capitalism in hand, what *particular* religion might have supported such features of capitalism? If successful capitalism demanded disciplined hard work, what religion preached the transcendental value of self-denying labor, for instance? If successful capitalism required workers to see their labor as a calling or vocation, what religion spoke of human life in terms of calling or vocation? By asking such questions, Weber eventually understood both the mechanism that made capitalism successful as well as the religious environment that selected for the moral qualities demanded by the new capitalist order.

In a way analogous to Weber, I seek to replace abstract talk of "Myth" or "myth" with concrete talk of "myths" — myths that can be said to "perform" in public discourse and life. Given a particular political or social situation, for example, what *particular* myths contributed to actors "doing things" of consequence in that situation? And, by means of what specific mechanisms? In the new nation of the mid-nineteenth-century "Germany" of Müller's time, what particular mythical narratives appealed to young German nationalists to establish the legitimacy of their new nation? As it happened, the vogue for the idea of old Europe being settled by an Aryan migration from the subcontinent was so considerable that young German nationalists looked to the vigor of the ancient India that Müller and other Indologists revealed in Indian mythology as their forebears. By associating themselves with ancient Aryan migrations out of India, German ethno-nationalists felt that they distinguished Germans historically from other peoples around them — Latins, Slavs, and Jews, in particular. Only Germans descended from the noble Aryan migrants who had dominated ancient India and then chosen to migrate to Europe. Although Müller may not have recognized what Hindu myths were "*doing*" for heightened German ethno-nationalism at the time, the myths of ancient India "*performed*" powerful legitimation operations for the German Aryanists. Indeed, they contributed to making a distinctive Aryanist racist political culture, culminating in the human calamities of the Nazi period and its fellow-travelers that Hubert sought to combat in France.

When I wrote *Four Theories of Myth in Twentieth-Century History*, I was dismayed by the lack of critical, conceptual self-awareness among highly touted theorists of "myth." What instead impressed me was their tendency to take the word "myth" and the folk concept of myth "off the shelf," with all taken-for-granted meanings that attend the word "myth" in everyday speech. The moral of this story is that if we restrict our theories of myth to what common sense or theoretical fancy have to say about lowercase "myth," we get a chaotic Rorschach inkblot of meanings. Here, the reader is left to pick up the pieces. Instead, the scholar of myth needs to *act*, to take responsibility for some concept of "myth" or "myths" and be prepared to say why it is a notion worth "owning." One might change one's mind about this decision, given new knowledge and so on, but being open and corrigible about our conceptual and theoretical commitments seems to me a sign of intellectual maturity.

How to Be Critical of and/or Responsible for a Concept of "myth" or "myths"?

Being critical about the use of words like "capitalism or "force" — and "myth" and "myths" too — means *assuming responsibility* for a particular sense of the term. Not each and every use of the term will do. For "myth," along with Segal, we might begin delimiting the sense of "myth" by citing the concept of "story."[6] I take ownership of a notion of "myth" by declaring that "story" is a notion central to the definition of "myth(s)," as I shall use it. But why "story"?

To answer this question, I refer readers to my discussion of Robert A. Segal's attempts to define myth in section of the next chapter titled "Segal Saved by Equivocation." Looking forward slightly, one must start somewhere — and that *somewhere* is ordinary, everyday speech. There, I shall appeal to the idea that in order for us to be understood as talking about myth, we first need to recognize its common, ordinary, everyday sense. In large part, although not exclusively, "myth" means, at least, a "story." But as both Segal and I agree, definition only begins there. Conceiving "myth" *merely* as "story" does not suffice to *define* it in any clear sense. It hardly distinguishes myths from among the many kinds of stories. I would describe this status of "myth" in ordinary, everyday common usage as being *theoretically* uninformed.

Now, there is nothing tragic about thinking of myths merely as stories. But being pre-theoretical means it cannot do some of the jobs we want a term to do, such as help explain things. This everyday sense of myth includes too many referents to be a useful notion. Thus, referring to myth only as "story" would be like only using the word "force" in its ordinary language sense when we really wanted to explain matter in motion in precise Newtonian quantitative terms. Defining myth in a strong sense would be like Newton defining "force" within his physical *theory*. Therefore, taking responsibility for a concept of myth, owning a concept of myth, would be analogous to locating "force" as a technical term particular to Newtonian physics. Here, just as the "force" of Newtonian physics is the mathematical *product* of the "mass" multiplied by the "acceleration" of an object, the *theory* of myth for which I am responsible *conceives* "myths" as "important" stories or derivatives of "important" stories. In the same way, as we will see, Segal eventually conceives myths as stories that are "significant" and "weighty."[7]

Of course, simply being responsible for one's concepts does not guarantee that one's concepts will be well formed. Some scholars — Joseph Campbell, for example — have taken responsibility for a hypostasized, metaphysical notion of *myth* — the uppercase Myth — as in the series *The Power of Myth*, for instance. But what if Campbell has misallocated responsibility? If, as I have argued, no such *thing* as uppercase Myth exists, buying into and thus seeking to own "Myth" would be analogous to being sold a false bill of goods. At best, Campbell deploys a rubric, headline, or shortcut, not a durable or fruitful concept of myth. Being responsible for a particular use of the word "myth" or "force" would then mean requiring us to defend or justify that usage.

Conceiving "Myths" Pragmatically, Not Empirically

In conceiving or defining "myths," most myth theorists mistakenly proceed as if myths were *given, objective realities* to which the word "myths" *corresponds*. But there are no things with the name "myth" written on them. We, the myth theorists, take our chances and *decide* what we *should* call "myths." Instead of imagining that defining the word "myth" consists in discovering an objective reality thus named, the theorist *decides* what things in the world should bear the name, "myths."

Richard Rorty's pragmatist approach to conceptualization thus commends itself for our consideration because it reflects the activity of the knower in the creation of concepts.[8] It replaces the "myth" of passivity of knowledge and concept-formation with an appreciation for the subjective element in practical category-formation. Reflecting the mental activity directing inquiry, we define the word "myth" in terms of the tasks we wish its use to achieve. In terms of Malinowski as a myth theorist, does the sense of "myth," as he conceives it, "*do anything*" to make a difference to actual practices? Does it "*do*" anything useful for solving any problems? What does it "*do*" to move our understanding of culture further along? Malinowski's concept of "myth" is, thus, a practical tool for our getting certain projects "*done*."

Rorty's general epistemological approach superficially resembles Malinowski's pragmatic approach to myth. When defining "myth," Malinowski may have become familiar with *classifying* stories from his youthful experiences assisting his father's folklore studies. He would, then, have recognized how central classification of stories was in his early fieldwork in the islands off New Guinea. Reflecting his commitment to Dilthey's methodology of empathy, when Malinowski wanted to know how to sort out the stories collected there, he listened to the way the islanders themselves *classified* their own stories. That empathetic perspective taught him what a "myth" was in the minds of the Islanders.

But Malinowski differs from Rorty in one key respect. Unlike Rorty (and the present author), Malinowski still imagined that in learning from the Islanders, he had also discovered an *objective* reality to which the word "myth" corresponded. As I have shown in the preceding chapter—see especially the section titled "Malinowski: Conflicted Empiricist and Reluctant Rationalist"—Malinowski did not fully appreciate the extent to which native Trobriand *theorizing* itself *created* a special category of story that Malinowski identified as "myths." Malinowski's theory of myths remains a pragmatist effort, but his epistemology is still caught in the illusions of empiricism—namely, that reality "out there" imprints itself on a passive mind. As an empiricist, however inconsistent, Malinowski thinks that he thus knows *objectively* what to look for in seeking "myth" in his fieldwork in the Trobriand islands. What he says about "myth" is true to the extent he believes that it *mirrors* the objective reality of *myth*. That the Trobrianders name these special stories *lili'u*—and not "myths"—does not faze Malinowski. He simply *dictates* that the Trobriand word *lili'u* means what the European word "myth" means to him. The problem is that Malinowski did not recognize his own mind's legislative act in so doing. He *decides* that the *lili'u* are "myths," all the while laboring under the illusion of having some profound cross-cultural discovery about this odd thing called "myth."

Thus, despite his many virtues in representing the folk about whom he wrote, Malinowski overlooked the full extent to which the islanders exercised their own conceptual and theoretical creativity in classifying stories. They spoke like veterans of battles against naïve empiricist ideas of concept-formation, since they behaved as if they knew that the classification of their stories depended upon them! Stories did not come with their names written on them! The folk *gave* stories certain names. In the case of the *lili'u*, that meant that the islanders *actively* probed their own culture by *asking themselves* which, if any, of their stories were more, or most, *important*. The islanders didn't sit back like *passive* empiricist *tabulae rasae* and absorb the range of stories in their culture. They made judgments at every step of the way and, in effect, claimed "ownership" for particular classes of stories.

Specifically, "myth" named a special class of "important stories," the *lili'u* that Malinowski then decided should be rendered as "myths." Now, we do not know how the Trobrianders decided the "importance" of the *lili'u*—or indeed whether *every* society would separate out a class of "important stories" in the same way. Nor do we know that each and every Western ethnographer would follow Malinowski and "translate" *lili'u* as "myths." We do not know, for instance, whether all such decisions were made by males, to the exclusion of women, by the rich and powerful to the exclusion of the poor and weak, or *vice versa*? Nor do we know if the choice of what story belongs to the *lili'u* class reflected any culturally designated differentials of beauty, influence, power, virtue, wisdom, and so on? For *whom*, for instance, are the *lili'u* thus designated "important"? Nonetheless, we do know that some segment of Trobriand society judged the *lili'u* as "important" stories of island society. Malinowski reports that the islanders did so because they believed the *lili'u'* were useful in justifying certain important practices and authorizing certain institutional arrangements—in *performing* certain critical tasks for their island culture. While Malinowski made moves toward appreciating native creativity in classifying their stories, he failed to go *far enough*.

Becoming "Important"

If given a choice for guidance about conceiving "myths," the Trobrianders offer us admirable models for doing so. They defined their myths as special or important stories. Starting with such a *minimal* concept of "myth" as an "important" or marked story. A "myth" is a story, a narrative, that a given society regards as standing out from others, as having a special role and place, and so on. This suggests certain further lines of inquiry, such as what stories are judged important because they make people laugh—jokes. Or we might follow the existentially sensitive Trobrianders and Malinowski, who sought the stories that provided fundamental legitimation and justification for various social arrangements. Such a view becomes attractive since "myths," like all good stories, may catch on or tap into a society's deep imagination. As marked stories, they may be told and retold in different versions.

Another line of inquiry along the same trajectory of defining "myths" as "important stories" comes from today's Russia, as we will see at length in chapter 10.[9] There, an industry deploying "alternative histories" of the nation's place in the world thrives. Published in immense tomes, these alternative histories sell by the thousands. Yet, because they are both massive and technical, few people actually read them! Nonetheless—and this is where myths come in—it is said that *everyone* knows their stories. The public has distilled core stories, capturing what they take to be the cardinal, important points of these bulky, unread alternative histories. What matters is not these massive volumes in and of themselves but the "myths" they relate.

Nonetheless, those narratives I call "myths" are not static tales or legends. Instead, as Malinowski decided, myth "comes into play when rite, ceremony, or a social or moral rule demands justification, warrant of antiquity, reality, and sanctity"[10]—when there are "*things to do.*" "These stories live not by idle interest, nor as fictitious or even true narratives, but they are to the natives a statement of a primeval, greater, and more relevant reality by which the present life, fates, and activities of mankind are determined."[11] In Rorty's language, a Malinowskian could defend the use of the word "myth" as "warrant," "charter," etc. because in doing so, he achieves certain desired ends. This is then why Bruce Lincoln claims that in Hesiod and in Homer, *mythos* means "a blunt and aggressive act of candor, uttered by powerful males, in heat of battle or agonistic assembly."[12] The Greeks apparently had something they wanted "*to do*" in having stories like that. We need not be stuck thinking about the word just as the Greeks did, even if it can be a point of reference. But this mention of *mythos* as a strong discursive act, as saying something that *matters*, is useful. I am saying that a defensible *minimal* definition of "myth" is as such an "important story," recalling Greek *mythos* as the robust "act of candor" that it was.

It is notable that Rorty defends his approach as consistent with the classic approaches of the great scientists, such as Isaac Newton. While it is true that Newton still operated in the Platonic epistemological world, his theoretical conclusions can be explained from Rory's pragmatist viewpoint. Thus, Newton's conception of "force" succeeds, for example, because it provides him a tool to accomplish a number of desired ends: explaining the laws of motion and universal gravitation. It does quite adequately in accounting for the movement of the planets, the ocean tides, the trajectories of comets, and so on. But Newton's physics is useless for explaining reality at the atomic and sub-atomic levels. It is the wrong tool for use in splitting the atom. For that tool, we need to wait for the likes of Niels Bohr and the Copenhagen School, Albert Einstein, and the theory of general relativity.

We know how Newtonian "forces" are measured. But the measure of its location within a coherent view of reality or theory emerges when we see how Newton committed himself to the understanding of "force" as the product of "mass" times "acceleration." These conceptual interrelations imply that Newton had assumed responsibility for a total picture of reality in the process—what we call the theory of Newtonian physics. Likewise, when we mark "myth," we too are implicated in theory, even if we may resist articulating it further, even if we resist pursuing the entailments of conceiving myth in a certain way. Any conception of "myth" will share the same conceptual space with other interrelated terms. Like any significant choice in human affairs, conceiving myth in a certain way has consequences—regardless of whether or not we wish to pursue them. In the past, for example, some theorists conceived "myths" as occupying the same conceptual space as dreams, symbols, or rituals. These notions were theoretically linked as surely as "mass," "acceleration," and "force." A theory of myth would simply articulate how these notions were related.

Weber too explicates his project in *The Protestant Ethic* in terms of its use in serving the larger purposes of promoting an overall idealist theory of culture, expressly articulating a viewpoint of the way values, legitimations, and beliefs make a difference to the formation of societies. The religious roots of capitalism are grounded in a larger vision of the way ideas legitimize, and thus ground, social institutions like, for example, economic systems. Likewise, students of myth theories need to ask into what larger projects does "myth," as variously conceived, fit? Someone like Bruce Lincoln, for instance, situates myths within his more encompassing vision of discourse and its destiny, which in turn would serve as a tool for furthering Lincoln's neo-Marxist worldview of the good.

Finally, religious studies is a discipline that is supposed to be about something in the world—what the Kantians called a "synthetic" discipline. Therefore, the ultimate worth of criticism of its categories, such as "myth," does not lie in the act of criticism itself. Criticism of categories in "synthetic" endeavors shows its worth if they serve as efficient tools for promoting fruitful understandings and explanations of the world. Yes, one does accrue moral merit for being responsible for one's concepts. But merely to have taken responsibility for one's concepts is not the end of the story. We still would need to show that the risk in so doing was worthwhile—that it makes a difference. How does a concept of myth, thus critically constructed, help us make consequential claims about the world? What value would Weber's theorizing of capitalism have had, if it had no practical value? Agree or disagree with Weber, the "Weber thesis" has borne abundant fruit.

"Important Stories": A Basis for Conceptual Consensus?

As I shall elaborate in chapters on myth in France and Russia (chapters 9 and 10 respectively), I have lately been working in the opaque world of mythically and religiously inflected politics. Circulating in today's Russia, for instance, is that entire literature of "alternative histories," well-documented as if they were works of erudition.[13]

These heavily documented tomes generate certain ready-to-hand narratives of Russian history, both ancient and modern. Examples? Russia single-handedly saved Europe from the Nazis, who moreover are attempting to re-emerge in Ukrainian rightist movements like the Right Sector militia. As we will see in chapter 10, signs of the resurrection of the once discredited "Myth of Moscow, Third Rome," and thus the true center of the Christian world, once more inform political rhetoric here and there. Or, as if to affirm Russia's unique place between East and West, she asserts her place as a Eurasian power, but not only that. Russia's long domination by the Mongols indelibly shaped her deepest political and social identity. These Eurasianist narratives, thus, proudly identify Russia with specifically Mongolian formations, leaving its European character adrift.

What matters for understanding "myth" in the sense I seek to elaborate is these oral and/or less-than-formal tellings of the major theses of formidable alternative histories. Even though the brisk sales of these "histories" indicate a large readership, we must imagine that in reality, only a few people carefully read these weighty tomes that spell out theories of Russian history. But everybody knows their *stories*. Everyone knows what "myth" the books deploy in the form of ready-to-hand narratives that can be easily recited or presumed as part of the repertoire of *legitimations* for a certain vision of the nation.

In this, the relation of these Russian "myths" to the massively documented works of scholarship of Russia's Eurasian past, for instance, follows a widespread pattern. In apparent agreement with my thesis, one of my colleagues recently told me that he had found evidence in modern-day politics of the same mythmaking. He cited the example of Turks who claim that Ottoman responsibility for the 1915 Armenian genocide is a "myth." I quickly made myself better understood by explaining that I was not using "myth" as a label for a falsehood, as his example did (and as is commonplace still). Rather, the "myth" was in the retelling, in the casting and recasting in an endless string of variants, in the circulation and popularity of a ready-to-hand story. The "myth" was in the "stories" told and what those stories effected in their audiences, not the documentation amassed, even if myths drew upon such documentation (or, of course, pseudo-documentation). So, as well, the stories of Armenian survivors and offspring were "myths"—the ready-to-hand or remembered narrative accounts of the horrors of being separated from family, of summary execution, of expropriation and certain death in inhospitable deserts. It would be left to a later generation of scholars to *document* the details of what these stories tried to convey together with the results of heroic work in archives and others stores of official memory. I am, thus, putting forth the notion that "myths" and such scholarly "documentation" are two different things, even if claims made in "myths" may be documented. The oral, or less than formal telling, retelling, writing, and rewriting of an endless stream of variants—"myths"—do not document important events. Only histories, ethnographies, or statistical surveys do. "Myths" *tell* about them, and in doing so ideally often "*do things*" that make a difference in political life.

Now, because these stories are marked by their widespread "importance," I have been tempted to mark them as well. I think they might be usefully organized under the rubric of "myths." Religious studies may have something special to offer treatments of the phenomenon of alternative histories, because existing treatments seem noticeably, and familiarly, deficient. Some historians seem unable to admit the recrudescence of such narratives as the hypernationalistic "Myth of Moscow, Third Rome," for instance. It does not seem to fall into the model of progressive modernization they tacitly assume, even in the face of Putin's determined remaking of the Russian soul. Others fall back on psychoanalytic models. For them, these alternative histories are simply "therapy" for the sick post-Soviet mind seeking solace for the loss of empire.[14] Russians are simply mentally ill or irrational, in massive numbers!

Students of religion should find that such dismissive discourses have a familiar ring. How often we meet in both learned and mass media the libel that various religious phenomena are pre- or illogical, crazy, or, irrational! Just think of the portrayal of cults like David Koresh's Branch Davidians, Jim Jones's Peoples Temple, Heaven's Gate, Scientology, Karen Brown's Voudon, so-called suicide bombers, and now ISIS! Our best response to this kind of dismissive analysis has been to bring out the hidden logic in so-called illogical beliefs and practices. We can do this because many of us have been trained in the kind of rigorous methods of understanding spelled out by Charles Taylor and other scholars.[15] Taylor takes to task both the hardline position that the insider always enjoys a privileged, incorrigible access to their actions and motivations, and the soft thesis that understanding is a product of empathy, conceived as a kind of mind-reading. Most important of all, he forces attempts to grasp the point of view of others to argue for their conclusions, to give an account of themselves. Attempts at understanding must be seen, then, as corrigible, and thus testable.

Let me suggest that these alternative histories might be understood as "myths." Like other marked stories—jokes, for example—they are told and retold in an endless number of versions. They circulate and have currency. These sorts of stories either exist or they do not. Determining whether they do or do not is a straightforward job of mainline empirical social research. Do societies judge certain stories to be "important" or not? Determining how and why is something done by normal procedures of social research. Part of an answer—worth testing—for example, is why a given story is judged "important," and thus rises to the level of a "myth." It might be that these "myths," like all good stories, tap into the resources of the imagination and memory. But our work only begins here. What does it mean that the myths win their importance by tapping into the imagination or memory, exactly, and how do they do so? As marked stories, one is tempted to argue that they also *circulate* in society and have a life of their own; they are told and retold in many versions. (But, again, by what mechanisms do they circulate?) Like good jokes, they catch on. But again, how do they do so? Furthermore, they provide a sense of wholeness—for instance, a story of the nation's past history and future destiny—from beginning to middle and end. Or they recall that the nation's story is open-ended and lacks a neat picture of its end. In either case, the constructed nature of stories might enable people to achieve a complete and/or defensible sense of their nation's place in the world. But again, and finally, how do they do so? These are only a few of the reasons that I find the notion of a marked or "important" story—a "myth"—an intriguing heuristic tool. Despite confusion about definition and a history of ramshackle scholarship—the term still has uses, perhaps indispensable ones—for a variety of research projects.

A Rich Trove of Myths: The Mythical Politics of the Two Brutuses

Let me offer some examples of how important stories, or "myths," can "do things," typically within the parameters of their political cultures. One is a story popular in both Elizabethan England and revolutionary France, and the other, comes from the years of India's struggle for independence.

Everyone knows the Shakespearean version of the assassination of Julius Caesar by Brutus and his fellow conspirators. Critics note that Shakespeare conveys a warning against trying to achieve social change by violence, just as he does in "Hamlet."[16] One could say that Shakespeare's version of the death of Caesar has become a "myth" for Anglo-Saxon political culture—a story warning that using violence to overturn lawful authority eventuates in chaos or backfires on the protagonist. Not only does Brutus come to a nasty end, but Hamlet too creates chaos by killing the king.

Commentators have argued that the Brutus/Julius Caesar myth is told as the conservative, Elizabethan, anti-revolutionary political culture that surrounded Shakespeare required it to be told.[17] Compare, for instance, Shakespeare's telling of Caesar's death with the version that emerges from France, which has a tradition of violent revolution. Indeed, in France, what Anglophones call "the Caesar story" is better known as the *Brutus myth*. Dead set against monarchy and autocrats, the French revolutionaries often looked to Marcus Junius Brutus—not Caesar—as a model of the "neo-Roman ideal of patriotic sacrifice."[18] While the Elizabethans sat uneasily on the throne, fearing uprisings, the Jacobins were inspired by the image of Brutus and his revolutionary courage. In fact, the proper name "Brutus" took on a generic meaning connoting heroic championship of freedom. Originally, it applied chiefly to the ancient Lucius Junius Brutus (c. 500 BCE), who slayed the tyrant king Tarquin in order to establish the first Roman republic. To a lesser extent, they also celebrated our Marcus Junius Brutus for his desire to save the Republic in Caesar's time.[19] Notably, Plutarch praises Marcus Junius Brutus in a spirit of moral engagement for his selfless devotion to nation.[20] Interestingly, these two self-sacrificing "Brutuses" merged into a single image of the heroic freedom fighter. In the French and republican Roman telling of the Myth of Brutus, the two Brutuses, although separated in time by five centuries, are experienced as a single Brutus.

Both Brutuses showed the same selfless heroic devotion to liberty, regardless of their resort to violence. Plutarch tells us how the Roman republicans of 45 BCE tried to rouse Marcus Brutus to action against Caesar by recalling the myth of our Brutus's ancient ancestor of 500 BCE before! "The tribunal upon which he [Marcus Brutus] sat as praetor," says Plutarch, "began to be covered day after day with writings which read, 'Brutus, are you asleep?' or 'Brutus, you are no true Brutus.'"[21] Brutus, they said, you are not conforming to the *mythic model* of your ancestral namesake! Unlike the cautious Shakespeare, the Revolution sanctified violent actions of loyalty to the nation by celebrating the violent deeds of both Brutuses against their own contemporary monarchs. Historian Edith Flamarion has shown how some of the success of the Brutus myths relied on the deliberate "confusion" of the two Brutuses, producing a symbolic "identification" of the two into one expressive "Brutus."[22]

In 1730, Voltaire published his play about Lucius Junius, "Brutus," followed immediately in 1731 by one about Marcus Brutus, "La Mort de César."[23] In a fit of revolutionary mythomania, the Committee of Public Safety decreed that both plays were to be performed *weekly* by all the theaters in Paris![24] Of Voltaire's two Brutus plays, scholars of the period claimed that citizens who had seen the plays were ready to "stab the villain who might attempt to enslave his country."[25] Admiration for the great ancestor of the "noblest Roman of them all" even called forth the creation on 22 September 1793 of the "Feast of Brutus" in memory of Lucius Junius.[26] The Brutuses were further memorialized in the mass production of busts of "Brutus." A 27 August 1792 decree required that all public buildings and associations should be adorned with such busts of Brutus.[27]

India's Genius for Manipulating Political Myths

Although controversial, the principal modern "myth" told repeatedly about the Bhagavad Gītā is its promotion of non-violent social reform. As a 1986 anthology overwhelmingly reveals, most contemporary commentators on the Gītā see it advocating non-violence.[28] But given its literal prescription of righteous violence, that is what the Gītā itself teaches. But the ideologically popular Gandhian ethic of *ahimsā* has until recently so dominated the reading of the Gītā that its myth of nonviolence overwrites the very words of the text.²⁹ In the Gandhian myth, passages referring to battle in the Gītā are seen as part of an "epic *against* war," thus only referring to symbolic struggle.³⁰ Krishna's urging Arjuna to *fight* as his warrior-*dharma* dictates belongs, like Gandhi believed about Krishna's supposed divinity, to the realm of the theological imagination.³¹ In its mythical Gandhian reading of the Gītā, Krishna really just wants Arjuna to be virtuous. Thus, as Gandhi confesses, "The *Mahābhārata* is the story of a bloody war. But I have maintained in the teeth of orthodox Hindu opposition that it is a book written to establish the futility of war and violence."³²

Taking exception to the Gandhian "myth" of the Gītā, the Indian nationalist Bal Gangadhar Tilak (1856–1920) embraced the strategic use of political violence in his battle to win India's independence from Britain. Known as a "relentless fighter," and the "father of Indian unrest," the British journalist Valentine Chirol captured the essence of Tilak's character and moral vision.³³ Tilak read the Gītā for a "myth" more amenable to his own notion of what "important story" the it was really telling. For Tilak, the Gītā narrated a "myth," advocating "rational violence," to borrow terminology from Marxist Eric Hobsbawm.³⁴ Both Tilak and Hobsbawm agree that morality permits a code of proportionate retaliation and should govern uses of political violence. Instead of turning the other—*Gandhian*—cheek, Tilak defended the use of sanctioned forms of violence. "All acts of violence outside the domain of sanctioned violence in this theory are criminal acts."³⁵ Like Hobsbawm, Tilak's *swarāj* entailed moral self-control—a disciplined pursuit of national independence permitting the use of force. As Mithi Mukherjee argued on Tilak's behalf, the so-called (non-violent) "constitutional modes of protest (*swadeshi* and boycott)" failed because colonial authorities had violently crushed them. Significantly, for Tilak such "sanctioned forms of violence" could theoretically include those in conflict with the statutes of positive law. Thus, in revolutions, Tilak cited "legitimate ends…in so far as its purpose was not to infringe law but to establish new law…" In fact, in doing so, "this violence had a lawmaking character."³⁶ Tilak's slogan for defending Indian dignity with force became "militancy, not mendicancy."³⁷

In the interest of Indian dignity and honor, Tilak's ethic of "rational violence" did not only mean that morality *permitted* righteous violence, but in some cases, positively *enjoined* it in the pursuit of justice. He subsequently coined the term "*swarāj*" for this political use of "sanctioned forms of violence," employed positively for winning self-rule for Indians.[38] So successful were Tilak's efforts that the term, *swarāj* became synonymous with Indian national independence itself.[39]

Nevertheless, Tilak's view of the ethical use of force had to compete with the greater prestige of Gandhi's non-violent political *nationalism*. In order to prevail over the Gandhians, Tilak felt that his policies of *swarāj* needed even more traditional Hindu "communal" supporting legitimacy.[40] This, Tilak thought he found in the cycle of traditional Hindu myths surrounding the life and exploits of the early modern Mahārāshtrian resistance fighter, Śivāji.[41] The seventeenth-century Marāthi hero Śivāji (1630–1680) had notably succeeded in leading Hindu armies against Muslim domination, just as Tilak wished to lead Indian independence fighters against the British.

Twentieth-century Indian demography, however, complicated Tilak's task of adapting the Śivāji myth to resistance against the British. Although an excellent "important story" in its own terms, the Śivāji myth was flawed for the uses to which Tilak would finally put it. Realistically, the success of Indian resistance to the British required *both* Muslims and Hindus to unite in common effort. But the Śivāji myth embittered Indian Muslims, since it casts Muslims as enemies of Hindus.[42] If the Śivāji myth were ideally to channel Tilak's political imagination in a productive way, it needed to overcome what seemed the impossible obstacle of Muslim resentment.

As well, Tilak's Śivāji myth had to make violence legitimate in a context where the Gandhians had made it virtually illegitimate. Perhaps it was just the wrong kind of myth to sway Indian imaginations in Tilak's direction? Nevertheless, Tilak made that attempt in 1906. Tilak's newspaper, *The Mahratta*, began a series of articles designed to celebrate Śivāji's heroic renown in mythical terms. Conventional opinion, marked doubtlessly by Western notions of heroism, held that he was "the only hero to be found in Indian history."[43] Śivāji exemplified the profile of an *ethical* warrior. He enforced a disciplined use of violence and was the epitome of honor and magnanimity for his followers and himself. All these factors won for Śivāji the classical mythic reputation of "hero" – a "chivalrous lover of liberty."[44] Even though Tilak may have sought deeper traditional Hindu support for the mythical profile of Śivāji, like the chivalrous heroes of British literature, such as in Sir Walter Scott's novels, myths told about Śivājī recalled those same Occidental manly codes of honor and discipline regulating the use of violence. Śivājī's myth even had him, Ivanhoe-like, saving "damsels in distress" or defending the womanly "honour" of those fearing the predations of villains.[45] Best of all for an Indian audience of the Śivājī myth, the great hero showed supreme devotion to his mother.[46]

Try as he might to get Hindus to embrace his telling of the Śivājī myth to use against the British, Tilak encountered difficulties. Some say that Tilak's glorification of Śivājī was so exaggerated that it effectively undermined the myth. Gandhi attacked Tilak's appeal to the Śivājī myth with the simple objection that Śivājī's patriotism was "misguided."[47] Some of Tilak's other foes even began undermining Tilak's mythical glorification of Śivājī by circulating myths designed to deflate Śivājī's reputation. Some of these myths cast doubts on Śivājī's honor, heroism, and discipline by skillfully retelling Tilak's version of the Śivājī myth, especially the details of the death of Afzal Khan. One such countermyth cast Afzal Khan as intending to trick and kill Śivājī, all the while giving the impression of wanting to negotiate peace. Another reversed the roles of Śivājī and Khan and narrated details of Śivājī's dishonorable treachery in scheming to assassinate Khan.[48] So successful were the various countermyths in circulation that Tilak's reliance on the Śivājī's myths weakened. Myths battled myths, and Tilak's version of the Śivājī myth often lost.

Making matters worse, undisciplined outbursts of violence by Tilak loyalists against Muslims undercut the ethical thrust of Tilak's telling of the Śivājī myth. Clearly, undisciplined violence failed to conform to the paradigm of rational, "constitutional," *ethical* violence. Nevertheless, despite such criticism, Tilak tightened his grip on the Śivājī myth instead of retelling it anew as circumstances dictated. Tilak's greatest critics even suggested that Tilak deliberately chose the Śivājī myth because in many tellings, it permitted him to *both* appeal to the Marathi leader's noble qualities *and* exploit Śivājī's unsavory qualities.[49] Frustrated, Tilak nevertheless pressed on with Śivājī and was finally forced to make excuses for the moral ambiguity of Śivājī's myth by admitting that even "great and responsible persons, who have to live in society and to do these duties consistently with righteousness and morality often find themselves in such circumstances."[50]

Tilak's critics succeeded and were similarly busy retelling the Śivājī myth for their own purposes. Some found just the parts of the story that raised the greatest doubts about the ethics of killing the Mughal general Afzal Khan.[51] Most tellings agree that the strength of Afzal Khan's army threatened the annihilation of Śivājī's forces. Feigning peaceful intentions to negotiate a truce, as some of these retellings go, Śivājī prevailed upon a certain trusted Muslim general to arrange a peace conference between himself and Afzal Khan. Afzal Khan agreed. Prominent countermyths, however, say that while Khan kept his word, arriving unarmed to parley with Śivājī, the treacherous Śivājī came armed, ready to murder Khan. Indeed, that is what the myth says Śivājī did at his first opportunity. The Mughal army, now leaderless, dispersed, leaving Śivājī the victor, however ignoble and *un-dharmic*. This myth, however, caught on to such an extent that Marathi patriots celebrate this victory as their community's foundational myth. At the same time, Tilak's critics, including the bulk of the Muslim community, recall the myth bitterly as proof of the illegitimacy of Hindu hegemony.

No longer offering an unambiguously plausible model of *dharmic* honor and virtue, this telling of the myth of Śivājī's treachery has only deepened alienation between Hindu and Muslim communities in Mahārāshtra. Within vast areas of subcontinental culture, the Śivājī myth is thus tarnished, and at worse yet, soundly demythologized by critical versions of the story of Khan's assassination. Whether Tilak betrays mythical illiteracy or simple perversity, he never stops defending Śivājī—tellingly by citing the Bhagavad Gītā! This creates ethical problems that complicate Hindu-Muslim relations and are not easily overcome.

> Did Shivaji commit a sin in killing Afzal Khan, or how? Its answer lies in Shrimad Krishna's advice in the Gita to kill even our teachers and our kinsmen. No blame attaches to any person if he is doing deeds without being actuated by a desire to reap the fruit of his deeds.[52]

What is more, in defending Śivājī so, Tilak does so on the basis of—for all things—his dharmic *honor* for killing Khan! At times even reverting to myth as "Big Lie," many of Tilak's supporters contort the details of the myth so that Afzal Khan is depicted falsely as attacking first, leaving poor Śivājī to defend his own life. Tilak's partisan re-mythologizers even leave out of the myth key elements of the original, such as Śivājī's concealment of his murder weapons!

Were these manipulations of the Śivājī myth relegated to a small coterie of Tilak's "True Believers," the politics of the Śivājī myth would scarcely merit attention. Yet further re-mythologizing of the Śivājī myth by Tilak's followers took on a life of its own—at least among those favoring Tilak's kind of politics. As a result, Tilak's critics argue that Tilak exploited the very same moral ambivalence of the retelling of the Śivājī myth for his own purposes. Why else, his critics demand to know, was Tilak indifferent to the assassination of colonial administrator, Walter Charles Rand, if Tilak were not trading on his partisans' re-telling of the Śivājī myth?[53] While Tilak may feign being repelled by political violence, his critics accused him of playing fast and loose with it, just as the Tilak re-mythologizers did of the Śivājī myth.

A regrettable upshot of Tilak's duplicity about telling the Śivājī myth? It deprives modern India of a *dharmically* unambiguous myth guiding those who seek a mythical rationale for a use of force. The myth as Tilak tells it cannot "do that thing." One can appeal to the Tilakian version of the Śivājī myth, but too many Indians know that re-mythologizing it only undermined the idea of a dharmic use of violence. At the very least, it rendered the Śivājī myth morally confusing. Other available textual candidates for such an ethic, such as the Arthaśāstra and Bhagavad Gītā likewise fail because they are either otiose in contemporary India or read from the Gandhian perspective of *ahimsā*.

Tilak's (and his opponents') use of the Śivājī myth shows how myths "do things" in different ways than standard prosaic speech. Myths and stories present special species of communication by insinuation, indirection, and suggestion. This does not mean the same people are incapable of straightforward prosaic speech, only that the matters about which they speak are better addressed indirectly through suggestion rather than baldly and explicitly. Many concerns at the heart of a society are not the kinds of things about which people willingly speak prosaically and directly. They must be inferred or left open to broad interpretation rather than narrowed into a simple statement. Perhaps this means that societies, nations, for example, do their business tacitly, just as individuals do. Stories, *important* stories, or "myths" is where that business is done, tacitly.

Chapter 8

Conceptual Problems for Robert A. Segal and Jonathan Z. Smith

Segal, Müller, and Mythical Stasis

If the arguments of the previous chapter have established anything, I trust they demonstrated *both* the complexity of arguments needed to "own" a defensible concept of myth, as well as the relative economy of the results. I have proposed a relatively tidy, *economical* definition of myths as "important stories," but the process of reaching this conclusion involved many moving parts. How does my definition resist being dismissed as idiosyncratic or merely relative? What makes my concept of myth *compelling*, instead of just something personally appealing to the present author? I think, however, that the trenchant argumentation I offered makes a good case for adopting the idea of myths as "important stories" as serviceable in many situations where a notion of myth is sought. Yet perhaps it is the very trenchant intensity of the process of justification — and its ever-possible futility! — that encourage myth theorists simply to avoid taking responsibility for their concept of myth? Acting in good faith, these reluctant myth theorists resist the process needed for taking ownership of their concept of "myth," simply because they think the exercise unnecessary. After all, doesn't everyone *know* what a myth is? Why then do we need all the justifying procedures when everyone agrees? The problem is, of course, that the idea of "myth" is obscure or just scattered hither and yon all over the place. No consensus exists about what *should* be called a "myth."

Resistance to the laborious justification procedures involved in deciding how to conceive myths defensibly is thus not surprising. What, however, is surprising is that resistance to taking responsibility for one's concept of myth should be found in the work of great myth theorists of our own times, like Robert A. Segal or Jonathan

Z. Smith. Not only that, but the same illustrious colleagues also seem to retain significant features of myth theorizing going back to its beginnings in the mid-nineteenth century with Müller. Segal and Smith's maintenance of central aspects of Müller's concept of myth is remarkable for a number of reasons besides Müller's relative intellectual antiquity. Despite Segal's desire to distance himself from Müller, for instance, both he and Müller agree that myths are essentially *static* cultural entities—symbolic narratives, preserved in texts. And while the efforts of pioneer nineteenth-century myth theorist Müller would seem a long way from prominent twenty-first-century theorists, Jonathan Z. Smith's theorizing is not as far away from Müller's as one would expect. Significant affinities persist between of Müller's *concept* of myth, on the one hand, and those of Segal and Smith on the other. While known chiefly for his psychoanalytic appreciations of myths, Segal aligns himself remarkably well with the philological and literary conceptual and theoretical views that characterize Müller's *oeuvre*.[1] In his own way, Jonathan Z. Smith joins Segal in carrying on the study of myths, for the most part, as if they were static *texts*. These affinities do not by any means imply that Segal and Smith simply rubber stamp Müller's work. In Segal's view, Müller's theory of myth is "at best quaint" and "nowhere accepted today."[2] Smith, in turn, objects to three features of Müller's thought: the "positivism of his appeal to 'science,'" "the presumption of generality," and a "presumption which some perceive as a sort of imperialism."[3] Yet, Nancy Levene balances Smith's dislike of Müller by claiming that Smith also "can be refreshingly idiosyncratic in his sourcing, leaning on older figures we thought were long passé,...lifting the veil of disinterest in or scorn of Max Müller."[4] My purposes in this chapter are not only to bring out these continuities across the centuries but also to highlight how both Segal and Smith struggle to resist taking what I believe is that all-important responsibility for their concepts of myth. In the process of avoiding the task of conceptual ownership, both Segal and Smith do not seriously entertain the performative possibilities of myths, a notion to which this book is dedicated.

From the outset, Segal does not consider conceiving myths ("Myth", or myth) as actions, as "doing things"—*pragmatically*. Related to this, the question of the conceptualization of myths never arises. Segal seems to believe that he can remain scot-free of conceiving *and* theorizing myths entirely. He casts himself as a humble reporter of the vast array of concepts and theories of myths, not anyone's hopeless advocate. Unlike the vision I am trying to advance, Segal does not view myths as agents, performing in distinct social venues. Or, as critic, Robert Frazer, claims, Segal sees myths as socially-untethered — even timeless — stories:

> Throughout, what is more, the debate is conducted in the present tense; no concession here to the past historic. "Myth" therefore, it's not simply a single topic but a synchronous one, in the discussion of which all contributors, whatever their age or period, must be deemed to be contemporaries.[5]

Conceiving myths in this way, as virtually autonomous symbols or representational iterations, bypasses anything that may be pragmatic about myths. Neither Müller nor Segal say anything, for instance, about what or whether myths can be *defined* as things that "*do*" anything. Indeed, because both Segal and Müller eschew involvement in extra-textual — historical, cultural, and sociological empirical — data, they cannot do so, in principle. This in itself does not constitute a criticism of Segal's approach to myths. It is merely an observation of intellectual difference.

Yet, despite his many declared differences with Müller, Segal, like Müller, finds "symbolic," rather than "literal," readings of myths most agreeable. Segal rightly notes Müller's belief that myths ultimately refer to the "infinite [but]…symbolized by the grandeur of celestial bodies and events."[6] There is something "significant" or "weighty" about myths.[7] Stories are thus accounts of physical entities that typically often stand for spiritual ones. Unlike Müller, who emphasized nature in myths, Segal sees the *significance* of myths in their recounting of stories with *weighty* psychodynamic references and meanings, such as Freudian readings of the myths like that of King Saul.[8] Segal joins Müller in seeing mythmakers as "poets," as opposed to producers of dull, leaden prose.[9]

Does Segal Define Myths or Not?

Nevertheless, Segal's devotion to the study of myth ought to be celebrated, as indeed it has been by many readers. But do we (or Segal) really understand Segal's fundamental conceptual and theoretical commitments about the identity of myth or myths? I think not. Nor do I think that Segal finds taking "responsibility" or assuming "ownership" for a theory of myth compelling—at least not as much as I do. It was in 2000 that Segal's position on definition emerged in tense debate with Bryan Rennie. There, Segal said he neither had nor needed to own a "definition"—a "concept"—of myth, or indeed a theory thereof. Segal effectively declined to "take responsibility" for his use of "myth."[10] Segal thus declared himself a kind of journalist of theorists and theories of myth. Being a good reporter required no conceptual commitments of Segal. Indeed, such commitments would have biased his reportage. How could Segal claim to be a critic of concepts and theories of "myth," if he could not, or would not, tell us what counted for him as "myths"? How would he even know whether or not the concept or theories he was reviewing were *about* "myths," if he himself admitted to having no concept or theory of myths? Resistance seemed in conflict with Segal's role as critic.

Bryan Rennie argued that Segal does not, therefore, abide by the standards of scholarly inquiry. "Contrary to Rennie, I never conclude that myth is 'not this, not this,'" Segal proudly said.[11] Turning to Karl Popper, Rennie recalled how the philosopher demonstrated the inescapability of conceptualization or definition. Popper would bluntly ask students "to observe," and then report their findings. When his students realized they had nothing to report, Popper emphasized that observation required a specified *object*. One needed to know *what* to "observe."[12] Rennie turned Popper against Segal. Like Popper's students, in the absence of a concept of myth, Rennie claimed Segal was trying to *observe* (theories of) myths without actually saying what *myths* were. Rennie chided Segal to "to come down off the fence."[13]

Rennie seems to be correct in saying that Segal's dismissal of Müller's concept of myth presumes *some* definition of myths. How else could Segal disagree with Müller, unless they already had, implicitly or explicitly, *agreed* what to identify as myth? Segal knows well *what* to "observe." He need but define it. More than a journalist of theories of myth, Segal does more than merely "observe." He knows *what* to observe. Later in the course of this chapter, I shall try to identify both what I take to be Segal's actual definition of myth, and his theory thereof—even as he denies having one. Segal further confuses matters by failing to distinguish concept or definition from *theory*. While speaking of *concepts*, for instance, Segal writes "of eliminating theories. Quite the opposite: I am trying to show what disparate theories accomplish. I am trying to show how varied are the ways that myth can be approached" — all the while conducting debate about definition.[14] Confusing as this is, Segal effectively reaffirms his conceptual innocence on myths and, in doing so, "owns" or assumes "responsibility" for a concept of myth. Just why Segal *ultimately* does not want to define myth remains a puzzle. Segal's scholarly integrity as critic is above question. Neither would Segal risk compromise, were he to reveal how he *conceives* or *defines* "myth." Neither would sharing his preferences for a *theory* of myth — even if only as a "working" definition — put Segal's critical integrity at risk. Such revelations would only help us understand how Segal *selects* "myths" from among the many objects of inquiry he might have chosen.

Segal Finally Defines Myths: First Impressions

Decades after his refusal to define myth for Rennie, Segal seems to have reversed course, defining myth as "story."[15] He twits Joseph Campbell for missing how essential story is to defining myths: "For all Campbell's deserved fame as a masterly storyteller, he is, as a theorist, surprisingly uninterested in myths as stories."[16] This apparent about-face led me, in turn, late in 2022, to ask Segal to explain.

I must report that Segal remains diffident about definition, about "owning" a concept of myth. The self-image of objective reporter, far above the conceptual fray, still holds Segal in its thrall.[17] Thus, in correspondence, Segal admits no conversion from his claims in 2000, despite his apparent reversal in 2023's *Myth Theorized*.[18] Let us look closely then at these new arguments of Segal's.

Problematic though it may be, Segal does *minimize* (even reject?) the importance of his 2023 definition of myth as "story" in *Myth Theorized*. Explaining, Segal adds that "I wouldn't mind having changed my mind about myth, if I have done so."[19] Segal claims that what he really meant was something else: "What I have done over the years…is to introduce the distinction between myth as story and myth as belief."[20] Nevertheless, even though Segal says he was only pondering the myth-as-belief *versus* myth-as-story distinction, he reverts to his 2000 refusal to take any responsibility for his concept of myth. Maddeningly, he says, "I now grant that I was wrong to limit myth to story."[21] What Segal means is that "I don't think that characterizing myth as either a story…amounts to a definition."[22]

This at first stumped me. Perhaps "story" *defines* "myth" weakly? But even weak definitions are definitions! Why the problem? Segal's answer: "myth"-as-story just repeats everyday speech, not scholarly or scientific language: myth as "story may seem self-evident...most of us think first of stories about Greco-Roman gods and heroes."[23] Or, in discussing Tylor's theory of myth, Segal says "myth functions to explain the world. But unlike the rest of religion, myth does so in the form of stories...."[24] Why elevate the obvious to academic levels? Says Segal, "myths undeniably tell *stories* rather than give arguments."[25] In effect, Segal asks, "so, what?" Indeed, why then does Segal devote an entire section of a chapter in *Myth Theorized* to "Definition of Myth," repeating what I have already noted about making "story" a key to defining myth?[26] The answer? Segal saves himself from certain contradiction by equivocating on the meaning of "definition."

Segal, Saved by Equivocation

At work in Segal's discourse are, in fact, *two* senses of "definition." "Definition" can mean *weakly marking*; but it can also mean the strong sense of *demarcating*, being *definitive*. In the discourse of philosophy of science, myth-as-story defines myth as ordinary language does; but saying more beyond ordinary language pushes us toward special scholarly or scientific language. In Segal's words, "this distinction" — myth-as-story — "is so basic as to stand prior to a definition, which would specify the nature of the story....I myself am open-ended about myth as a story...."[27] So, the natural question arises for Segal, *what kind* of story counts as a "myth"? Ready with his answer, Segal says that he defines "myth as simply a story about something *significant*."[28] To say myth is "a story about something *significant*" means for Segal that a real myth is a "weighty" story. In Segal's own words, he adds,

> I note only that for all the theorists the function is weighty — in contrast to the lighter functions of legend and folktale. I thereby assert that myth accomplishes something significant for adherents, but I leave open-ended what that accomplishment might be.[29]

Farhang Erfani, in reviewing Segal's *Myth: A Very Short Introduction*, also catches Segal's willingness to define "myth" as a "weighty story." Therefore, continues Erfani, for Segal,

> ...a myth is at least a "story".... Not all stories are myths, of course. Myth is a type of story that has discernible main characters, with a "weighty" function... — as opposed to the case of literature or folklore; and it is a type of story "held in conviction" by its adherents.[30]

Like the ordinary language use of "force" in physics, conceiving myth as story is "so basic as to stand prior to a definition, which would specify the nature of the story."[31] Part of "specifying" the "nature of the story" would be analogous to locating "force" as a technical term particular to Newtonian Physics — linking the *concept* of myth-as-story to a *theory* of myths. As he tells it, myth-as-story only seemed like a *definition* of myth. For Segal, "defining" "myths" requires they be defined as *special kinds* of stories — "important stories, or derivatives thereof," analogously as I do, or as "a blunt and aggressive act(s) of candor, uttered by powerful males, in heat of battle or agonistic assembly," as Bruce Lincoln does.[32]

After all this struggle, it is distinctly odd that in 2023 Segal still resists even recognizing his having *defined* myths as "significant" and/or "weighty" stories! Astonishingly, he adds, "I was wrong to limit myth to story."[33] The only way I can explain the continued resistance to admitting having conceptualized myths as "weighty" lies in Segal's — unduly — chivalrous dedication to maintaining scholarly evenhandedness and objectivity. However noble the instinct, I think Segal's commitment to some unspecified notion of objectivity has compelled him — mistakenly, in my view — toward extremes. Why should he still resist assuming responsibility for defining myths as "significant" or "weighty" stories? I say this because using the word "myth" is to utter something special. Merely naming something "myth" has often ignited controversy — implying thereby that not "everything" is "myth." Enlightenment critics of Christianity called the stories in the Bible "myth" because they felt they were *not* "history" or "science." Biblical myths were false — hardly an uncontroversial matter in the Christian West! On the other hand, Romantic talk of "myth" simply reversed Enlightenment iconoclasm. But bizarrely, in another place Segal seems to reverse himself. Clearly, something is at stake in naming things "myths." For that very reason, scholars of myth like Segal should declare how and why they do so.

The Cost of Resistance

Although Segal's equivocation about "definition" saves his position on conceiving myth, Segal's continued refusal to admit that he does so creates needless confusion. Why does Segal seem to delight in Joseph Campbell's mystagoguery that "everything is myth"?[34] Furthermore, resistance to definition also raises the critical question of how Segal sees concept in relation to theory. Segal sometimes minimizes differences between *definition*—"myth is 'not this, not that'"—and *theory*—"trying to show what disparate theories accomplish," i.e., kinds of explanations.[35] But this doesn't much help. In reply to the specific question of the relation of concept/definition to theory, Segal, in effect, claims they cannot be separated logically. "Twentieth-century theorists give outright definitions of myth...."[36] In doing so, they "doubt that definitions come first for any theorist."[37] This 2023 statement of the internal relation of concept to theory actually recalls Segal's own statement in 2000:

> Definitions are rationalisations for the kinds of entities that theorists wish to call myths. If I may quote from my book, "Theories of myth purport to cover all kinds of myths. In practice, few do." At the least, every theory is best suited to a particular kind of myth. The subject matter determines the suitability.[38]

The history of the social sciences does not necessarily support Segal's accusation that theorists, in effect, cut their definitions to fit their cloth. Were that true, how could Segal *compare* theories and/or concepts of myth? Since each concept of myth would then be specific to a given theory, different theories and their concepts would be *incommensurable* with each other. Segal would not even be able to compare theories of myth, as he has done countless times, because, strictly speaking, the theories are not about the same things, the same concepts. Theory of myth A is about concept of myth A. Theory of myth B is about concept of myth B, and so on…, *ad infinitum*.

Fortunately for the progress of science, we have superb examples of how the logical distinction between theories and concepts produces results. Max Weber, for instance, went to extraordinary lengths to carefully *define* "capitalism" at the beginning of his *The Protestant Ethic and the Spirit of Capitalism*.[39] But is Segal claiming that Weber's theory of the rise of capitalism as legitimated by a certain revolution in Christian religious values was already necessarily contained in Weber's concept or definition of capitalism?

Was all Weber's effort to sharpen what he understood as critical to capitalism merely a "rationalization" for a theory he had secretly concocted? No doubt, Weber identified religious values that have a definite "elective affinity" for certain values of capitalism, as he defines it.[40] But Weber might not have *theorized* that those particular Calvinist Pietist *religious* values had critical causal influences upon the rise of capitalism. Some other sources of legitimating and/or motivating values other than religion, whether Pietist or not, might have spurred capitalism! Marxism, anyone?

Add to this that Segal has already committed to *defining* myths as significant and/or "weighty" stories. If concept and theory are in some key sense inter-definitional, is Segal in effect also admitting to a theory of myth? And, in that case, what is Segal's *theory* of myth? Concepts like "force" or "acceleration" have meaning independent of that given them within Newtonian physical theory. They begin their lives in Newtonian physics as terms of ordinary language, later to be given precise theoretical meaning by Newtonian mechanics. For instance, the Newtonian *concept* of "mass" makes a particular technical sense within Newtonian mechanics. Newtonian "mass" is not the "mass" of everyday common speech any more than myth as significant and weighty story is the "myth" of story alone. Newtonian "force" is the rather extraordinary "product" of the quantity "acceleration" multiplied by "mass."

To some degree, Segal and I agree about the internal relationship between concept and theory. Theory and concept of myth are mutually related, so much so that theories select for their own definitions of myth, and definitions of myth fit only with certain theories. Lévi-Strauss's structural theory of myth, for example, selects only *structured* narratives as "myths."[41] Similarly, Segal's real definition of myths as "stories" has a pre-theoretical life in ordinary language *before* Segal conceived—defined—myth scientifically as weighty, significant story. All good. But what then is Segal's corresponding theory of myth, fitting with his concept of myth as significant and weighty story? Now, that we know what "rationalizations for the kinds of entities that theorists wish to call myths" Segal offers, what is the theory they inhabit?

Conceptual Problems for Robert A. Segal and Jonathan Z. Smith 155

Segal's Theory of Myths?

Segal scatters many clues about the identity of his *theory* of myth. For example, Segal thinks that we explain myths by reference to the deep—often unconscious—workings of a relatively universal human psychology. Understood in this psychological way, myth can then be used to explain human behavior, or at least the way myth-makers choose to record how people behave. Myths reveal the encoding of the psychological templates that channel human thought, emotions, and action. Another clue leading to Segal's *theory* of myths emerges from Segal's practice of capitalizing "Myth" or referring only to the singular "myth." Reviewer Robert Frazer dryly notes in his critique of *Theorizing about Myth* (1999), "Grammatical habits have thematic consequences. Consider the title and style of this book. 'Myth' is in the singular, denoting one subject, not many. 'Myth,' we are told is a field; myths probably not."[42] Segal continues this use of "myth" in the singular scores, if not hundreds, of times in his most recent book, *Myth Theorized*. The singular word myth clearly has resonance, even if Segal lately claims that "my use of the singular MYTH is a mere convenience. I use it to name a category, much as I would, say, SCIENCE."[43] Denials to the contrary, "Myth" in the uppercase would seem to suggest an extra special resonance. Here, Segal is in excellent company using "Myth" in the uppercase, given how many myth theorists of the past did as well. Consider Ernst Cassirer's *The Myth of the State*, Mircea Eliade's *Myth and Reality*, Bronislaw Malinowski's *Myth in Primitive Psychology*, Claude Lévi-Strauss's *Myth and Meaning*, and so on. Without concluding what special resonance capitalizing "myth" had for each of these authors, what resonance has "Myth" for Segal?

Capitalizing "Myth" is like capitalizing "Science" to Segal. And if this is true, then Segal assumes that, like Science, "Myth" indicates some sort of cognitive unity—a "category." For Segal, opposing Myth to Science roughly means contrasting approaches to nature—myth as a special ("poetic"?) etiological alternative to science. Both may purport to serve "the same function" of explanation.[44] Both offer "etiological" answers to questions.[45] Both endeavor to explain "how things came to be."[46] But Segal does not doubt that science explains the world truly, while myth does not. At best, myth is a "primitive counterpart to science."[47] As such, myth and science are ultimately "mutually exclusive" because mythical explanations of nature are "religion" in a theistic sense—a *god* acts in the world...as in the nineteenth-century theories of Tylor and Frazer.[48] For them, "Myth and science...are incompatible."[49] Segal rejects those who prefer the biblical Flood myth account of human origins to those of the natural sciences. "Want to learn about the history of the earth?" asks Segal rhetorically. "Study geology, not the Bible."[50] Taking this position puts Segal squarely in the camp of Enlightenment critics of myths. Myths do not give us "knowledge" about nature. They weave poetic wreaths about nature. But they are not competing explanations about the natural world. Beautiful, mysterious, or deifying though they may be, myths just do not explain the world of nature, whatever the intentions of the mythmakers. But if Segal's theory of myth disallows it offering competition for the natural sciences, does it explain anything else?

Segal's "Garden-Variety" Jungism

Segal's enormous output of observations of theories of *myth*, *Myth*, and *myths* points toward a definite theoretical preference. Can it be accidental that in his 184-page *Myth Theorized* that Joseph Campbell and Carl Jung should garner over 250 mentions *each*, Freud and the Freudian Otto Rank over 200 each, and finally Lord Raglan over 100? Is it also accidental that other great modern theorists of myth register comparatively paltry totals—Malinowski (57), Müller (27), Lévi-Strauss (25), Ernst Cassirer (24), Durkheim (11)? Notably, Henri Hubert, Marcel Mauss, and Segal's contemporaries Bruce Lincoln and Jonathan Z. Smith receive *no* mentions *whatsoever*.

Numbers, of course, can lie. But for Segal, Campbell and Jung merit *five times the attention* that Malinowski does, and considerably more than Müller, Lévi-Strauss, or Ernst Cassirer. If Segal himself does not find psychological or psychoanalytic theorizing more compelling than other kinds, why do Campbell and Jung merit *so much more* attention than Malinowski, Müller, Lévi-Strauss, or Ernst Cassirer? Why, does Segal also completely omit engagement with notable contemporary myth theorists like Bruce Lincoln or Jonathan Z. Smith, the neo-Jungian Mircea Eliade is mentioned 188 times? Segal might not want to take ownership of any particular theory of myths above all others, but his dedication to a complex of psychoanalytic theories says otherwise.[51]

In a cautious vein, the *Modern Language Review*'s Robert Frazer sees Segal's dedication to Jung in, at least, as garden-variety or generic. Frazer says that Jung is "evidently something of a courtesy uncle" for Segal.[52] Arguing circumstantially again, Frazer concludes that Segal marches in step with Jung because in Segal's work, Jung "is given more elbow-room, his thoughts carefully and respectively explained" than any other theorist of myth.[53] Concluding, Frazer says that, "From the tone of the…essays, one infers that the Jungian view is as close to precision as one is likely to get" to Segal's actual theoretical viewpoint.[54] At the very least, Segal's theoretical approach is deeply colored by the Jungian character of Campbell and Eliade—and Jung himself—even if the evidence is admittedly circumstantial. So, yes, unless critics can offer a more plausible alternative, Segal's theory of myth can best be described as *generically* psychoanalytic. Moreover, on Segal's own terms Segal's psychoanalytic theoretical orientation marries well with his conceptualization of myths as significant and weighty. What else does psychoanalysis employ but the "significant" and "weighty" stories that analysands narrate to their therapists? Later in this chapter, we will see how Segal uses Freudian theory to decode the story of King Saul as "Myth." What then of Jonathan Z. Smith, earlier linked with Segal as continuing some of the defining features of maxmüllerism?

Back to Boas and Ahead to Lévi-Strauss…at the Same time

Jonathan Z. Smith endeared himself to his many readers and students in countless ways. A popular teacher and much sought after commentator and critic, Smith's generosity of spirit shone forth in his lighthearted but vehement public performances. Smith's writing effortlessly crossed disciplinary boundaries and brought insights from the cross-cultural, comparative study of religion to far-afield specialized areas like biblical studies. His interventions into current academic debates about method and theory in the study of religion were often featured by academic journals and gatherings.

Among Smith's wide-ranging endeavors, Segal singled out "classification" and category formation as focal areas of his intellectual passion.[55] Smith indeed developed interests in *classification* across a range of subjects, prominently *myths*, beginning in 1969, with an Eliadean article, "Earth and Gods,"[56] and in 1970 with "Birth Upside down or Right Side up?"[57] Then, with Eliade's star dimming, Smith shifted loyalties to the structuralism of Claude Lévi-Strauss—a move he had been preparing for since graduate school. Smith's 1972 publication "I Am a Parrot (Red)" and the 1973 iconoclastic "When the Bough Breaks" took on the venerable subject of his PhD dissertation at Yale: J. G. Frazer.[58] Now, however, Smith set about to disenchant Frazer's memory.

But readers waited until late in Smith's life for his more consequential theorizing about myth. These came in a trio of essays on anthropological studies of myths contained in "Conjectures on Conjunctures and Other Matters: Three Essays" (2017) and in two major books, *To Take Place* (1990) and *Drudgery Divine* (1992).[59] These pieces consist essentially of critical and expository studies featuring Smith's critiques of major myth theorists like Lévi-Strauss, Franz Boas, and others. Like Segal, Smith too resisted declaring theoretical commitments, reserving that for the very end of his career, when he celebrated Lévi-Strauss in his two book-length studies, *To Take Place* and *Drudgery Divine*.[60] Instead, Smith surprised dedicated readers by touting unfashionable figures like Boas and extending his reputation for eccentricity by applauding the nineteenth-century Pan-Babylonian theorists!

Although Smith rode the meandering currents of myth theory, he always maintained respect for Mircea Eliade, even after shifting to structuralism in the mid-to-late 1960s. But staying abreast of the latest myth theorizing left Smith something of a conceptual and theoretical eclectic. From structuralism, Smith adopted a heterogeneous set of insights, yet he was still too much a phenomenologist to represent himself as an orthodox structuralist. Like Lévi-Strauss and Segal, Smith seized on Freud, concluding that myths do not tell the truth about *external* reality, but they do reflect the "unconscious." To the extent myths are stories, says Smith, and "insofar as we think with stories," they are "parallel means…of 'making sense' alongside discursive reason."[61] Smith believes that "the structures and processes of sense-making share in this unconscious extension."[62]

But even in bending Freud to his purposes, Smith actually *adapted* his earlier Eliadean orientation to myth to Lévi-Strauss's formalism. Smith's nostalgic affection for conceiving myths as defined by their repetition of Eliadean stock motifs, types, and archetypes—e.g., "Birth Upside down or Right Side up?"—suggests that Smith never entirely graduated from his doctoral obsessions with Frazer's *The Golden Bough*, either. Granted, Smith may have broken with Frazer with his 1973 "When the Bough Breaks." But even in his eighty-page "Conjectures on Conjunctures and Other Matters," Smith maintains the spirit of a Frazerian devotee of literature or folklore, equally well associated with Segal and maxmüllerism.⁶³

As for Eliade, Smith never risked disturbing collegial relations, despite increasingly troubling revelations about the great man's rightist politics in 1930s Romania. In the mid-1980s, revelations about the rightist ideological features of Eliade's theory of myths came to light along with news of Eliade's relationships with the intellectual leadership of Romania's fascist Iron Guard.⁶⁴ But, immediately after Eliade's death, Smith published *To Take Place* and *Drudgery Divine*, both of which are more critical of Eliade than anything Smith had published since 1972's "The Wobbling Pivot."⁶⁵ Bryan Rennie charges that these books constituted "Smith's 'most incisive criticism' against Eliade."⁶⁶ Indeed, Smith admitted reticence at criticizing the living Eliade. Concealing his distaste for "scholarly approaches to the study of myth" (like Eliade's) that promoted "a conservative, ideological element," Smith confessed to "often using Adolf Jensen as a stalking horse for Eliade."⁶⁷

Briefly, Smith's orientation to myths retains the same maxmüllerist bias as does Segal. Myths are texts, rather than as tools, functions, or performatives. Even when Smith embraces anthropological data, he, like Segal, continues to lean on literary critics like Kenneth Burke. Affirming his dedication to *text*, Smith says, "there is no privilege to myth….[Myths] must be understood primarily as texts."⁶⁸

Even when Lévi-Strauss writes of wanting "to do things with myths," Smith maintains loyalty to literary conceptions of myth. So, while Smith may note how the Tsimshian and Cree First Nation folk "adapted the same myth to recent history, with the manifest intention of *justifying* a development in the making and of *validating* one of its possible orientations—collaboration with the white man,"⁶⁹ Smith again retreats to thinking about myths in explicitly literary terms. Emphatically, Smith concludes that "myth is best conceived…as a limited collection of elements with a fixed range of cultural meanings which are applied, thought with, worked with, experimented with in particular situations."⁷⁰ That Smith resists performative readings of myth remains a puzzle in his intellectual history.

J. Z. Smith's Structuralist Moments

Urged by Lévi-Strauss to regard myths as literary objects, Smith focuses on "the relations in myth [that] are within myth."[71] Like any other treatment of literature for literature's sake, "we need not turn to external relations, whether these be in nature, in society, or within other cultural formations," — even to rituals.[72] In perhaps his most deliberate attempt at defining myth — and in structural terms, no less — Smith reasserts his linguistic focus.

> ...insofar as mythmaking is a linguistic activity, it is both a human and a social activity. In this sense it is correctly viewed as generated by, organized by, structures that are largely unconscious in the sense specified above. This lack of consciousness extends beyond grammar and transformations to the level of worldview.[73]

Interestingly, Smith's affection for Lévi-Strauss has its own peculiar history. While he wrote his Yale dissertation on Frazer and the *Golden Bough*, Smith was guided by Lévi-Strauss's advice from *The Savage Mind*. Lévi-Strauss's attack on Wilhelm Mannhardt (1830–1881), the great nineteenth-century "naturist" German folklorist and mythologist, made a great impact on Smith. There, Lévi-Strauss claimed Mannhardt mistakenly claimed that "natural phenomena are what myths seek to explain."[74] Like Segal argued, myths should not then be likened to science, as explanations of nature.[75] "But actually rather than seeking means to explain realities," Lévi-Strauss continues, myths "seek to explain matters that are not of the natural order, but of logic."[76]

"Insofar as we think with stories" (and myths),[77] Smith follows Lévi-Strauss in seeing mythic thinking as another, seemingly autonomous means of cognition. Myths or stories, says Lévi-Strauss, are "the parallel means we have of 'making sense' alongside discursive reason — the structures and processes of sensemaking share in this unconscious extension."[78] With myth as story at the center of Smith's concept of myth, his focus naturally dwells on the essentially thematic, poetic, literary, or linguistic nature of myths. Smith credits this literary approach to myth, in turn, originally to Paul Ricoeur, first encountered as an undergraduate from 1955 to 1960.

Smith Gets Metaphysical: Myths, Tragedy, and Incongruity

For Smith, literary notions like Ricoeur's "incongruity" have formed Smith's approach to myths: "the incongruity of myth is not an error, it is the very source of its power."[79] Critic Allan Sun says that for Smith, "Myth is a 'strategy for dealing with the situation' that fails. It is a kind of 'self-conscious category mistake,' which plays upon the incongruity between traditional modes of thought and the prevailing historical circumstances."[80] Sun thus sees Smith better conveying the tragedy embedded in numerous myths from indigenous folk. Instead of celebrating harmony, their myths bespeak native tragedy. The folk attempt—perhaps futilely—to reconcile the incongruity of the colonial encounter between the indigenous peoples and the Europeans."[81] By contrast, Eliade sees myths as benign agents of centering and foundation. In this way, Eliade offers an anodyne, while colonial predation persists.[82] Salutary here for Smith was Ricoeur's *The Rule of Metaphor.* It "may well have had more influence on me than I presently recognize, certainly, given my interest in metaphoric 'tension'" and "the dimensions of incongruity that exist in religious materials."[83] In his 1974 inaugural lecture at the University of Chicago, "Map Is Not Territory," Smith adds that "there is no pristine myth; there is only application"; and "that myth is...a self-conscious category mistake."[84] This means that "the incongruity of myth is not an error, it is the very source of its power. Or (to borrow Kenneth Burke's definition of the proverb) a myth is a "strategy for dealing with a situation."[85] Thus shining the harsh light of reality on Eliade's neo-romantic mythic harmony, Ricoeur forces Smith to see the incongruity in myths. Preferences for such tropes like "tension," and "incongruity" puts Smith's literary sensibility on display.[86] Smith's attention to the Trickster as jokester, for instance, shows how "the power of myth depends upon the play between the applicability and inapplicability of a given element in the myth to a given experiential situation."[87] Jokes, says Smith, "neither deny nor flee from disjunction, but allow the incongruous elements to stand."[88] So, as well do myths, claims Smith![89]

So decisive are such literary properties as incongruity in myth that they suggest a definition of myth in terms of a "collection of elements," "the play between the applicability and inapplicability of a given element."[90] Or literary properties like incongruity "neither deny nor flee from disjunction but allow the incongruous elements to stand."[91] And, further, "they seek, rather, to play between the incongruities and to provide an occasion for thought" — again, all literary properties.[92] The upshot of such an orientation draws us a close as possible to Smith's definition of myth:

> ...myth is best conceived...as a limited collection of elements with a fixed range of cultural meanings which are applied, thought with, worked with, experimented with in particular situations....They seek, rather, to play between the incongruities and to provide an occasion for thought.[93]

Embracing disjunction and opposition, Smith rejects the "replication model" of myth first taught him by Lévi-Strauss "in 1960 when [he] first read Lévi-Strauss's 'Four Winnebago Myths.'"[94] There, Lévi-Strauss said — with Durkheim doubtless in mind — that "anthropologists have often simply assumed that a full correlation exists between the myths of a given society and its culture....[But] it does not follow that whenever a social pattern is alluded to in a myth [it] must correspond to something real."[95] Like Ricoeur, Smith too challenges the

> ...notion of the myth as mirror: whether that which is reflected be expressed as social situation (as some functionalisms as well as the seminar has sometimes formulated it), infrastructure (as in some materialisms), or as divine archetypes (as in Mircea Eliade).[96]

Following Lévi-Strauss's lead, Smith goes on to burnish his literary credentials by celebrating the mythological works of Franz Boas. In *Drudgery Divine*, notably, Smith puts Boas to good use on biblical myths, believing he detects in them novel meanings in classic myths, such as those that magnetized Smith's ancient mentor, J. G. Frazer. Consider alone Frazer's ambitions about the discovery of the so-called "dying and rising god" mythical motif.[97] "The notion of comparing stories, of constructing *vitae parallelae* is not, of course, foreign to early Christianity"; one such example is "the double infancy stories of John the Baptist and Jesus in Luke 1–2, a duality later elaborated in Mesopotamian Christian accounts of Jesus's twin brother."[98] The Bible recalls these and other classic mythic themes.

But especially when it comes to myth in the biblical materials, Smith is particularly alert to the apologetic interests of scholars from the Reformation tradition. In the early years of the twentieth century, various notions of myth facilitated comparisons between Christian and non-Christian motifs. These included titles such as *Jesus the Solar Deity*, *The Astral Myth of Jesus*, *Did Jesus Live 100*

BC?, *The Pre-Christian Jesus*, *The Christ Myth*, and others.[99] Of these, Smith judged the more "influential and theoretically interesting" to be Otto Pfleiderer's (1839–1908) use of Jesus's resurrection story as myth, claiming its parallels with pagan myths of the "dying and rising god," also featured prominently in Frazer's *The Golden Bough*.[100] Pfleiderer concluded that the resurrected Jesus was the same myth as those of the dying and rising Osiris, Adonis, Demeter, Persephone, and Dionysius.[101] Once Smith tips his conceptual hat toward literary-textualist conception of myths, he argued that what matters most is not the possible dependence of the Christian myth upon the pagan. Instead, Smith claims that their "common dependence" resolves into a literary matter.[102] "The question is not," says Smith, "which is first?" Instead, their textual resemblance is *the* issue—"'why both, are more or less the same?'"[103] Supporting the literary reading of the resurrection myths, Smith notes that for the ancients, "there has never been a claim for the rising of Mithras in any Late Antique document."[104] Moreover, even the "notion of the 'dying and rising' Marduk is based on a misreading of the ancient Near Eastern sources."[105] On the Christian side, dying and rising is totally absent from Q; nor, like Mark, do significant early Christian martyrology documents consider the dying Jesus resurrected.[106] Otto Pfleiderer, as well, thought nothing of linking the Jesus myth to the Eleusinian mysteries, Smith suggests, in part because doing so served his polemic against the Roman theology of eucharist.[107] In sum, the resurrection myths make good stories or good apologetics but bad history. Here for a moment, Smith seems to approach myths as performative in mentioning how myths act in dealing with a situation or the power of myth. But such forays into performative theory are short-lived. Smith beats a hasty retreat into conceiving "myths" as a standard literary trope.

The Case for Smith's Methodology of "Play"

Smith's involvement in the details of literary tropes over, say, political or social complements to myths has led some commentators, like Allan Sun and me, to suspect that Smith seeks to distract from his failure to declare his own conceptual or theoretical commitments. Here, Smith and Segal-the-reporter seem to share the same reluctance to declare where they stand. Allan Sun pads that "Smith is deliberately evasive about his own normative commitment."[108]

Citing Smith for his own purposes, Sun notes that Smith says, "'I am an essayist, which makes me more elusive and indirect than a writer of monographs. I tend to do my work in relation to others. I tend not to speak my mind.'"[109] Others, like Sam Gill, says Sun, indeed believe that Smith thereby reveals himself at "play"—but as a Trickster rather than an earnest "essayist" or even a Segal-like "reporter."[110] Without delving speculatively into Smith's psychology, his intellectual eclecticism, flair for style, and strategically outrageous presentation of his public self do say "Trickster." Many will recall Smith of the wild hair, shaggy patriarchal beard, extravagant gesticulation, holding forth in ringing stentorian tones, all the while grinning gap-toothed and broadly, steadying himself with his Tolkienish gnarled tree-root of a staff! This is not to diminish Smith's integrity in the slightest; Smith could always be counted upon to put on an unforgettable *show* in public, the absence of which has left us all vastly poorer. If Smith used "play" as the secret sauce of his own survival, I would not gainsay him for it. If Sun is correct that Smith's affection for "'play', 'absurdity' and 'incongruity'" do not easily accommodate "issues of ethical significance," they at least make a good case for how to confront life's absurdity. Some, at least occasional, detachment from moral seriousness in the study of religion may, at worst, make forays into the incorrigible issues thrown up in political culture easier to endure.[111] R. I. P., J. Z. S.

From Smith to Segal's "King Saul"

It is by contrasting Smith to Segal that circumstantial evidence mounts to support my view of Segal's *generic* theoretical psychologism—featuring Jung and Freud. Although Segal shies away from commitment to any one theorist, he virtually advertises his affinities for psychoanalytically-inspired myth theorists such as Northrop Frye, Kenneth Burke, Otto Rank, Lord Raglan, and Joseph Campbell. It is hard not to see in Segal's attention to this class of theorists his own preferences, as indeed, I will argue that his treatment of the myths of Saul shows. This is yet another reason to see Segal's theoretical inclinations recalling Müller.

It is no fault of Müller's that he had little or no data about Vedic India to justify his interpretations of ancient Indian myths. Likewise, I shall argue that Segal would need quality extra-textual data to justify his psychodynamic readings of the myths surrounding Saul in the time of the Bible itself. Not to get ahead of myself, but while Freud's models may be "applied" with equal ease to any case one's imagination offers, Freudian analysis may not apply to every historical situation, so to speak. Given the vast differences of time and space between ourselves and the biblical other, we should realize that while psychoanalysis provides a much-admired interpretive tool for prying open the secrets of the modern Western psyche, we cannot assume ourselves to be the measure of human cultural possibilities. For good or ill, their dearth of empirical data throws both Segal and Müller back onto the texts as texts, as literature. I have been arguing, however, that in cases where empirical data about the contexts in which myths occur, the attractiveness of performative option increases.

No one would argue that Robert A. Segal has not written a brilliant, trenchant, and deeply researched typological-cum-psychological analysis of the biblical narrative account of the life of King Saul, found in 1 Samuel 8–31.[112] Segal extends himself beyond his own special training and informs his treatment of Saul with the latest biblical scholarship—a tall order in itself. Controversial, however, will be Segal's attempt to bring psychoanalytic theory to bear on biblical materials. In Freudian Lord Raglan's case, Segal notes how Raglan defines hero myths according to their conformity to a twenty-two-part typological schema! But my difficulties with Segal's application of psychoanalytic theory to the King Saul story have more to do with Segal's perpetuation of a severely handicapped literary approach to myths, familiar to us from the work of Müller. Indeed, it is even unclear whether the story of the Saul–David rivalry actually was a *myth* for ancient Israel, or for later generations? Segal also automatically takes the Saul stories to be "myths." I am much less certain. Thus, our opposing conceptions of myths will lead us down different paths of myth interpretation.

Red Flags: Fits, Paradoxes, and More

Segal begins by showing how Rank, Raglan, and Freud read the King Saul story as conforming to classic mythical themes. Notable for Segal is the Freudian Oedipal pattern of a son's desire to kill his father. Segal devotes major attention to the psychoanalyst Otto Rank and myth-ritualist Lord Raglan, showing how they work over the biblical text to show how their perspectives reveal patterns certifying the story's mythical nature. Appealing to classic Freudian psychoanalytic tropes, the "life of Saul is at heart a fight, one rooted not in deed or circumstance, but in biology, between a father and a son."[113] Saul's story is a story of struggle. But first, let me clear the way by unburdening myself of what may just be quibbles about Segal's efforts, but which, nonetheless, raise some red flags.

Do patterns in the Saul story actually match those spelled out by the Ranks, Raglans, and Freuds? Here I must say I find Segal's analyses forced. Speaking broadly, Segal says of mythical heroes: "the hero is heroic not because he dares to win a throne but because he dares to kill his father."[114] But can that be said of the story of Saul as the ancient Israelites conceived their heroes, if indeed that notion makes sense in biblical times? Samson was surely a hero, even comparable to the Greek model. But his heroism has to do with standard bravery and prowess in battle. Samson's heroism has nothing seemingly to do with father-killing. Why, therefore, should it come into play in the King Saul stories? Nor are there indications that the prospect of David killing Saul would make David a hero, nor of Saul killing Samuel, his symbolic father. Indeed, David displeased God by seducing Bathsheba, the wife of Uriah the Hittite, and then effectively sending Uriah to his death by having him placed in the front lines of battle. Thus, 2 Samuel 11:27 concludes, accordingly: "But the thing David had done displeased the Lord." Are we to believe David a hero for killing his own (or symbolic) father? Then Segal also says, "For Jonathan's military feats, the people praise him over Saul (see 1 Sam. 14:45), just as they later do David over Saul (see 1 Sam. 14:43–46)."[115] Indeed, military prowess would plausibly make one a hero in any number of cultures. But killing one's own father [sic] seems hardly a good reason for establishing oneself as a hero, even in such an oft-paradoxical vehicle of lore as myth.

A second questionable device is Segal's delight in paradox, thus making it easy to get snarled in the words. Ultimately, no matter how clever the inversions in Segal's paradoxes, is their result falsifiable? Example. Segal tries to connect divine kingship with god. In one place, he says that people make God, so to speak, by being strong. Thus,

> But the trio do not fail because God deserts them. They are not weak because of God. On the contrary, God is weak because of them. The strength of God depends on the strength of him in whom God resides.

God repeatedly fails to defeat Israel's enemies not because he will not but because he cannot. The fault is not God's.[116]

So, Segal inverts humans (those "in whom God resides") and God as sources of power. Fine, but how to falsify this claim — of unspecified generality and application in the Hebrew Bible — that God's power is limited by "the strength of him in whom God resides"?[117] What would need to be true to make this a false statement? What would need to be true to make the claim that God's power is limited by the human mediation a false claim? Is it not true that the Bible tells us God created heaven and earth? Doesn't that falsify the claim that God's power depends on "the strength of him in whom God resides"? Is Segal saying that this required human embodiment of God, even before Adam and Eve came to be? And which humans made it possible for God to make the first couple? The bottomless pit of infinite regress yawns open before us. Clever is good but being "too clever by half" is not.

An additional problem — also related to "fit" — is that Segal also asserts just the opposite relationship of dependence as immediately above — God makes the king divine:

> This infusion of God in Saul (see 1 Sam. 10:9-13) even certifies Saul as king. In both the anti- and the pro-Saul material, whenever God is with Saul, the "spirit of God", "comes mightily upon him" (see, for example, 1 Sam. 11:6). God's abandonment of Saul means the departure of God's spirit, or at least of God's "good" spirit, from Saul (see 1 Sam. 16:14, 23; 18:10).[118]

Finally, were this possible, Segal combines both propositions in one, thus having it both ways, right out in the open.

Undeniably, 1 Samuel taken straightforwardly makes God the cause of the strength or weakness of the ruler. But one might ask why, when even the ruler has not sinned, success for Israel still proves elusive? Why — at least in the pro-Saul sources — cannot the dutiful Samuel, with God always behind him, defeat the Philistines? If God has to appoint Saul to do Samuel's job, then God depends on Saul for success. I love paradoxes because they signify quick wit and cleverness. But here and in other places, they do not do the work that Segal would like them to do. Again, paradoxical thinking here could be said to be too clever by half. In other words, the conclusions do not really make good sense.

A third universe of questions left untended by Segal is whether a psychoanalytic reading of the stories of King Saul matters as much as other possible connections the myth might have with Jewish life. What connections does the King Saul myth have with Jewish liturgies, rituals, or religious institutions—connections that show that the story has a kind of power attached to many conception of myths? Does it have a pragmatic or performative life in addition to its literary or psychological one? Why, of all the readings of the King Saul myth, should we pay as much attention to a psychoanalytic reading as Segal wishes so to do? What are the larger considerations that would incline us to elect Segal's priorities in approaching the Saul myth? Are there particular rival interpretations that Segal's Freudian reading serves to correct? And so on…

Reading the Bible with a Psychoanalytic Eye

Although Segal's mastery of the relations in the King Saul text is impressive, those with more sociological interests might wish he had indicated whether there was any cultural or social payoff for these complex exercises? Until he does, my interest will be drawn more to theoretical questions that surround the text, rather than engagement with its content. I feel pressed to put to Robert Segal a number of questions arising from this extra-textual perspective. Segal chooses Rank and Raglan for their prowess as theorists. Yet, one oddity in the initial sketch of Segal's argument seems to cast doubt on their qualifications as the theorists of Segal's ardent desire. Segal notes that the first scholars of myth "limited themselves to finding a pattern and, despite their own theoretical inclinations, did not seek to answer the main theoretical questions: What are the origin, function, and subject matter of hero myths?"[119] Segal then points to Otto Rank and Lord Raglan as "the most important" of those who "considered these theoretical questions."[120] However, I find it difficult to see Rank and Raglan as the paradigmatic theorists that Segal does. How, specifically, can Raglan and Rank qualify as credible theorists if they cannot hope to answer questions about the origin and function of the Saul stories beyond the projections of psychological or literary motifs upon them? In the absence of social and/or cultural data, such questions are unanswerable. How, for example, can we know how these stories function in the cultural or social world without considerable historical knowledge of the contexts surrounding them? How can we say they speak authoritatively of *origin* when we have so little factual knowledge of Saul's ancient Israel? We simply do not know how ancient Israelites—or those in the many different contexts of the past 3,000 years—*read* the Saul stories—nor, as pragmatist Bronislaw Malinowski might say, how they "worked." Are these myths a kind of literal history of the days and works of Saul? Or, alternatively, are they to be read as fictional hero epics like *The Lord of the Rings*? Indeed, what did the myths themselves *do*? Without the factual knowledge to which I refer, how can we answer any of these queries?

Segal's confidence in the explanatory power of psychoanalytic approaches is so immense that at times he seems to believe they can answer these cultural or social questions. But psychoanalytic theories cannot step in where history leaves us empty. For instance, Segal claims that a psychoanalytic point of view assures us that these myths of Saul are "fantasy."[121] A consummately intriguing suggestion, to be sure. But whose fantasy is it? And how can we be sure? And, as for Raglan, what ritual—as he would inquire—was linked to them, as fantasy or as something else to be specified? Raglan cannot know this from the biblical narrative alone.

And, with a Literary Eye

Now as strictly literary analyses, I do not gainsay Segal's creative readings. Indeed, they bring out how possibly rich and multivalent these biblical stories can be. But they tell us nothing, nor can they, about origin and function in any cultural, social, or historical sense. Given their extra-clinical setting, they are, more precisely, literary entities—and thus not even authentic subjects for psychoanalysis. While Rank writes as if he were equipped to answer such questions of origin and function (and thus qualify as a "theorist"), if we adopt Segal's view, I am not persuaded. Raglan may be celebrated for his imagination, but he fails as a theorist in any way but as a literary theorist. To be a theorist about human historical phenomena entails being more than a theorist of what folks have narrated or written. And, as rich a source of human wisdom as psychoanalysis has been, it cannot create its own factual reality. Here's why.

Psychoanalytic theories purportedly address questions of origin and function by assuming that the patterns of familial strife are rooted in a common, universal human nature. But, given the gap of millennia between Saul's life and the Occidental lives familiar to Rank, Raglan, or Segal, we cannot assume any universality of experience. In support, I cite anthropologist Bronislaw Malinowski, who, despite being a great devotee of Freudian ideas, was also a great critic of Freud. Notably for the case of Saul, Malinowski attacked the universality of Freud's Oedipus Complex.[122] Malinowski felt that Freud's ideas had to be adapted to suit different cultures. Malinowski, for example, felt that Freud wrongly assumed the universality "of a patriarchal family with a tyrannical and ferocious father who repressed all the claims of the younger men."[123] Per Freud, in the struggle between fathers and sons, eventually the younger men, denied possession of sexual partners by the father, kill him. But Malinowski discovered that in Melanesia, families did not correspond to the Victorina Viennese patriarchal. Different forms of families generated different individual psychologies. In Eastern New Guinea, for example, Malinowski testified that

> the mother and her brother possess...all the legal *potestas*. The mother's brother is the "ferocious matriarch," the father is the affectionate friend and helper of his children....In fact, none of the domestic conditions required for the sociological fulfilment of the Oedipus complex, with its repressions, exist in the Melanesian family of Eastern New Guinea....[124]

Segal has not taken account of the effects of such cultural variants in the psychological realm.

Psychoanalyzing Myths and Religion Done Better: The Marian Cult in Context

A persuasive example of a psychoanalytic approach that integrates universal Freudian themes with cultural variation is Michael Carroll's *The Cult of the Virgin Mary*.[125] First, Carroll's work is steeped in the history of the time of the rise of the Marian cult. It is not just a literary or typological study, as I think Segal's approach to Saul is. Second, Carroll offers a plausible account of the historical and sociological facts that shaped the Marian cult. This required Carroll to locate the origins of the Marian cult in a particular period in the late Roman Empire—not in some timeless universal Never-neverland where Segal's Saul exists. Before that time and in that place, Carroll shows that no cult of the Virgin Mary was known to exist. Carroll then aligns the rise of the cult with specific events—namely, the

Councils of Ephesus and Chalcedon, where Mary was certified as both worshipful and ever virgin. The councils, in effect, conferred theological legitimacy on the Marian cult. Third, Carroll shows further how the new cultists shared common sociological characteristics that made them prime candidates for cult membership. The absence of mature men, due to wars and other social disruptions, left behind domestic units ruled by women. Absence of male role models combined with strong women leaders of familial units provided the sociological conditions for the particular kind of socialization of young men favoring identification with Mary, mother of God. This match of theological legitimacy with a particular kind of socialization accounts for what has come to be known as the cult of the Virgin Mary. Mary not only had ready devotees conditioned by their upbringing, but ecclesiastical approval as well.

When compared with Carroll's factually informed viewpoint, Segal's treatment of the King Saul story reveals a dearth of historical and sociological data. Without such data, one cannot treat the King Saul myth as any more than a literary item. In this book I have been arguing that it is no particular virtue to assume a Freudian tradition of inquiry that effectively discounts cultural contexts and differences in the formation of the human psyche. Less is not more. Segal's otherwise sparkling interpretations, therefore, need, like Carroll, to seize these myths with a firmer bite. Having only the texts of the Bible to hand, we cannot reasonably expect to apply Viennese psychology to the Hebrew religious life of 1000 BCE or so.

Our inability to answer at least the questions of historical origin and function is one reason that I argue for moving further out onto the territory of giving myths their life, and thus currency. Just as vital is understanding the thought-worlds of the myth theorists themselves. In other publications, I have emphasized certain questions about myth and myth theorists—namely, why a given story becomes a myth, as well as why a theorist would bother creating such a theory. Why did theorists think they were right to say what they said about myth? Segal and others dealing with myths originating in historically remote eras—ancient Greece, biblical times, etc.—are unavoidably disadvantaged. But given our knowledge of the historically accessible world, we have data to make good hypotheses about such problems—theories that consider salient features of a theorist's time and place in the world. This discrepancy makes it all the more important to realize how the availability of empirical and/or historical data, or lack thereof, unwittingly determines the kinds of theories of myth appropriate for use in making sense of mythical materials. Psychoanalytic genius cannot make up for lack of empirical or historical data. We just do not know whether Saul's world was alike enough to Freud's to lend itself to psychoanalytic interpretations of the myths of Saul's world.

In the next two chapters, I shall show by contrast how detailed *knowledge* of the historical and cultural situations in which myths really "do things" critically informs the appreciation of myths performing in certain political cultures. My admiration for Hubert's work on French Aryanism, for one, shows how we can achieve consequential understandings of myths in action *without* imposing *a priori* theoretical templates, such as Freudian psychoanalytic theory, on the data. In some cases, the data—Aryanist mythic propaganda—speaks for itself. Hubert teaches us that paying heed to Aryanists myths, informed by a theory of myths as powerful propaganda, can yield real understanding. Similarly, in chapter 10, we learn how a modern-day, complex theological geopolitics can seize control over an old myth like that of Moscow, Third Rome to create a lived mental reality in which many Russians will try to do their politics.

Chapter 9

Henri Hubert Undoes Aryanist Political Myths

Durkheimian Remoteness

Durkheimian sociology can give the impression of a certain scientific, impersonal remoteness. Several reasons account for this impression, regardless of it is warranted. Durkheimian thought does tend to pursue general explanatory *principles* such as "elementary forms," that can give an impression of emotional detachment from the issues at stake. Durkheim also favored viewing modern society from the distant perspective of its being an evolutionary development from long-extinct archaic forbears. Finally, Durkheim's commitment to scientific objectivity ruled out making concessions to existential, moral, or other expressions of subjectivity.[1] This declared ideal of scientific objectivity and Durkheim's practical orientation toward remoteness both raise further questions. Durkheim sincerely believed in a science of morality: a sociological approach to morality that discounts subjectivity.[2] Nonetheless, present-day critics have judged Durkheim epistemologically naive — or perhaps disingenuous — in this regard. No one doubts Durkheim's sincerity as a scientist. But was his intention to create a *science* of morality, given the subjective nature of moral viewpoints? Few scholars believe that human nature could permit such intentions, however noble, to be realized.

Whatever Durkheim may have *believed* about the value-neutrality of his science of morality, his deeply held, personal, moral commitments inspired some of his most important research projects. Close collaborator Celestin Bouglé once said of Durkheim, "Behind the scientist, the moralist still lives."[3] Despite the fact that Durkheim said virtually nothing about the personal and political moral motivations behind his sociological work, we generally think more of

Durkheim and Durkheimian sociology today the more we learn of Durkheim's constructive humanism. Durkheim's interventions in the Dreyfus affair—indirect, scholarly, and remote as they may have been—showed how seriously he took his role as both scholar-scientist and moralist. No one can accuse Durkheim's "Individuals and the Intellectuals" of either moral flaccidity or deficiency in social and historical scientific rigor.[4]

Durkheim stood aloof from conspicuous political activism, even if he could not resist *thinking* profoundly about the political implications of the events of his day. (Alexander 1988; Durkheim 1975c, 1905, 1915, 1975a, 1885, 1975b) Durkheim did, after all, classify politics as a division of other choice areas of study such as morals and law.[5] Thus, Durkheim knew that what he wrote and taught about morals often had unavoidable political implications, even though he resisted exploiting them publicly or converting them into political activism. W. Paul Vogt describes this ambiguity well, saying that although the Durkheimians "usually *said* that their work was not to be taken prescriptively, they *hoped*, and not always tacitly, that it would be so taken."[6] Thus while Durkheimian texts may appear or purport to be removed from values, and thus scientific, their *subtexts* often spoke to moral concerns both personal and political. In the particular case of Durkheimian opposition to Aryanist antisemitism infecting scholarship about myths, I shall show how the Durkheimian mythologist Henri Hubert tried to balance scientific objectivity with his own moral and political subjectivity.

A Socialist Ethnographer of Europe's Primitive Religions

Until fairly recently, little was known about Durkheim's mythologist, Henri Hubert.[7] But along with Mauss and Durkheim, Henri Hubert formed the vital "nucleus" of the original Durkheimian *équipe*.[8] From that vantagepoint, Hubert engaged some of the larger political and social issues of his day—sometimes even pseudonymously—as his professional training in European archeology, ancient history, comparative ethnography, and myth permitted him. But the Roman Catholic Hubert also deliberately sought to study critical Church history under the liberal historian Abbé Louis Duchesne.[9] Often considered a precursor to the Modernist movement, Duchesne may well have informed Hubert's sympathy for Alfred Loisy, the most prominent Roman Catholic Modernist, and others.¹⁰ In a review of Loisy's *L'évangile et l'église*, Hubert, like Durkheim, steers clear of the public controversy surrounding Loisy and Modernism. But he nevertheless gives Loisy and his work a fair and hospitable treatment, despite its confessional, theological character. Instead, they take Loisy's work seriously from a methodological and theoretical standpoint in their reviews, leaving aside any derogatory comments about its theological character.¹¹ Specifically, Hubert notes how well Loisy and the Durkheimians agree on religion's social nature. Both the Durkheimians and Loisy had made the "life" of the actual, evolving community primary in their conceptions of religion.¹²

As we know from chapters 3 to 5, Hubert too found particular professional pleasure in archeological and museum work. He joined excavations at major paleolithic sites including Les Éyzies in Perigord and managed France's prehistorical holdings as Conservateur at the Musée des Antiquités nationales in Saint-Germain-en-Laye. But a scholarly temperament did not prevent Hubert and other younger members of the *équipe* from rallying to the Dreyfusist moral revival. The plight of Captain Dreyfus captured the moral imaginations of Hubert's generation, many of them graduates of the École Normale, where the main librarian, Lucien Herr, held court as a kind of *spiritus rector*. Meeting this great socialist luminary daily, Hubert could hardly have resisted the idealistic socialism that suffused the École.¹³ The *haute-bourgeois* Hubert was also rumored to have been an original stockholder in Herr's socialist successor to *La Société Nouvelle de Librairie et l'Édition*. Hubert similarly collaborated with Francois Simiand on *Notes critiques*, a journal of review that Steven Lukes wittily tagged the "'socialist' *Année sociologique*."¹⁴ Little more, however, can be said on the subject of Hubert's precise connections to socialist ideas and values.

During this period of rising antisemitism, coincident with the Dreyfus affair, Hubert took special care to join forces with his many Jewish colleagues and friends: Durkheim and Marcel Mauss, above all, but also scholars like Hartwig Derenbourg, Israel Lévi, Sylvain Lévi, and Isidore Lévy. Hubert complemented these personal relations by exploring his own scholarly interest in Near Eastern studies and Jewish religious history. In addition to the Dreyfus trial, sensitivities about antisemitism had been set on edge by the spectacular 1886 publication of Édouard Drumont's *La France juive*.

Here Mauss tallied his interests in bolshevism, co-operatives, financial support for socialist publications, L'Humanité and Notes critiques.[15] In such a state of political awakening, Hubert eagerly joined the *gauchiste* fellowship of the *équipe* led by Mauss. From 1898 until the outbreak of the Great War, Mauss and Hubert—rather than Durkheim—spearheaded and sharpened the thrust of a Durkheimian approach to religion with monographs on sacrifice, magic, prayer, sacred time, and, notably, *myth*. As his career advanced, Hubert developed both teaching and research specialties in the primitive religions of Europe, especially those of the prehistorical Celtic and Germanic tribes. Inevitably, these historical studies led Hubert into meditations on the deep nature of differences between modern France and Germany—and in particular, the German political mythology we will deal with in this chapter. The Great War interrupted Hubert's civilian career, as it did for many of his contemporaries. From 1914 to 1919, Hubert served with considerable distinction on socialist minister Albert Thomas's diplomatic missions to Russia. After the war ended, Hubert supervised the repair of historic monuments in France's recently restored territories, winning the *Croix de la Légion d'honneur* for his service in 1920. Although the war had remade Europe, Hubert resumed his university career in 1919, focusing increasingly on European prehistory and what lessons it might hold for understanding the present.

The worrisome ascent of racism and hyper-nationalism after the war slowly began to inform Hubert's scholarship. At about the same time, Mauss too refocused his research on nationalism.[16] Mauss argued, notably, that nations needed their own stirring national histories—their political myths.[17] These myths, in turn, demanded close attention because of their ability of generate powerful emotions not easily tempered by rational argument. Given Hubert's earlier training and professional interest in ethnic mythologies, he was well placed to address the challenge of understanding how archaic myths and pseudo-historical origin stories could play such an influential role in modern nation-states.

Hubert's Uniqueness: From Fact to Value to Myth

Although Hubert was not the first to approach the social problem of race from a Durkheimian perspective, he did so in his own way. Durkheim first launched a critical polemic against the pretensions of *anthroposociological* race scientists in *The Division of Labor* (1893). In *The Rules of Sociological Method*, published a year later, Durkheim once again condemned similar movements.[18] Another Durkheimian, Célestin Bouglé, also ventured into the normative area in 1899's *Les idées égalitaires* and 1904's *La démocratie devant la science*. Bouglé's earlier practical politicking for the Radical-Socialist Party made the appearance of such books more consistent with the tenor of his career. Nevertheless, he continued with his conventional academic criticism of anthroposociology, exposing it as an anti-democratic ideology masquerading as social science.[19]

Hubert was no less sincere a critic of race sciences like anthroposociology than the overtly political Bouglé. But for the most part, Hubert eschewed explicit attacks on racism. Instead, he undermined the principles grounding anthroposociology's racism. His critiques of Friedrich Max Müller flirtations with the "Aryan origins" of Europe are one example of how Hubert did so.[20] The Aryanist ideas of Müller had progressively penetrated European public discourse by the mid-nineteenth century. But their greatest impact in France did not come until the final decade of the century when rising anti-semitism unsettled France. Not only was the era of the Dreyfus affair (1894–1906) in full swing, but influential Aryanist agitators like Georges Vacher de Lapouge were at their height of their prominence, often stoking anti-Semitic public opinion.

Both Müller and Lapouge admired the Aryans, but they did so in very different spirits. Müller saw the Aryan migration from their homeland in Bactria as peaceful.[21] Lapouge could not abide the idea of Europeans deriving from Asian Bactria. Instead, he declared — falsely, as it happens — that it is "today pretty well agreed to regard central Europe as the region in which has occurred the evolution of the Aryan languages and institutions."[22] Then, Lapouge substituted a violent, dystopian view of Aryan origins, casting them as caught in a Darwinian struggle among similar groups vying for superiority. The Aryan migration into Europe was then — in Lapouge's false view — a violent affair of barbarians at the gates, "a process of selection [that] eliminated the weaker and gave a broader extension to the stronger."[23] Contemptuous to the end, Lapouge boasted — absurdly — that "Max Müller's theory has now only one serious advocate — himself."[24] Durkheimian sociology and maxmüllerist historical linguistics differed immensely. Yet Müller never lost the respect of the Durkheimians as Lapouge did.[25] In Lapouge, Hubert spotted a recrudescence of political mythologizing that merged *racial* identity with *national* identity. Lapouge was not just an idle storyteller. Lapouge's ethno-nationalist mythologizing *did* perverse things. It *performed* a role in shaping European political culture by appealing to Aryanist myths of a violent, ethnically pure, warlike European history.[26]

As spelled out in chapter 7, "Taking Responsibility for the Concept of Myth," by "*myth*" I mean important stories or derivatives of such stories. Contrary to their common understanding, myths need not be stories about the gods. They may instead focus on other realities regarded as *important*, such as their politics. Political myths differ from standard religious myths *not* only in subject matter—being about the folk, nation, people, polis, political movement, or racial ancestors, rather than about the gods. They also differ in that political myths constitute and spur *action*, just as ideology, propaganda, and such do. Myths as *performatives*—as *doing* something—naturally gravitate to the domain of politics in the form of political myths. As derivatives of full-blown political myths, we often do not even require meeting myths whole and entire. Quite often, we meet fragments or allusions to political myths or stories, such as the idea of savior or *Führer*. These are sufficient, nonetheless, to appreciate the ubiquity of myths or mythological elements in our political world.

By marrying progressive politics to professional competence in ancient European history and myth, Hubert positioned himself well to counter racist mythologizing like Lapouge's. But besides countering the way Aryanist myths *implemented* racist ideology, Hubert was equally well prepared to construct myths that *performed* in an anti-racist way. By mythmaking himself, Hubert expanded the application of Durkheimian moral discourse to include new ways of using imaginative narrative forms of discourse. By embracing what myths could *do*, Hubert saw myths not only as potentially dangerous in the hands of racists but also good for lifting modern society from its periodic troughs of depression. Political myths are particularly interesting in this respect.

The Aryans, Lapouge and "L'Anthroposociologie"

Ever since the mid-nineteenth century, European academic discourses about language, race, and national identity have been entangled with one another. One field that arose from the intersection of these elements was "anthroposociology." Evidently unaware of anthroposociology's unsavory features, the Durkheimians reviewed publications under this rubric for a short while. From about 1901 until 1906, a section of *L'Année*, "L'Anthroposociologie," hosted reviews of publications by social Darwinist authors as well as Aryanist race scientists (*Rassenkunde*). Indeed, in a short editorial introduction to the new section, Durkheim introduced *L'Anthroposociologie* and its new principal reviewer, Henri Muffang—incidentally, one of its chief advocates, as well. Somehow, the latent moral implications of anthroposociology, as well as Lapouge's racialism, had escaped Durkheim's attention. Perhaps it was Durkheim's well-intentioned editorial policy of scientific openness that allowed Muffang entry to the pages of *L'Année sociologique*? Durkheim once said that he hoped that something valuable would emerge from a fledgling science like anthroposociology: "One never knows in advance," said Durkheim, "what kinds of results might emerge from a scientific movement."[27] And so Henri Muffang had editorial command over the reviews appearing in *L'Année sociologique* under the heading of "L'Anthroposociologie" for three years.[28]

Eventually, and quite abruptly, Durkheim eliminated both Muffang and the *Anthroposociologie* section from the *Année*. Durkheim announced his decision to eliminate the rubric in a 1900 letter to Bouglé but did not provide a rationale for doing so.[29] Perhaps Muffang's outspoken advocacy for ethno-nationalist Aryanism finally pushed Durkheim beyond his liberal tolerance of difference. Once dismissed, however, all ties between Muffang and the *Année* were cut. Oddly, though, even though the rubric, "anthroposociology," had been banned from the *Année,* Durkheim still maintained interest in the field. He assigned Hubert editorial command over any publications remotely related to it and kindred titles. What could have accounted for Durkheim's sudden and unexplained decision to dismiss Muffang and his new science?

A comparison of Muffang's reviews of Lapouge's work with those by core Durkheimians suggests an answer.[30] As the Dreyfus affair proceeded, Durkheim reassessed his open welcome to all contributors to the *Année*.[31] For one thing, anthroposociology's social Darwinist, fascist-adjacent worship of power became evident, as had its biological reductionism. In a review in 1901, Hubert savaged the pretensions of anthroposociology's appeal to inherited biological traits:

> These simplistic theorists ask biology to answer all our questions. For a certain kind of inquisitive person, "heredity" has functioned like "electricity" for peasants—a word which covers a lot—but really relieves us of the responsibility of understanding anything at all and, at the same time, seems to explain different sorts of incomprehensible things. In fact, heredity explains nothing in social life...[32]

Furthermore, under the pseudonym "Henri Pierre," Hubert roundly mocked Lapouge's scientific ambitions. It is nonsense, said Hubert, for Lapouge to claim that the physical dimensions of a person's cranium provided any *social* information. Examining skulls taught us nothing, for example, about the relationship of Aryans to Jews.[33] Lapouge's *L'Aryen: son rôle social* is thus nothing but an absurd "last gospel of anthroposociology—the epic of the Aryans."[34] Writing again pseudonymously as Henri Pierre for Gabriel Monod's *Revue historique*, Hubert denounced Lapouge's "false science."[35] Hubert reduced Lapouge to the clownish figure of a "prophet and seer," chanting a "hymn to the glory of the Aryans."[36] Not only is Lapouge's book guided by a "method...vicious in its principles," adds Hubert.[37] But its arguments are "only scientific in appearance," and rest on "really scanty statistics."[38] As if further evidence of the poverty of Lapouge's scholarship were necessary, his comparison of the ethnic psychologies of Jews and Aryans reeks of anti-semitism.[39] Concluding his review of Lapouge in the *Année*, Hubert unleashes his puckish talent for withering scorn:

> ...the Anglo-Saxons, the world's hope, inherit the heritage of the pure Aryans; they subdue the earth. But an Anti-Christ arises, the Jewish race, dolichocephalid and brown, which threatens to subjugate and incorporate the brachycephalids, and oppose the plans of the blond dolichocephalids.[40]

Hubert continued elsewhere in this critical vein for other work like Lapouge's. For instance, Hubert applauded Louis Manouvrier's indictment of anthroposociology as "pseudo-sociology" and also reviewed Manouvrier's book in the same spirit of "ridicule and spirited good humor" as its author.[41]

In sum, Hubert's reviews of anthroposociology reveal him to be more of a passionately engaged partisan than a neutral representative of an objective, remote Durkheimian science of society. They further reveal Hubert as unabashedly engaging an un-Durkheimian *politics of myth* through the medium of scholarship. This politics features the demythologizing of "race" as one of its choice weapons against the racist mythologizing of the day. Hubert's demythologizing of "race" exposed it as a notion "in appearance more precise" than in reality. Race is too simplistic a notion to account for the social facts it claims to explain: "In a given 'race,' the most varied set of its individuals," points out Hubert, also "share the best characteristics of that race."[42] Not only is race too simplistic an idea to account for the facts of Europe's population, but the "populations of today's Europe are products of mixtures which date back too far, have lived lives too complicated, represent too many traditions, and have been subjected to too many influences to furnish convincing examples of specific aptitudes of the *brachycephalids* and *dolichocephalids*."[43]

With the pretensions of anthroposociology safely deflated, Hubert took his demythologizing wrecking ball to German Aryanist ethno-nationalist mythologizing. First to go was the myth that German Aryanists told about being aboriginal speakers of an Aryan mother tongue, "Indo-European." Not so, said Hubert. Germans, instead, were a northern European people who later *became* "Indo-europeanised or…adopted an Indo-european language."[44] The same goes for other European tongues claiming to represent an Indo-European *Ursprache*. The linguistic term "Indo-Germanic," favored by the German Aryanists, thus, had no basis in history.[45] Second, although the Germans plausibly claimed an ancestral homeland in the Baltic basin, the Aryans originated elsewhere in Central Asia, e.g., Turkestan.[46] These facts meant that the anthroposociologist myth of pure Aryan-German blood conflicted both with the Asian origins of the Aryans and the relatively later Indo-European character of German language.

Durkheim's Mythologist

Hubert's subsequent work with myth charted new territory for the Durkheimians, effectively making him "Durkheim's mythologist."[47] Nearly ten percent of Hubert's reviews for the *Année*, some 40 out of 410 total, were about myth, while only about seven percent—30 of 460—of Mauss's dealt with myth. More than this, myths figured in so many of Hubert's works that the tedium of so doing prevents me from listing them here. As we have already noted earlier in this volume, Hubert wrote what seems to be the consensus Durkheimian statement on theory of myth, although he probably did so in collaboration with Mauss.[48] Thus, if there had been any official Durkheimian theory of myth, it would have been Hubert's. Even without such distinction, Hubert's novel approach to myth can be found in many Durkheimian publications. Particularly notable is Hubert's "Préface" to his student Stefan Czarnowski's *Le culte des héros et ses conditions sociales: Saint Patrick, héros national de l'Irlande*, in which he advances three theses about myths. First, myth is society's way of *doing* something to regenerate itself. By imaginatively representing itself and its ideals in mythical form, a society sets its own collective imagination aflame with images of its own distinction. As a "collective representation," it thus seeks to *accomplish* something for a society. A myth of a hero, like that of Saint Patrick, collectively imagines *actualizing* its own highest ideals or values for its own consideration. Agentive in a way even a colorful chronicle of pseudo-history is not, Hubert urges us to see such a myth as Ireland's Saint Patrick myth *performatively* — as it *endorses* the community's values and, hence, stirs the community's emotions.[49]

Hubert also means that myths are better seen in terms of their social dynamics. A person *becomes* a "hero" as much by *being mythologized* as by having performed exceptional deeds. This is because being mythologized is, at the same time, being socialized — being made current within the community, say, by creating a reputation. Myths thus *make* the hero into a "hero" by celebrating their exploits within their home community. What person can be said to be a hero if their extraordinary exploits remain obscure or ignored? None can attain heroic stature without social repute and collective awareness, no matter how objectively remarkable their deeds may be.

In the case of the hero myth of Saint Patrick, Hubert sees heroic Saint Patrick as enveloped by a particular collectivity. Such collectivities range from small groups and tribes through to nations. Saint Patrick's identity, along with his myths, represent a political identity belonging to a particular polity.[50] Rituals, then, become the occasions when communities enact and revive their collective natures and the sites where myths are recalled. Thus, Hubert became a different sort of historian than he would have been had he remained complacent in the established positivist camp of skeptical French *historiens historisants*. But Hubert's adaptation of Durkheim's sociological theory of the autonomy and functions of myth led to myths as agents endorsing social values and dealing power.

Czarnowski: Political Myth in Text and Subtext

Hubert's introduction to Czarnowski's *Le culte des héros et ses conditions sociales* seems to stand out as Hubert's first venture into the domain of expressly political myths. In 1914, Stefan Czarnowski, a Polish political *émigré*, found himself in Paris. An encounter with Durkheimian sociology led him to write his doctoral dissertation on Saint Patrick and Irish national identity under the direction of Hubert and Jean Vendryes. Thus, myths fascinated Czarnowski because of what myths *did* politically, leading him to discover how ancient Irish hero myths *sustained* a modern nation's struggle for its own identity. The archaic hero myths were not just idle legends of the fantastic deeds of ancient times. Hubert explained this to the French public in two articles in the *Revue d'histoire des religions* (1914–1915), in which he introduced Czarnowski's *Le culte des héros et ses conditions sociales*.[51] Hubert even argued in his "Préface" that Czarnowski should have made even more of the agency of myths than he did. Hubert twits Czarnowski for falling back into the commonplace view that "hero" status consists of merely having performed extraordinary deeds—neglecting the agentive role of myth in making a person a *hero*. After all, for Hubert, it is the hero's repute—the social respect—that makes a person a "hero," not just objective accomplishments.

In the midst of agitation for Irish independence, Hubert noted how Czarnowski's book showed how an ancient myth can *act* as a potent *subtext* in contemporary politics. The archaic Saint Patrick myths drove their share of Ireland's contemporary *political* struggle. Czarnowski's vision deepened as he realized how the Irish materials spoke to his own contemporary Polish political concerns for independence. Although Czarnowski's text bears a plain enough reference to Ireland, its subtext meditates on modern-day Poland's politics. François Isambert argued that the Patrick's "struggle to unify an Ireland torn between rival clans is the image of what Czarnowski wanted for his native Poland."[52][53] Ancient Irish myth thus had the potential to *do things* contemporary Poland's politics as well as for modern Ireland's. I shall argue further that, as Czarnowski used remote ancient mythology to *do things* for contemporary purposes, so too did Hubert try to put similarly archaic mythologies to work for modern France.

184   *How to Do Things with Myths*

In particular, Hubert exploited a version of French republican reliance on the political mythological discourse known as *Celtisme*, notably celebrated by Ernest Renan in 1854. For French patriots like Renan, the ancient Celts mythologically symbolized the core values of the liberal, cosmopolitan France beloved by Hubert and other Durkheimians. These Celts—*les Gaulois*—competed for national mythical identity with the Franks in what came to be known in Hubert's time as the "Controversy about the Two Races."[54]

The Controversy about the Two Races: Political Myth as Subtext in France

Who were the French? From whence did they originate? Were the French really just Romans who had assimilated the vanquished *Gaulois*? Or were they, rather, really still *Gauls*—Celts—who had superficially adopted Latin language and political institutions? Indeed, the name "France" also indicates ancient origins of a quite different, and alien, kind—the (Germanic) Franks! In the fever of *fin-de-siècle* patriotism, this raised the disturbing question whether the French were actually—mythically [sic]—their ancient enemy, the Germans! And, if the French were Franks, what became of their Roman and Celtic origins? Did archaic Celtic origins live on as much as their Frankish counterparts? Words like *franchement* (frankly), *franchise, affranchisement* (enfranchisement), and even *franc*—in all its senses—seemed to evoke from the depths of the folk memory a certain string of lofty associations with freedom, forthrightness, and success.[55] Was there no competing non-Germanic myth, rooted in other French ancestors, to *do the work* of informing French national identity? These were the terms of myth-inflected discussions between republicans and rightists known as "The Controversy about the Two Races." Across the Rhine, German scholars were also creating their own prehistoric mythological identity as a distinct, superior ethnicity. As Lapouge implied in his critique of Müller's myth of Aryan origins in Asia, German Aryanists of Hubert's generation insisted Germans were the true Aryans—indeed, the modern-day representatives of the mother-race of a uniquely northern European civilization. "*Indo-germanisch*" was the *lingua franca* of their mythical Aryan Eden. Impressively, German Aryanists supported their claims with formidable historical and comparative linguistic erudition. Hubert faced the Aryanist challenge of whether

French prehistory was informed by a more appropriate national myth — Celtism?

Hubert thus effectively thus engaged in a mythological cultural politics similar to that of Ernest Renan's "La poésie des races celtiques"[56] — the "The Controversy about the Two Races." As Czarnowski had adapted Saint Patrick's mythology for use in contemporary Poland, Hubert wanted to cast French social and political dramas in equally potent mythologies of prehistory. Antagonisms between Germans and Gauls (later, Jews and Slavs) sprang to life again in the mythology Hubert engaged about modern Europe. Defending French aristocracy, French partisans of a mythic Germanism celebrated their Frankish ancestors as noble survivors, both of the Revolution and the original Frankish ruling classes.[57] Republican thinkers claimed the opposing Celtic mythical origins as the true basis of French identity. A century earlier, liberals like François Guizot, Augustin Thierry, Jules Michelet, and Henri Martin, accordingly, wove myths of the rebellious third estate's love of freedom as the Celt within, defying their Germanic Frankish masters.[58] From the mid-nineteenth century, these liberals deployed the myth of a democratic, republican, and cosmopolitan *"celtisme" working* to counter the aristocratic and aggressive, often racist, antisemitic German (and Anglo-Saxon) mythology of Aryan/Frankish supremacy. Armed, then, with the latest results of archeology and history, Hubert contributed his flare for myth to this republican Celtic mythologizing effort. In addition to criticizing *"l'Anthroposociologie"* and *Germantum*, Hubert traded in mythologies of his own. Like his republican *celtiste* political forbears, Hubert too imagined a Celtic world fit to edify republican France.

Durkheim's Mythologist Meets the Celts and Germans

Hubert imagined such a Celtic world with the aid of a version of the liberal *celtiste* nationalist myth. Because in republican political imagination, the French are really — *mythically* — the Celts, they are less Romans. "Celtic civilisation is basically our own," Hubert pleaded. Furthermore, "the nation which the Celts of Gaul started to form is basically our nation [and] remains... Celtic."[59] In declaring this identity, Hubert also deliberately countered fascist-adjacent Action Française mythologizing of the Romans as Europe's sole civilizers. As the French are Europe's civilizers, so also should the Celts rightly own that title in ancient Europe.

> The Celts have been the bearers of the torch of civilization in the ancient world; we have succeeded them. Lovers of beauty and precise thought, in Europe we have been the intermediaries of ancient, mature and lofty civilizations—by virtue of which we have contributed to making "civilization" itself.[60]

After all, the Celts dominated all of old western Europe, while the archaic Germans never did. Indeed, every western European nation bears the traces of a Celtic element in its foundation. By contrast, the Germans came relatively late to Europe and then remained confined to the shores of the Baltic. Furthermore, Celtic influence concentrated in the moral dimension of national identity—in its *civilizing* quality, not in the ability to make war or dominate others. Implicitly, so soon after France's crushing defeat in the Franco-Prussian War, Hubert seemed intent upon consoling his fellow French patriots of the proposition that, while Germany may be perpetual, eternal France will always survive.[61]

In terms of the major themes of this book—myths as performative, as "doing things"—Hubert's discussion of the Celts tells us that his myth of Celtic-French identity is not just an idle "story." It is an *important* story, purposed to *do something* to stir French national self-confidence. As a performance, the Celtic myth of French identity actually *does*, then, make things happen by contributing to French political *culture*. For Hubert, myths are active—they *accomplish things*, not just represent things.

Myths *do things*, in effect, says Hubert, by creating "a 'world of... figures, sensible images,'" contributing to the funding of political culture.[62] While this mythically-informed political culture lives in the realm of "the imagination" and hence "freely surpasses the limits of perception," it is nonetheless real.[63] As a dynamic source of inspiration, mythology is meant to "replenish" and "nourish thought" notably,[64] as the Ireland of Czarnowski's Saint Patrick myth stokes thoughts of national revival. In his foreword to *Les Celts*, historian Henri Berr calls attention to this central role of imagination in Hubert's thinking:

> Imagination is a dangerous thing when it lets itself go on insufficient evidence; but, as I have often said, it plays a legitimate part when it comes in to crown a long piece of analysis, when it is inspired by a wealth of

learning, when it completes and vivifies a synthesis by a sort of spontaneous generation of images which have arisen to the inward eye. Here precisely is the historian's gift of recreating; he is, as he has been called, "the seer of the past." Hubert sees and makes you see.[65]

As Hubert waxes poetic about the noble Celtic identity of the French, Berr again senses the way Hubert feels that the French mythically participate in the Celts of the past:

> ...the essential survival of Celticism [Hubert] finds and shows us in Romanized Gaul, in the France of all ages. We cannot conceal the fact that this historian, with all his devotion to objective science, seems to have a sort of tenderness for the Celtic genius. I do not think that it leads him astray, but it infuses emotion into many pages of his work, particularly those which tell of the effects of Celticism on the history of the French nation.[66]

For Hubert, Durkheim's mythologist, France and the Celts are then *mythically* one. The historical pathos of the Celtic twilight is *mythically* annulled in this realization of what—for a Durkheimian and a patriot like Hubert—was surely a merging of different historical moments in the long life of one nation. As Hubert says in his "Conclusion" to "Introduction aux mythes," "mythical acts continue, repeating themselves without end...or they endure in their effects."[67] In the Celtic mythological mirror, Hubert sees modern France as he and other progressives wished her to be: a generous, all-embracing, cosmopolitan, racially mixed, broadly European people living in sometimes tense, but also equally vital, symbiosis with her German neighbors. Yes, Hubert did maintain some degree of Durkheimian remoteness as a social *scientist*. Yet, he also kept faith with his republican political values in the face of social problems like chauvinism, inequality, and racism. He did his politics in his own unique way—according to his own academic specialties in the primitive ethnography of Europe and the study of myth.

In the next chapter, we update investigations into the way myths "do things" in recent Russian history. Here, the story casts a cabal of Russian Orthodox divines and sympathetic mid-nineteenth-century *intelligentsia* as reclaiming how a fundamentally forgotten ancient myth can "do things" to shore up the Russian state.

Chapter 10

The Myth of Moscow, Third Rome: What It Seeks to Do

The Power of Myths: Some Concluding Remarks on Myth and Method

In my 1987 book *Four Theories of Myth in Twentieth-Century History*, I tried to show how the dizzying array of meanings attached to "myth" challenge any coherent use of the term. In chapters 7 and 8 of that book, I tried to sort out a defensible concept of "myth," fully recognizing what a tangle of semantic controversy bedevils the term.[1] However, once the critical mind had been applied to the term "myth," I was convinced of the continued utility of the term on one condition: assuming ownership or taking responsibility for its uses. In seeking a *deliberate*, well thought out, critical sense of the concept of myth that I could henceforth own and find compelling, I joined Bruce Lincoln and others who did likewise. The existing conceptual chaos surrounding the term neither caused despair nor furnished adequate excuses for endlessly tearing up the conceptual foundations of "myth."[2] "Myth" *could* be a usable notion, *provided it was defensibly conceptualized*. In offering the concept of myth as an "important story, or a derivative of an important story," I think I have done that without, notably, determining in advance what counts as importance for any and all future cases. There are simply too many reasons people value their stories to declare a monopoly on the question of importance. This open approach also resists the common tendency to mystify myth by alluding to some sort of arcane basis of importance, such as myths mysteriously being capable of communicating what words cannot, etc. If someone claims that a story is particularly *important*—that a given story is a *myth*—I think readers are justified in knowing why.

While this definition in terms of importance would seem unlikely to spark controversy, it has nonetheless. Some opposed to committing to a concept or theory of myth, like the late Robert A. Segal, have subsequently settled down into a similar conceptual space to mine, but only after considerable indecision. Segal, for instance, also concluded that myths conveyed what is "significant" and "weighty."[3] In 1999, Lincoln jumped into the lead by defining a myth as a narrative making "powerful—and highly consequential—assertions... about its relative level of validity and authority vis-à-vis other sorts of discourse."[4] Lincoln further argued for his more colorful phrasing of the definition by indicating that by *mythos* the Greeks literally meant "a blunt and aggressive act of candor, uttered by powerful males, in heat of battle or agonistic assembly."[5] Although my abbreviated definition of myth reflects more reticence about ideological orientation than does Lincoln's, his conceptual decisions about myth are completely congenial.

The essays in this volume have, in sum, attempted to provide such a defensible and compelling concept of myth while charting the genealogy of what I have called a *"performative"* concept of myths. In these two final chapters, I show how such a performative concept of myths can then produce the result that all scholars everywhere and always seek: greater knowledge of our world.

The myth theorist who first led me to think about myths as "important stories," as I have spelled out in chapter 6, was Bronislaw Malinowski. His analyses of the Trobriand stories in his first, and perhaps greatest book, *Argonauts of the Western Pacific*, led him to observe that the Trobriand Islanders *themselves* mark a particular class of stories as *important*. They were "sacred"—cultural "treasure," to trade on Maurice Godelier's theory of the sacred.[6] Accordingly, Malinowski recorded that the Trobrianders designated their *important* stories with a special name, *"lili'u."*[7] The *lili'u* of the Trobrianders became prime examples, for Malinowski, of myths.

When I read Malinowski, I was not yet aware of Lincoln's work and its stress upon *power*.[8] Had I been so, I might have focused on a question Malinowski did not ask and thus pursued my investigations of Malinowski into the area of power, as had Lincoln. Namely, *for which* Trobrianders were the *lili'u* a marked category of important story? For *whom* are certain stories *important*, sacred, a "treasure," and why? Yet, even bracketing out how power gave the *lili'u* importance, I was able to explore a wider range of dynamics that shaped why and how particular stories became important. Power is surely among them. But, whether power is the *only* criterion of importance in a story — and power of a particular political or economic sort — remains an open question. A story's importance may well have to do with social dominance, political *power,* and such, but other species of power, e.g., esthetic, ethical, emotional, sexual, etc., cannot be dismissed out of hand.

Moscow as Third Rome Is Not the "Myth" of Moscow, Third Rome

While power in the sense of political power matters, this chapter on the Myth of Moscow, Third Rome (hereafter MMTR) shows how political power relies on its situation in an overarching political culture, providing the discursive, historical, psychological, and sociological conditions that make an iron-fisted politics possible in a particular context. Here is the story of that myth and some ways it might be undone.

Religious beliefs and practices, social memory, oral or written histories, conventional wisdom, and so on have many different political uses. The Magna Carta has had dubious influence on the shape of British politics. The myth of the Magna Carta has *done things* — it fueled political resistance to the Stuarts, and 500 years later, it was instrumental in Supreme Court Justice Samuel Alito's arguments in the Dobbs decision that undid *Roe v. Wade*.[9] In France, we saw how Hubert's appeal to the myth of the civilizing Celts performed an undermining of the myth of the lordly Franks and conquering Romans, and thus eventually implemented the role of endorsing the nascent Third Republic's liberal self-image against the authoritarianism of Catholic France.[10]

The origin of the MMTR dates from an account about a prophetic letter presumed by some to have *performed* an act of certifying the the historic role of Moscow as direct successor to Constantinople as capital of Eastern Christendom. The dubious historicity of that story — *Legend of the White Cowl* (or *Mitre*) — recalls similarly fraudulent documents such as the "Donation of Constantine," long thought to have *performed* the act of certifying Vatican hegemony in Western Europe.[11] The *Legend of the White Cowl* relates how Emperor Constantine granted Pope Sylvester I (285–335 CE) sovereignty over the West and marked the occasion by presenting the pontiff with a white monastic cowl. The story goes that the white cowl remained hidden until the fourteenth century, when it was transferred to the Patriarch of Constantinople, Filotheos. Shortly thereafter, the Patriarch dispatched the white cowl to Novgorod to prevent its capture by the invading Ottomans in the mid-1400s. According to the *Legend*, it remained there in Novgorod before being transferred to Moscow, where it signaled the symbolic shift of Christianity's leadership to Muscovy. The relocation to Moscow, though, remains clouded in obscurity. Nonetheless, once in hand, the court at Muscovy asserted that the cowl's transfer to Moscow from Rome and through Byzantium had world-shaking consequences. Moscow had now succeeded Byzantium as the center of Christianity.[12] A monk of Pskov, Filofei, eventually issued a prophetic letter forming the basis of the modern political myth of MMTR.[13]

The letter's meaning remains rather questionable. In a possibly muddled state of mind, Filofei mixes references to church and state, making it unclear whether his message was political, religious, or some hybrid of both.[14] As a religious document, it can be read to warn the tsar to remain loyal to the Orthodox Church. Thus, addressing the tsar on fidelity to Orthodoxy, Filofei writes,

> Now I beg you and beg you again, please remember what I have said. For God's sake, please also remember that now all [Orthodox] Christian kingdoms have merged into your tsardom. Henceforth we can expect only one kingdom to come. That kingdom is eternal. I have written this because, admiring you as I do, I have appealed and have prayed to God that He may bless you. Change your stinginess to generosity and your inclemency to kindness. Comfort those who cry and moan day and night. Protect the innocent from their tormentors.[15]

Following these lines in the prophecy come the *political* words that have sparked controversy ever since: "Two Romes have fallen. The third stands [firm]. And there will not be a fourth. No one will replace your Christian tsardom…."[16] Filofei's words might not be conceived as myth, strictly speaking, but rather as prophecy. In a political sense, Filofei declared that Roman imperial succession now resided in Moscow, since the Second Rome—Byzantium—had fallen to Ottoman conquest. Striking an apocalyptic tone, Filofei prophesies sternly that no other realm will succeed Moscow as a fourth Rome. If the tsar remains faithful to Orthodoxy, Moscow will rule Christendom until the end of time. If not, no other city will succeed Moscow.

Ivan III's Romism Is Not the MMTR

The circumstances surrounding MMTR are however easily confused with another history of the late fifteenth- to eighteenth-century tsarist imperial courts' appetites for all things Italian Renaissance and Roman. Here suggesting a powerful narrative of spiritual succession from Rome, the MMTR would be a religio-historical *myth*. But for the tsars, the historical attraction of Renaissance Italy and Rome seems chiefly to have been a preoccupation with imperial regalia and fashion. The making of a myth and the pursuit of fashion need to be untangled. The Russian court simply lined up along with other Eastern European regimes in pursuit of the sartorial, architectural, and other cultural splendors of Renaissance Rome. The place of the city of Moscow in universal Christian history seemed less important than "the look" of the Russian court and capital. It, in fact, took another 400 years before the Myth of Moscow as Third *Rome* focused on the city of Moscow as the third Rome. Yet, of course, the Russian court's attraction to the Renaissance splendors of Italy cannot be cleanly separated from the later developing MMTR.

Let me explain. To understand Renaissance Russian Romism, we need to focus on the machinations of Tsar Ivan III (1440–1505 CE). Van den Bercken and Østbø and both argue that Ivan III appealed to MMTR on the occasion of his campaigns against Kazan.[17] But those efforts were rather half-hearted. Ivan III had more pressing concerns. Glorious military victories a century earlier, such as Alexander Nevsky's defeat of German and Swedish Catholics, had boosted Russian pride and deepened a Muscovite sense of independence from the West. But Ivan III felt he needed other sources of reassurance when he ascended the throne in 1462. He began his reign on an auspicious note with the withdrawal of the Mongols. Moscow finally controlled her own territory after centuries of Mongol domination. Yet, contrary to expectations, "as Russian expansion continued throughout the next centuries, the Third Rome concept faded into oblivion, no longer invoked as an argument by the tsar regime."[18] This neglect of the MMTR prevailed even though Constantinople fell to the Ottomans in 1453 and the

Russian Orthodox Church declared independence from the Greek church in 1470.

One ought not to then mistake Ivan III's infatuation with Renaissance Rome with being in thrall to the MMTR. Clearly, Ivan's marriage to Zoe Paleologos, the niece of the last Eastern Emperor, Constantine XI, then living in Rome under the protection of the pope, begs to be read as an affirmation of MMTR?[19] It is not. Perhaps more important to Ivan than Zoe's lineage was her residence in the Vatican where he could satisfy his Italian tastes.[20] In returning to Russia, Ivan brought not only Zoe, but more to the point, a team of Renaissance Italian architects to renovate the Kremlin we see today.[21] Italian architect Pietro Solari (1445–1494 CE) built six of the Kremlin's present towers, including the clocktower and Spasskaya Tower, which serves as the citadel's main entrance.[22] Further, virtually every fifteenth-century gateway, *parterre*, roof, wall, terrace, and turret is owed to Ivan's Italian Renaissance architects, including Solari, Aloiso de Carcanno, Marco Ruffo, Rodolfo "Aristotele" Fioravanti , and others! Fioravanti rebuilt the Dormition Cathedral, even going so far as to use bricks of his own original manufacture.[23] But oddly enough, even with this Italian influence on the capital and his marriage to Zoe, Ivan III never claimed the title of Moscow as "Third Rome." Actually, Ivan III had been more motivated to declare Muscovy the new Israel or "Third Jerusalem," than the new Rome.[24] It was left to the geopolitical theological strategies of Metropolitan Zosima to ascribe the title of Moscow, Third Rome to the city in the 1490s.

Making Ivan III's attitude to Moscow, Third Rome less compelling, little or no evidence of Ivan III's desire to import major Byzantine state institutions can be found either. Ivan III did nothing to incorporate Byzantine institutions, such as a Roman legal system, into Muscovy. Given law's natural complement to morality and its critical role in ordering society, one would expect Ivan III to have made Byzantine law his own. He did not. Even after the Mongol retreat, Keenan argues that Mongol influence lingered for years in Muscovy. This, in turn, created a deep "political culture" in Russia, inhospitable to a Roman regime of codified legal rights system, and even some semblance of a rule of law — all features of Byzantium's rule under Justinian's *Corpus Juris Civilis*.[25]

Furthermore, Muscovite history challenged the coherence of MMTR's narrative. If Moscow as Third Rome were claimed to be real rather than *mythical*, how good an account could be given of that reality? No date of the first mention of Moscow as "Third Rome" is certain, with an early possibility being Filofei's letter from between 1524 and1526.[26] If any Slavic capital were to claim the title of Third Rome, in Ivan III's time and earlier, that capital would more likely to have been Kiev. In 1049, the Metropolitan Ilarion of Kiev preached in a sermon, "On Law and Grace," about Kiev as modeled on Jerusalem, the "city of glory." However, with Kiev still unable to reassert its ancient primacy in the fifteenth century, Moscow moved to capitalize on its new strength and "appropriated" Kiev's more credible talk of ecclesiastical primacy.[27]

History, to the contrary, tells us a Slavic prince—Prince Voldomar I of Kievan Rus—did actually forge real links to Byzantium nearly *five* centuries earlier than Ivan III *could* so have done! Initial contacts between Kievan Rus and the Byzantine empire date from 18 June 860 CE, when a Varangian-Rus army raided Constantinople.[28] Once this initial confrontation passed, trade between Rus and Byzantium took over. Byzantium then made concerted efforts to covert Rus to Christianity. After a series of minor treaties dating from the early 900s, in 944 CE, official diplomatic relations between Kiev and Constantinople commenced, and movement between the two polities became regular.[29] But it was not until 988 CE, however, that a prince of Kievan Rus, Voldomar I, converted to Greek/Eastern Orthodoxy. In 1011 CE, Voldomar commissioned the construction of his own version of Constantinople's Hagia Sophia on the site of Kiev's present-day *barokaziert* cathedral, Saint Sophia's. In 1011, Voldomar I joined the Byzantine hierarchy of "Christian princes" and was assumed into the Byzantine imperial family ("*genos*") by taking as his wife Princess Anne Porphyrogennete, daughter of the Byzantine Emperor Romanos II. Voldomar I's actions constituted "the ultimate phase of the incorporation of Rus into the Byzantine *oikumene*" and—in terms of actual relations governing kinship and succession—contrasted with the dubious mythologies concocted by the Muscovite clergy.[30]

In practical terms, during the tenth and eleventh centuries, the Kievan court was party to political quarrels in Constantinople, even coming to the brink of possible military action. Nevertheless, despite decades of material connections between Kiev and Byzantium, Kiev was never cast as Constantinople's eventual successor as Third Rome, should Byzantium fall.[31] Enjoying membership along with other Christian princes in the imperial court, the Kievan princes maintained a presence in Constantinople until the Mongols conquered and occupied Kiev in 1240.

Back in fifteenth-century Muscovy, Ivan III obsessively continued to hone his romance with Rome. He continued importing the superficial trappings of Roman and Byzantine liturgies and court ceremonies. He even adopted the title of *Caesar* as tsar, along with the double-headed eagle regalia of Byzantium. While Ivan III did acknowledge the Byzantine origins of Russian Orthodoxy and gave shelter to Byzantine refugee notables after the Ottoman conquest of Constantinople,[32] he made little or nothing of any spiritual succession of Byzantium by Muscovy. In a show of local self-assertion, in 1589 Ivan III declared Moscow an autonomous Patriarchate equivalent to Constantinople.[33] Yet despite these maneuverings, Ivan III never embraced MMTR.[34] At most, historians like Keenan, Ostrowski, Bushkovitch, and others conclude that Ivan III's flare for Greco-Roman fashions in architecture alone may have in some part led Russians "in later times, to *think* their traditions were 'Byzantine.'"[35]

MMTR versus the Time of the Emperors

From the Ivan III's tsardom through Peter the Great's *imperium* and well into the nineteenth century, MMTR received little or no attention. Instead, as Judith Kalb notes, in the interests of national identity and imperial Western European grandeur, Russia's leaders succumbed to decades of infatuation with imperial Romism. Kalb characterizes this "large scale Romanization" as a deliberate scheme of "self-mythologization."[36] As the classic style of Stalinist public architecture would indicate, Ivan III's Roman fashions persisted into twentieth-century Russia.[37] "Rome Envy" further continued to shape Russia's self-mythologization as a national identity throughout the period.[38] Recall that Peter the Great (1672–1725) took the Roman title "Imperator," not "tsar," effectively forgetting MMTR. With Peter in charge of the Russian Orthodox Church, from "the beginning of the eighteenth century," writes Kolstø, "the Russian state underwent a thoroughgoing secularization, leaving Filofei's religious apocalyptic without legitimating functions in imperial Russia.[39] The *Romanov* love affair with all things Italian meant that neither Peter nor Catherine had much use for the MMTR to support Russian imperial designs.⁴⁰ Accordingly, once he succeeded Catherine, Emperor Paul (1754–1801) constructed a bizarre, scaled-down version of Rome's St. Peter's—Our Lady of Kazan Cathedral—on prime real estate along Nevsky Prospekt in St. Petersburg. By contrast, in 1011 CE, when Kiev's Voldomar built his capital's cathedral, he modeled it on Constantinople's Hagia Sophia!

The 1860s: Russian Orthodoxy Flexes Its Theological Geopolitical Muscles

After a long period of suppression and secularization under Peter, Catherine, Paul, Alexander I, Alexander II, and Nicholas I, the Russian Orthodox Church succeeded in reasserting itself in the 1860s. It was here under Church initiative that "The Third Rome concept was taken out of mothballs…by conservative thinkers seeking to reestablish an Orthodox foundation for Russian tsardom."⁴¹ Launched in the midst of the nineteenth century, a new politics of Orthodox geopolitical piety, armed with MMTR, began.⁴² Between 1861 and 1863, the purportedly original medieval sources of Filofei's prophecy appeared in print. The ecclesiastical push behind the MMTR's revival insured that Filofei's dire warning to Russian leaders was clear. Stray from Orthodoxy, and Moscow, Third Rome, would fall like Constantinople, and without prospects for a Fourth.

But the Church's leverage over the tsar would not be easy to sustain. After "a hiatus of more than 300 years, the historical links to Abbot Filofei's original exhortation had been largely lost."⁴³ Ambitious ideologues and geo-political theologians rushed in to take charge of the MMTR discourse, and something of an ideological free-for-all ensued. "Thinkers who picked up this idea were at liberty to interpret it much as they saw fit, without being overly concerned about historical accuracy"—which MMTR totally lacked. In the hands of enterprising propagandists, the MMTR took on "a life of its own, [and] the Third Rome idea started on its voyage through intellectual history"⁴⁴—unchecked.

Prominent among such enterprising MMTR propagandists was Vladimir Ikonnikov (1841–1923). He roused masses and intellectuals alike as author of *The Essay on Russian Historiography* (1891–1908), in which he made "vibrant usage [of MMTR] in new political and ideological conceptions in Russia."⁴⁵ Slavophiles, like "pan-Slavist Nikolai Danielevski" (1822–1885), symbolist writers, and well-known philosophers like Nikolai Berdyaev (1874–1948) and Vladimir Solovyov (1853–1900) promoted the MMTR.[46] These ideological entrepreneurs pressed their view throughout the early twentieth century and into the midcentury, only to be shunted aside by Stalin's governmental scheme (1943–1948) to "use the Russian Orthodox Church as a major agent for bringing Eastern Europe and the Middle East under Soviet control…" Creating "a 'Moscow Vatican,' Stalin sought a Moscow-centered transformation of the orthodox world."[47]

From then these developments in the late nineteenth and early twentieth century, MMTR would play an active role in Russian political imaginaries—on "how it is used."[48] With the use of MMTR at the center, focus naturally turns to MMTR as propaganda. Here, propaganda takes the form of a "myth" in my sense of "an important story," at least for certain segments of Russian society. As this volume's title suggests, what matters is not some will-o'-the-wisp original, "real" ancient prophecy.[49] What matters is what MMTR *does*! As Østbø notes,

> it is only here, in its "uses", that the notion of the Third Rome (as it appears in the discourse of Russian nationalism) has a meaning—not in any assumed perennial "essence"…[that is in] what functions the myth fulfils in each author's attempt to define what Russia "really is", and what the myth reveals about this image of Russia.[50]

Thanks to the machinations of the Russian Orthodox Church, the MMTR becomes a modern Russian political myth.

MMTR, Putin, and a Variety of Political Myths

In its *performative* sense as political myth, the MMTR has chiefly taken three recent forms of "incitement to action,"[51] each connected a different clusters of thinkers. In general, Østbø sees all three versions of MMTR as presuming Russia's leadership of all Eastern Orthodox Christians, and therefore, as heir to some formula of Roman/Byzantine imperial greatness. In the first cluster, MMTR has a nationalist and isolationist meaning. Its main representative, Vadim Tsymburskii (1957–2009) sees Russia as a separate realm, an "island," distinctly blessed by Providence for great things undertaken in "isolation" from the rest of Europe and Asia.[52] A second cluster traces back to the nineteenth-century pan-Slavist

Nikolai Danielevski (1822–1885). Today, this cluster includes neo-pan-Slavist Natalia Narochnitskaia (1948–). She relates the MMTR as Russia playing a role in an "irreconcilable struggle with the 'Roman-Catholic' West."[53] Moscow's status as Third Rome thus marks the Russian people for an eschatological, expansionist, and imperial career.[54] Like other imperial myths, it falls into a pattern of self-aggrandizing Muscovite mythology of imperial war, seen lately in the war against (partly Roman Catholic) Ukraine. The third cluster—a "Eurasian Third Rome"—recalls Berdyaev's romantic imperial expansionism. But in the early twentieth century, despite Berdyaev's opposition to Bolshevism, Sidorov suggests that Lenin's *Third* International also traded on the messianism of Berdyaev's MMTR.[55] But today the Eurasianist mythologization of Filofei's prophecy is led by Alexander Dugin (1962–). Dugin had previously regarded the USSR as "essentially a reincarnation of the Orthodox Third Rome Empire," but today Dugin represents a major branch of Third Rome-inspired expansionism beyond the historical Slavic world into Turkey, Iran, and India.[56] Generously included under the Eurasianist rubric are Anatolii Fomenko's (1945–) "'New Chronology'" and some "neo-Orthodox Communists," notably Gennady Zyuganov (1944–).[57]

Since the collapse of the Soviet Union, the myth has been readied to rally the nation to patriotic goals. Precisely how frequently such an appeal was considered useful to meet the political needs of the day, I have not been able to determine. Yet conspicuous occasions should be noted. Writing, for example, in the newsletter of the Russian Special Forces, *Spetsnaz Rossii*, Egor Kholmogorov, a MMTR partisan, declared that "Third Rome" captures the ideal of an exceptional, powerful, and even brutal Russia, perfectly.[58] During the chaos of the early post-Soviet period, ultranationalist groups like *Pamiat* appropriated it as a symbol of "Russian renewal and superiority."[59] More recently, in February 2015, the pro-European Ukrainian online newspaper, *Euromaidan* reported on an essay published in the *Novaya Gazeta* by Yulia Latynina, a commentator from the outspoken *Ekho Moskvy* radio station. Entitled "Moscow, 'The Third Rome,' May Suffer Fate of the Second Rather Than the First," Latynina argues that "it is becoming obvious that under Vladimir Putin, Russians are being encouraged to think of themselves as 'the heirs of spiritually rich Byzantium,' the traditional 'Second Rome' in Russian thinking."[60] First employed to justify Soviet expansionist international policies, Putin later enlisted it to strengthen his domestic authority.[61]

Even current domestic Russian mass media confirm the popularity of the MMTR. In 2008, Russian state-controlled station Rossiia (*RTR*) broadcast a film—followed by frequent *rebroadcasts*—*Gibel' Imperii, Vizantiiskii Urok*. Unhappily, however, not even Levada Opinion Research succeeded in reporting anything substantial in the way of empirical data on viewership.[62] Appealing to the fall of Constantinople as a historical precedent, the program warns present-day Russians to heed warnings about complacency and corruption.

According to the orthodox geo-political logic of MMTR, Putin urged Russia to assume the role of world leadership of Christianity in his notorious speech of July 2021, "On the Historical Unity of Russians and Ukrainians," in which he explicitly promoted the Russian nationalist-imperialist mythologized history that he now invokes to justify his war against Ukraine.[63] There, Putin elides the histories of modern Ukraine with Russia on the basis of a mythological unity between Kievan Rus and Muscovy. The two are "bound together," says Putin, in such a way that it "still largely determines our affinity today…between parts of what is essentially the same historical and spiritual space…"[64] Unsurprisingly, from as early as 2008, "*Gibel' Imperii, Vizantiiskii Urok*" had been "produced and directed" with some coordination with Putin's Kremlin via the activist monk Tikhon Shevkunov.[65] Rumor has it that Father Tikhon served as *duchovnik*—the equivalent of a personal trainer or father confessor in the "spiritual" life—to the conspicuously pious Putin.[66] Having such a spiritual advisor would not be out of line with what one knows of the history of Putin's family dedication to the Russian Orthodox Church. Local church archives from the village church, located some 125 kilometers from Moscow, where Putin's family lived continuously for 300 years, indicate their unbroken record of weekly church attendance through all that time![67] About the mass popularity of the MMTR, a note of caution might be lodged. Van den Bercken notes that, since its recrudescence after 1991, MMTR sometimes appears as kitsch. The new "Miss Third Rome" beauty pageant is not what Filofei, the pious monk of Pskov, exactly had in mind.[68]

Today, then, for some elements of the population, national identity is anchored by variants on the myth of Moscow as "Third

Rome." Dmitrii Sidorov even calls this a "re-emerging religious geo-politics" of Third Romism, wherein Russia's "current geopolitical imaginations" and sense of its "national uniqueness" are rooted in the MMTR.[69] While difficult to compare the present-day strength of the MMTR to its admitted heyday in the mid-nineteenth century, the MMTR is consequential to the sway of current Russian Orthodox geopolitics, now so much in evidence in Putin's Russia.

On the other hand, these days, the MMTR has become something of a conventional Russian nationalist factoid—something that everybody takes to be true, like George Washington's reputation for honesty or the celebration of the first Thanksgiving in Puritan Massachusetts. But, even in that folksy form, it matters. Historian Wil van den Bercken, concludes that the "doctrine of the Third Rome forms the ideological climax of the political and religious awareness of Moscow and its theological apotheosis," a conclusion that would doubtless please Bruce Lincoln's earlier cited conception of what myths *do*.[70]

In the post-Soviet period, the MMTR has been adapted to new political purposes, linked to nostalgias of a restored Empire. In Russian exceptionalist circles, the myth continues to promise restoration of the former glories of the Russian imperial and Soviet past.[71] President Putin's heavily mythologized theory of the war in Ukraine seems only to have kept this tendency alive.[72] For example, present-day neo-imperialist and "Russian Orthodox fundamentalists" like Kholmogorov confidently write and lecture about appeals to the MMTR resonating among the Russian intelligentsia.[73] Marcel De Haas also writes of "the so-called 'third Rome' *theory*" (as opposed to myth) as something that, in Putin's Russia, expresses a "feeling of superiority which is expressed in references to the unique status of Russia and its leading role in the world."[74]

Although I have not found explicit citations of MMTR in Putin's recent public statements, Niels Drost and Beatrice de Graaf claim that in their reading of over "11,000 speeches, statements, declarations, and interviews from 1999 until 2022," they can prove how Putin resorts to a "combination of history and Russian Orthodox theological, biblical tropes *as a usable pass to create his powerbase…*" With respect to the ideological thrust of Moscow, Third Rome,

> Putin has been inspired by those who once reign the Russian empire. He loves to read history books and admires the different rulers and thinkers

that played a significant role in Russia's past, especially those tsars that safeguarded the strength and stability of the state. And what was even more, represented not just earthly power but within the framework of Russian Christian Orthodox religion also embodied the eschatological purpose of Russia is the "Third Rome."[75]

The compelling power of this myth may thus be one reason that rightwing nationalists like Vladimir Zhirinovsky (1946–2022) and, however improbably, various Communists like Gennady Zyuganov, have appealed to the MMTR.[76] In his 1994 book, *Derzhava*, Zyuganov itemizes some of the necessary characteristics of the new Russian State. It should immediately reconcile the ancient past with the revolutionary future—the religious ideals of social justice with the new political goals of national statehood.[77] In particular, Zyuganov calls explicitly for reclaiming Russia's imperial Byzantine heritage and once more seizing the claim to be the Third Rome. Says Zyuganov, "Russia has long perceived itself as the successor and keeper of the great power imperial legacy. This was powerfully expressed in the designation, Moscow is the Third Rome, a phrase coined by the monk Filofei."[78] While noteworthy, the recrudescence of myths like the MMTR in contemporary Russia has precedents elsewhere. Kenneth Scott's classic account of Mussolini's conception of Fascist Italy as succeeding the Roman Empire recalls a similar rhetorical move.[79] Taking these various facts together, we can at least be sure that, as a creation of powerful actors, that the MMTR bears a thoroughbred elite political pedigree.

An Empty Inheritance?

As the Russia-Ukraine War (2022–) has gradually made many in the West aware, the histories of Kievan Rus and its Ukrainian successors differ fundamentally from Muscovy's. Depending upon what historical period serves as a baseline, their respective Byzantine inheritances vary. In the legal realm, Ukraine of the Polish-Lithuanian *Rzeczpospolita* of the sixteenth and seventeenth centuries, Ukrainians may have been exposed to different legal influences than the earlier under the Grand Duke of Lithuania, dating from the thirteenth to fifteenth centuries. Whatever else the case, the *Rzeczpospolita* was organized on the basis of rights, albeit limited to the gentry. Kiev was theoretically better positioned—from the time of the *Rzeczpospolita* with its connections to the Renaissance and

Reformation—to represent law or a legal establishment of rights quite unlike the autocratic system of the tsars of Muscovy. Since Muscovite Russian legal history fails to present a robust tradition of a regime of rights, rule of law, etc., Russian ecclesiastical history likewise does not offer examples of another major institution ready to challenge secular authority, and which, in turn, could leverage a regime of rights or a rational legal system. Both Kievan Rus and Muscovy lacked the kind of Gelasian pope who could behave as a counter-sovereign—who, on occasion, might stand against the emperor. Even given the predations of the post-Constantinian *imperium*, in the West, as early as 496 CE, Pope Gelasius I could articulate the famous "Two Swords" principle of the separation and interdependence of ecclesiastical and imperial authorities.

One brief suspension of this rule came with Metropolitan Philip's 1568 petition to Ivan the Terrible (1530-1589) concerning the tsar's failure to respect law. Ivan accepted Philip's petition, but—small comfort for Philip—executed him! As time passed, in the Greek East traditions of sacral kingship eventually overcame Gelasian notions of separation and interdependence, *opposition* or *tension*, between Church and Empire. When, in the late eleventh century, Pope Gregory VII (1020-1085) asserted ecclesiastical power and independence in the West, unsurprisingly, the estranged East did not follow. There, the principle of "symphony" between the emperor and church prevailed. Explaining this principle, Patriarch Antonios IV of Constantinople wrote to Prince Vasilij I of Moscow in 1393, "'It is impossible for the Christians to have a church, but no emperor. The imperial power and the church have a great unity and community, and it is quite impossible for them to be separated from each other.'"[80] Thus, Russia never saw an institution like the revolutionary papacy of Gregory VII. In setting the sacred and profane in opposition to each other, he asserted the sacred over against encroachment by secular institutions, such as the emperor—if necessary, even by force of arms.

Gregory's papacy thus contributed to the foundations of the West's legal system. Under papal patronage, in the later twelfth and early thirteenth centuries, scholars at the universities of Bologna and Paris reworked the Byzantine Emperor Justinian's *Corpus Juris Civilis*'s elaboration of Roman law for contemporary use. But Russia never incorporated Roman law in the same way until the nineteenth century. Nor despite a rich tradition of folk law, could it match the sophistication and tenacity of British Common Law. To the extent that a civilization's legal history informs basic societal attitudes toward concepts such as the rule of law, Russia maintains a weakness for autocracy. At an event in 2014, exiled Russian oligarch Mikael Khodorkovsky, who had recently been released from prison, reflected on the prospects for dramatic political change from autocracy in Russia: "It's not just Putin that needs to be replaced," he said. "The entire system needs to be changed."[81] Khodorkovsky called for a Russia where the "law protects the people and not the bureaucracy" and where human rights do not depend "on the mood of the tsar."[82]

The task that Khodorkovsky calls for will be difficult, given the degree to which MMTR has become conventional Russian wisdom. As such, it invites ethno-nationalist Russian "generalists and popularizers...to inflate and exaggerate the importance" of MMTR.[83] So, in one form or another, the MMTR remains widely believed, despite its many historical vulnerabilities.[84] William Keenan dryly observes that while there is little evidence "of influential links between modern Russian or even Muscovite political culture and that of [...] Byzantium," Russians have continued to like to "think that their traditions were 'Byzantine.'"[85] Perhaps *the* classic case of such powerful media-savvy mythologizing was Sergei Eisenstein's 1938 film *Alexander Nevsky*. Eisenstein later admitted that his depiction of thirteenth-century clashes between the invading Teutonic Knights and the Russian forces led by Nevsky was intentionally meant to raise public concern over Stalin's military vulnerability to the Nazis.[86] However, as our specific story goes, Sidorov points out that later Eisenstein traded on the MMTR in 1944's *Ivan, the Terrible*, depicting the tsar promising to unite all orthodox peoples under Muscovite leadership and solemnly invoking Filofei's Third Rome prophecy.[87]

Bruce Lincoln and "Swiftboating" the Swiftboaters

If historical demythologizing runs up against limits set by conventional wisdom, is myth criticism an impossibility? Is there no way the MMTR might be blunted, turned, or falsified? The final chapter of Bruce Lincoln's *Theorizing Myth*, entitled "The Pandits and Mr. Jones," offers an intriguing demonstration of how Hindu myths can be defeated—*as myths*, and sometimes by other *myths*—when other means fail.[88] The local pandits crafted a polemic crafted of traditional Hindu myths, in effect using their myths to argue that the British should leave India. This strategy proceeded in several stages. First, the rebellious pandits located the British within their own ancient mythical cosmology. Charmed by their acceptance, the British embraced the pandits' mythical vision of their place within a sacred geography. Flattered, the British did not realize that the pandits had simultaneously relegated them to the remote periphery of the subcontinent! While the British never fully grasped their classification as inferior, every knowledgeable Indian immediately understood their subordinate status. The haughty British imperialists had, in effect, been defined as polluting outsiders. Thus, colonial attempts to push into the (Indian) center by means of economic and military intrusions were not a conquest of India but the actions of a polluting or "dirtying" inferior. The British had unwittingly accepted designation as mythological pollution, dirt—matter out of place. Therefore, by means of *inclusion* in a Hindu myth, the Hindus essentially *excluded* the British from genteel society. Although the British may have acted the role of imperial superiors, the Hindus saw them as their inferiors.

Is some analogous mythical device available to counter MMTR? Let me suggest that another effort to unseat the myth might be to *tell a better version* of the myth. One way to displace a given story is to tell another, more compelling story. Modern politics gives us classic examples of how myths can be thus turned, blunted, or even hijacked, so to speak, by *another myth*. One device of myth criticism, employed to great effect during the 2004 US presidential election, was the so-called "swiftboating" of the myth of Democratic candidate John Kerry's war heroism. A myth arose about Kerry for his bravery and heroism in Vietnam. Those wartime tales—myths— had helped him gain national renown. The myth of Kerry's heroism entered the world of conventional wisdom with little effort on his part. His exploits became the stuff of myth, "important stories" told by his admirers and the media alike.

But when Kerry ran for president in 2004, he—and the myth of his heroism—was undone by a strategy of dirty-tricks politics that would come to be known as "swiftboating." The term derives from a class of motorized river assault gunships, "swifts." Part of Kerry's duties involved their command. In connection with his extraordinary heroic service on these "Swift Boats," Kerry was awarded three

Purple Hearts, each given for a separate case of being wounded in action, a Bronze Star for bravery in battle, and a Silver Star for another battlefield exploit. His fame as war hero spread widely. By any standard, Kerry's military record is impeccable and extraordinary, and since military awards involve rigorous official scrutiny, it was universally recognized as such.

As Kerry's campaign gathered momentum, a group of Republican operatives vowed to blunt Kerry's surge in the polls. A group of military veterans opposed to Kerry's candidacy launched a campaign to replace the myth of Kerry's heroism with a myth of Kerry's perfidy. Alleging (falsely, as it was later discovered) to have served alongside Kerry, these "Swift Boat Veterans for Truth," as they called themselves, concocted their own counter-version of the Kerry myth. Their myth turned what had been a celebration of Kerry's heroic record into its opposite. They, in effect, turned the Kerry myth on its head by charging him with ambitious opportunism in seeking high awards and military malfeasance in endangering his comrades. Kerry's honor and modesty betrayed him, at least, in the blood sport of American politics. Although the charges of the swiftboaters were later proven to be false, a sufficient enough portion of the public believed them to damage Kerry's chances for victory in the presidential race.[89] Kerry's attackers succeeded simply because their myth played better with enough of the voting public than did Kerry's real story. This counter-myth of Kerry worked in large part because many Americans remained suspicious of the patriotism of Democrats—an image that became popular because of Democrats' opposition to the Vietnam War. For just enough American voters, the myth of Kerry as coward *worked* better than the myth of Kerry as hero.

Since Kerry was indeed a true hero, modest, self-effacing, and allergic to boasting, he felt it beneath his dignity to defend himself against the swiftboaters' myth. But this played into the hands of Kerry's demythologizers. In refusing to defend himself, Kerry reinforced his patrician image of elitist aloofness and undermined his common man's heroism. The swiftboaters' counter-myth played on the stereotype that Democrats were not—and perhaps could not be—vigorous defenders of the nation. Indeed, hadn't Kerry prominently opposed the war? The swiftboat *version* of the original Kerry myth of heroism thus became its own counter factoid that everyone—at least everyone who opposed Kerry—knew to be true and that therefore required no further examination. Good patrician believer in the eventual triumph of reason—argument—that he was, Kerry could not fight myth with myth. But, like the similarly rationalist progressive Russian historians opposed to the myth of the MMTR, Kerry was powerless to engage mythological polemics. These failures suggest that myths can best sometimes be countered only with other myths. To counter a false story, critics need to be ready to tell a better story.

In terms of Russia and the MMTR, I do not know what such a "swiftboating" effort, an alternative narrative to the autocratic telling of the MMTR, might be. But thus far, calling attention to straightforward historical inaccuracies has not dented the myth's prestige. The MMTR survives both historical disconfirmation and falsification. Historians may know the reasons Muscovite Russia did not inherit Byzantium's rich traditions of legal science and jurisprudence. Historians note that Ivan III adopted the superficialities of Byzantine imperial culture but not Constantinople's Roman legal traditions and institutions. Had Moscow been the Third Rome since Filofei's letter, Justinian's *Corpus* would have been absorbed into the Russian legal system centuries before Tsar Alexander I (1777–1825) appointed the liberal Mikhail Speransky (1772–1839) to do precisely that. But Muscovy had not done so.

While historians like Keenan point out how empty Muscovy's claim to a direct Byzantine legacy is, in politics, myth and magic often overwhelm reason. In its frantic effort to gain the Roman legitimacy that Muscovy simply did not have, Moscow resorted to mythical, symbolic, and ritual magic. In consequence, Russians have continued to "think their traditions were 'Byzantine,'" to use Keenan's words. But they are not. Keenan even charges that continually saying so is really a form of "protective behavior."[90] The tsar is no *Caesar*, nor is the Emperor an *Imperator*. But this has not stopped Russians from being roused by neo-imperial rhetoric, whether regarding Ukraine, Crimea, or Novaya Rossiya. Thus, the MMTR, and all its attendant ramifications, live on. Perhaps the persistence of such a myth as MMTR confirms the view that the only thing that can stop a bad guy with a bad myth is a good guy with a better myth?

Notes

Chapter 1

1   Bronislaw Malinowski, *A Scientific Theory of Culture and Other Essays* (Oxford: Oxford University Press, 1944).
2   Jane Desmond, "Ethnography as Ethics and Epistemology: Why American Studies Should Embrace Fieldwork, and Why It Hasn't," *American Studies* 53, no. 1 (2014): 32.
3   Desmond, 33.
4   Desmond, 33.
5   Desmond, 33.
6   Desmond, 52.
7   Desmond, 32.
8   Friedrich Max Müller, "Forgotten Bibles," in *Last Essays: Essays on the Science of Religion*, vol. I, Collected Works of the Right Honorable F. Max Müller (New York: Longman, 1901), 1–35.
9   Ivan Strenski, *Thinking about Religion: An Historical Introduction to Theories of Religion* (Oxford: Blackwell, 2006); Ivan Strenski, *Understanding Theories of Religion: An Introduction*, 2nd ed. (Malden, MA: Wiley-Blackwell, 2015).
10 Henri Hubert and Marcel Mauss, *Mélanges d'histoire des Religions* (Paris: Librorium, 2021), e3753.
11 Malinowski, *A Scientific Theory of Culture*, 36.
12 Malinowski, 71.
13 Jardar Østbø, *The New Third Rome: Readings of a Russian Nationalist Myth* (Stuttgart: ibidem, 2016), 12.
14 R. Dean Davenport, "Patriarchy and Politics: A Comparative Evaluation of the Religious, Political and Social Thought of Sir Robert Filmer and Robert Lewis Dabney" (PhD diss., Baylor University, 2006).
15 Østbø, *The New Third Rome*.
16 Hubert and Mauss, *Mélanges d'histoire des Religions*, e136.
17 Østbø, *The New Third Rome*, ch. 2.
18 Bruce Lincoln, *Theorizing Myth: Narrative, Ideology, and Scholarship* (Chicago: University of Chicago Press, 1999), ix.

Chapter 2

1   Robert A. Segal, *Myth Theorized* (Sheffield: Equinox, 2023), 31.
2   Segal, 44.

3 Tomoko Masuzawa, *In Search of Dreamtime: The Quest for the Origin of Religion*, Religion and Postmodernism (Chicago: University of Chicago Press, 1993), 75.
4 Masuzawa, 8.
5 George Eliot, *Middlemarch* (New York: New American Library, 1964), ch. 3.
6 Ivan Strenski, "Misreading Max Müller," *Method & Theory in the Study of Religion* 8, no. 3 (1996): 291–96.
7 Sarah Barnette, "Friedrich Max Müller and George Eliot: Affinities, *Einfühlung*, and the Science of Religion," *Publications of the English Goethe Society* 85, no. 2-3 (September 2016): 191–203. https://doi.org/10.1080/09593683.2016.1224490
8 Barnette, 194.
9 Barnette, 194.
10 Barnette, 196.
11 Barnette, 196.
12 Barnette, 200.
13 Barnette, 199, citing Eliot, *Middlemarch*, 208.
14 Barnette, 195.
15 Segal, *Myth Theorized*, 39.
16 Friedrich Max Müller, "Lecture on the Vedas or the Sacred Books of the Brahmans (March 1865)," in *Last Essays: Essays on the Science of Religion*, vol. II, Collected Works of the Right Honorable F. Max Müller (London: Longman, 1881), 328.
17 Friedrich Max Müller, *Physical Religion* (London: Longman, 1891), 15, 54, 277.
18 Segal, *Myth Theorized*, 39.
19 Friedrich Max Müller, *Chips from a German Workshop*, vol. 1 (London: Longman, 1867).
20 Müller, "Popol Vuh," in *Chips from a German Workshop*, vol. 1.
21 Friedrich Max Müller, "On the Philosophy of Mythology (Lecture at the Royal Institute, 1871)," in *Chips from a German Workshop*, vol. 5 (New York: Scribner, 1890), chaps. 3, 5.
22 Friedrich Max Müller, "Comparative Mythology (*Oxford Essays*, 1856)," in *Selected Essays on Language, Mythology and Religion*, vol. I (London: Longman, 1881), 590.
23 Friedrich Max Müller, *Chips from a German Workshop*, vol. 2 (London: Longman, 1867), 143.
24 Hubert and Mauss, *Mélanges d'histoire des religions*, loc. 372.
25 Müller, "Comparative Mythology (*Oxford Essays*, 1856)," 451.
26 Müller, "On the Philosophy of Mythology," 56.
27 Müller, 56.
28 Müller, "Comparative Mythology (*Oxford Essays*, 1856)," 451.
29 Müller, "On the Philosophy of Mythology," 68.
30 Müller, *Physical Religion*, 294–95.
31 Friedrich Max Müller, *Natural Religion* (London: Longman, 1889), 54.
32 Müller, *Physical Religion*, 302.
33 Müller, 302.
34 Müller, *Natural Religion*, 218.
35 Müller, "On the Philosophy of Mythology," 57.
36 Müller, *Natural Religion*, 218.

Notes

37 Richard M. Dorson, *The British Folklorists: A History* (Chicago: Chicago University Press, 1968), 161.
38 Müller, *Natural Religion*, 138.
39 Émile Durkheim, *The Elementary Forms of Religious Life*, trans. Karen E. Fields (New York: Free Press, 1995), 80.
40 Müller, "On the Philosophy of Mythology," 53.
41 Müller, 53.
42 Müller, "Lecture on the Vedas," 135.
43 Müller, 112.
44 Müller, "On the Philosophy of Mythology," 75.
45 Müller, "Lecture on the Vedas," 129.
46 Müller, "On the Philosophy of Mythology," 48.
47 Friedrich Max Müller, *Introduction to the Science of Religion: Four Lectures Delivered at the Royal Institution, in February and May 1870* (London: Spottiswoode, 1870), 203; Barnette, "Friedrich Max Müller and George Eliot," 194.
48 Masuzawa, *In Search of Dreamtime*, 74–75.
49 Segal, *Myth Theorized*, 41.
50 Friedrich Max Müller, *Auld Lang Syne* (New York: Scribner, 1899).
51 Müller, "On the Philosophy of Mythology," 64.
52 Friedrich Max Müller, *My Autobiography* (New Delhi: Scribner, 2002), 196.
53 Müller, "On the Philosophy of Mythology," 83.
54 Müller, 97.
55 Müller, *Natural Religion*, 20.
56 Müller, 20.
57 C. Scott Littleton, *The New Comparative Mythology: An Anthropological Assessment of the Theories of Georges Dumézil*, 3rd ed. (Berkeley: University of California Press, 1982).
58 Nirad C. Chaudhuri, *Scholar Extraordinary: The Life of Professor the Rt. Hon. Friedrich Max Müller, P.C.* (London: Chatto & Windus, 1974), 364.
59 Chaudhuri, 364.
60 Müller, "Lecture on the Vedas," 112.
61 Müller, *Physical Religion*, 36.
62 Müller, *My Autobiography*, 68.
63 Müller, 68–69.
64 Müller, 70.
65 Müller, 70.
66 Müller, 70.
67 Müller, 70–71.
68 Müller, "Lecture on the Vedas," 113.
69 Léon Poliakov, *The Aryan Myth: A History of Racist and Nationalist Ideas in Europe* (New York: Basic Books, 1974), 214.
70 Müller, *My Autobiography*, 33.
71 Müller, *Physical Religion*, 264.
72 Müller, *My Autobiography*, 192.
73 Richard Hofstadter, *Social Darwinism in American Thought* (Boston: Beacon Press, 1955); Poliakov, *The Aryan Myth*, 214.
74 Robert A. Segal, ed., *The Myth and Ritual: An Anthology* (Malden, MA: Blackwell, 1998); Robert A. Segal, *Theorizing about Myth* (Amherst: University of Massachusetts Press, 1999); Robert A. Segal, *Myth: A Very Short Introduction* (Oxford: Oxford University Press, 2004); Segal, *Myth Theorized*.

75 Robert A. Segal, "Myth," in *The Wiley Blackwell Companion to the Study of Religion*, ed. Robert Alan Segal and Nickolas P. Roubekas, 2nd ed. (Hoboken, NJ: Wiley-Blackwell, 2021), 351.

76 Segal, 351.

77 Bronislaw Malinowski, "Myth in Primitive Psychology," in *Magic, Science and Religion and Other Essays*, ed. Robert Redfield (New York: Free Press, 1948), 79.

78 William Bascom, "Malinowski's Contributions to the Study of Folklore," *Folklore* 94, no. 2 (January 1983): 167.

79 Segal, "Myth," 2021, 354–56.

Chapter 3

1 Fritz Stern, *The Politics of Cultural Despair: A Study in the Rise of the Germanic Ideology* (Berkeley: University of California Press, 1961), chap. 1.

2 Philippe Alphandéry, "Albert Réville," *Revue de l'histoire des religions* 54 (1906): 401–23.

3 Albert Réville, *Les religions des peuples non-civilisés*, vol. 1 (Paris: Fischbacher, 1883).

4 Albert Réville, "Contemporary Materialism in Religion: The Sacred Heart," *Theological Review* 44 (January 1874): 138–56.

5 Franck Storne, "Le protestantisme libéral français au 19e siècle à travers l'engagement des Révilles, pasteurs réformés" (Diplôme d'études approfondies, Université de Reims, 1985), 52.

6 Alphandéry, "Albert Réville."

7 Réville, "Contemporary Materialism in Religion."

8 Réville.

9 Réville, 154.

10 Réville, 152.

11 Réville, 151.

12 Robert Alun Jones, "Robertson Smith, Durkheim, and Sacrifice: An Historical Context for the Elementary Forms of the Religious Life," *Journal of the History of the Behavioral Sciences* 17, no. 2 (April 1981): 184–205. https://doi.org/10.1002/1520-6696(198104)17:2<184::AID-JHBS2300170205>3.0.CO;2-J

13 William Robertson Smith, *Lectures on the Religion of the Semites: Fundamental Institutions. First Series*, 2nd ed. (London: Black, 1894), 53.

14 William Robertson Smith, "What History Teaches Us to Seek in the Bible (November 1870)," in *Lectures and Essays of William Robertson Smith*, ed. John Sutherland Black and George Chrystal (London: Black, 1912), 317, 24.

15 Smith, 324.

16 William Robertson Smith, "The Place of Theology in the Work and Growth of the Church (March 1875)," in *Lectures and Essays of William Robertson Smith*, ed. John Sutherland Black and George Chrystal (London: Black, 1912), 319.

17 Smith, *Lectures on the Religion of the Semites*, 440.

18 Desmond, "Ethnography as Ethics and Epistemology," 32.

19 Marcel Mauss, *A General Theory of Magic*, trans. Robert Brain (London: Routledge and K. Paul, 1972); Henri Hubert and Marcel Mauss, *Sacrifice: Its Nature and Function*, trans. W. D. Halls (Chicago: University of Chicago Press, 1964); Marcel Mauss, *On Prayer*, ed. W. S. F. Pickering, trans. Susan Leslie, Reprint (New York: Durkheim Press, 2003).

20 Ivan Strenski, *Durkheim and the Jews of France*, Chicago Studies in the History of Judaism (Chicago: University of Chicago Press, 1997).
21 Philippe de Félice, *Poisons sacrés, ivresses divines. Essai sur quelques formes inférieures de la mystique* (Paris: Albin Michel, 1936).
22 Félice, 363.
23 Félice, 317.
24 Félice, 317.
25 Émile Durkheim, "Review. 'Guyau—*L'Irréligion de L'avenir*,'" in *Durkheim on Religion: A Selection of Readings with Bibliographies and Introductory Remarks*, ed. W. S. F. Pickering (London: Routledge, 1975), 24–38.
26 Smith, *Lectures on the Religion of the Semites*.
27 Durkheim, "Review. 'Guyau—*L'Irréligion de L'avenir*.'"
28 Henri Hubert, "Préface," in *Le culte des héros et ses conditions sociales: Saint Patrick, héros national de l'Irlande*, by Stefan Czarnowski (Paris: Alcan, 1919), xxxix.
29 W. S. F. Pickering, *Durkheim's Sociology of Religion: Themes and Theories* (London: Routledge & Kegan Paul, 1984), 347.
30 Henri Hubert, "Le rituel: Introduction," *L'Année sociologique* 5 (1900): 247–48.
31 Durkheim, "Review. 'Guyau—*L'Irréligion de L'avenir*,'" 26.
32 Émile Durkheim, *Sociology and Philosophy*, trans. D. F. Pocock (New York: Free Press, 1974), 31–32.
33 Hubert and Mauss, *Sacrifice*, 77.
34 Sylvain Lévi, "Abel Bergaigne et l'indianisme [1890]," in *Mémorial Sylvain Lévi*, ed. Jacques Bacot (Paris: Paul Hartmann, 1937), 7–9.
35 Sylvain Lévi, *La doctrine du sacrifice dans les Brāhmaṇas* (Paris: Leroux, 1898), 9.
36 Lévi, 10.
37 Marcel Mauss, "Sylvain Lévi," in *Oeuvres*, ed. Victor Karady, vol. 3: Cohésion sociale et divisions de la sociologie (Paris: Éditions de Minuit, 1969), 539.
38 Louis Renou, "Sylvain Lévi et son œuvre scientifique," in *Mémorial Sylvain Lévi*, ed. Jacques Bacot (Paris: Paul Hartmann, 1937), xv.
39 Abel Bergaigne, *Abel Bergaigne's* Vedic Religion, trans. V. G. Paranjpe, vol. 3 (Delhi: Motilal Banarsidass, 1978), 283.
40 Bergaigne, 3:283.
41 Paul Mus, "La mythologie primitive et la penseé de l'Inde," *Bulletin de la Societé Française de philosophie* 37 (Mai-Juin 1937): 119.
42 Renou, "Sylvain Lévi et son œuvre scientifique," xxiii.
43 Poliakov, *The Aryan Myth*, 186.
44 Lévi, *La doctrine du sacrifice dans les Brāhmaṇas*, chap. 2; Marcel Mauss, "Review of *La doctrine du sacrifice dans les Brâhmanas*, by Sylvain Lévi," in *Oeuvres*, ed. Victor Karady, vol. 1: Les fonctions sociales du sacré (Paris: Éditions de Minuit, 1968), 293–95, 353.
45 Lévi, *La doctrine du sacrifice dans les Brāhmaṇas*, chap. 2.
46 Lévi, 27, 38, 54, 76.
47 Louis Renou, "Préface," in *La doctrine du sacrifice dans les Brâhmanas*, by Sylvain Lévi, 2nd ed. (Paris: Presses Universitaires de France, 1966), vii.
48 Mauss, "Sylvain Lévi."
49 Bergaigne, *Abel Bergaigne's* Vedic Religion.
50 Renou, "Préface," xxii.

51 Pierre Sorlin, «La Croix» et les Juifs (1880-1899), contribution à l'histoire de l'antisémitisme contemporain (Paris: Grasset, 1967), 138.

52 Sylvain Lévi, Une renaissance juive en Judée, Ligue des Amis du Sionisme, Tract no. 5 (Paris: Driay-Cahen, 1918).

53 Lévi, 22.

54 Lévi, 22.

55 Lévi, La doctrine du sacrifice dans les Brāhmaṇas, 9.

56 Johannes Voigt, Max Mueller: The Man and His Ideas (Calcutta: Firma KLM, 1967), 3; Poliakov, The Aryan Myth, 247.

57 Gabriel Monod, "James Darmesteter," in Portraits et souvenirs (Paris: Calmann Levy, 1897), 162; James Darmesteter, "The Prophets of Israel," in Selected Essays of James Darmesteter, ed. Morris Jastrow Jr., trans. Helen B. Jastrow (Boston: Houghton and Mifflin, 1895), 59. In 1886, Darmesteter Visited India to Study Oriental Languages.

Chapter 4

1 Émile Poulat, Histoire, dogme et critique dans la crise moderniste (Paris: Casterman, 1979), 19; Alec R. Vidler, A Variety of Catholic Modernists (Cambridge: Cambridge University Press, 1970), 66.

2 Louis Dumont, "A Modified View of Our Origins: The Christian Beginnings of Modern Individualism," Religion 12, no. 1 (January 1982): 1–27. https://doi.org/10.1016/0048-721X(82)90013-6

3 Henri Berr, "The Expansion of the Celts," foreword to The Rise of the Celts, by Henri Hubert (New York: Knopf, 1934), xii.

4 Henri Hubert and Marcel Mauss, "Introduction à l'analyse de quelques phénomènes religieux," in Oeuvres, ed. Victor Karady, vol. 1: Les fonctions sociales du sacré (Paris: Éditions de Minuit, 1968), 300.

5 Marcel Fournier, Marcel Mauss: A Biography (Princeton, NJ: Princeton University Press, 2006), 329.

6 Victor Karady, "The Durkheimians in Academe: A Reconsideration," in The Sociological Domain: The Durkheimians and the Founding of French Sociology, ed. Philippe Besnard (Cambridge: Cambridge University Press, 1983), 74.

7 Karady, 74.

8 Philippe Besnard, "The Année Sociologique Team," in The Sociological Domain: The Durkheimians and the Founding of French Sociology, ed. Philippe Besnard (Cambridge: Cambridge University Press, 1983), 25.

9 Steven Lukes, Emile Durkheim, His Life and Work: A Historical and Critical Study (New York: Harper & Row, 1973), 328 n34.

10 Marcel Mauss, "An Intellectual Self-Portrait," in The Sociological Domain: The Durkheimians and the Founding of French Sociology, ed. Philippe Besnard (Cambridge: Cambridge University Press, 1983), 151.

11 Mauss, 145.

12 Marcel Drouin, "Hubert (Henri)," in Annuaire (Paris: Association des anciens élèves, élèves et amis de l'École normale supérieure, 1929), 48; Salomon Reinach, "Henri Hubert," Revue archéologique 26 (1927): 176.

13 François A. Isambert, "At the Frontier of Folklore and Sociology: Hubert, Hertz and Czarnowski, Founders of a Sociology of Folk Religion," in The Sociological

Domain: The Durkheimians and the Founding of French Sociology, ed. Philippe Besnard (Cambridge: Cambridge University Press, 1983), 154 n7.

14   Mauss, "An Intellectual Self-Portrait," 145.
15   Drouin, "Hubert (Henri)," 46.
16   Henri Hubert, review of *Steinzeit Kunst und Moderne Kunst: Ein Vergleich*, by Wilhelm Paulcke, *L'Année sociologique* 1 (nouvelle série) (1924): 960–61.
17   Henri Hubert, review of *Cultes, Mythes et Religions, tome IV*, by Salomon Reinach, *L'Année sociologique* 12 (1909): 80.
18   Henri Hubert, review of *The Jew in London: A Study of Racial Character and Present-Day Conditions*, by G. Russel and H. S. Lewis, *Notes critiques. Sciences sociales* 1, no. 20 (n.d.): 310–11.
19   Drouin, "Hubert (Henri)," 46.
20   Louis Duchesne, *Christian Worship: Its Origin and Evolution*, trans. M. L. McClure, 2nd English ed. (London: Society for Promoting Christian Knowledge, 1903); Louis Duchesne, *Origines du culte chrétien: étude sur la liturgie latine avant Charlemagne*, 5e éd. rev. et augm. (Paris: Éditions de Bocard, 1920).
21   Drouin, "Hubert (Henri)."
22   Poulat, *Histoire, dogme et critique*, 19.
23   Claude Savart, *Les catholiques en France au XIXe siècle. Le témoignage du livres religieux* (Paris: Beauchesne, 1985).
24   Salomon Reinach, *Orpheus: A History of Religions*, trans. Florence Simmonds, Rev. ed. (New York: Liveright, 1930), 24–25.
25   William R. Keylor, *Academy and Community: The Foundation of the French Historical Profession* (Cambridge, MA: Harvard University Press, 1975), 8.
26   Henri Berr, "Les progrès de la sociologie religieuse," *Revue de synthèse historique* 34 (1906): 18.
27   Marcel Mauss, review of "Introduction à la traduction française" in *Manuel de l'histoire des religions* by Pierre Daniel Chantepie de la Saussaye, by Henri Hubert, *Notes critiques. Sciences sociales* 5 (1904): 177.
28   Henri Hubert, "Étude sommaire de la représentation du temps dans la religion et la magie," *Annuaire de l'École pratique des hautes études, section des sciences religieuses* 18, no. 14 (1904): 1–39. https://doi.org/10.3406/ephe.1904.19635
29   Hubert, "Préface," lxxxix.
30   Henri Hubert, *Leçons. St Germain-en-Laye: Archives* (Saint-Germain-en-Laye: Musée des Antiquités nationales, 1924).
31   Arnaldo Momigliano, "Georges Dumézil and the Trifunctional Approach to Roman Civilization," *History and Theory* 23, no. 3 (October 1984): 312–30; Fournier, *Marcel Mauss*.
32   Momigliano, "Georges Dumézil and the Trifunctional Approach to Roman Civilization," 315.
33   Momigliano, 314.
34   Fournier, *Marcel Mauss*, 329, chap. 5.

Chapter 5

1   Émile Durkheim, *Lettres à Marcel Mauss*, ed. Philippe Besnard and Marcel Fournier, Sociologies (Paris: Presses Universitaires de France, 1998); Besnard, "The *Année Sociologique* Team"; James Clifford, *Person and Myth: Maurice Leenhardt in the Melanesian World* (Berkeley: University of California Press, 1982); James Clifford,

"Power and Dialogue in Ethnography: Marcel Griaule's Initiation," in *Observers Observed: Essays on Ethnographic Fieldwork*, ed. George W. Stocking Jr. (Madison, WI: University of Wisconsin Press, 1985), 121–56; Jean-François Bert, ed., *Henri Hubert et la sociologie des religions: sacré, temps, héros, magie* (Liège: Presses Universitaires de Liège, 2015); Jean-François Bert, ed., *Marcel Mauss, Henri Hubert et la sociologie des religions: Penser et écrire à deux* (Paris: La Cause des Livres, 2012); Laurent Olivier, ed., *La mémoire et le temps: l'œuvre transdisciplinaire d'Henri Hubert (1872–1927)* (Paris: Éditions Demopolis, 2017); Henri Hubert, *Essay on Time: A Brief Study of the Representation of Time in Religion and Magic*, ed. Robert Parkin, trans. Jacqueline Redding and Robert Parkin (Oxford: Durkheim Press, 1999); Marcel Mauss, Henri Hubert, and Robert Hertz, *Saints, Heroes, Myths, and Rites: Classical Durkheimian Studies of Religion and Society*, ed. Alexander Riley, Sarah Daynes, and Cyril Isnart (London: Routledge, 2016).

2   Claude Lévi-Strauss, *Structural Anthropology*, trans. Monique Layton, vol. II (New York: Basic Books, 1976), 44.

3   Thomas M. Kando, "L'Annee Sociologique: From Durkheim to Today," *The Pacific Sociological Review* 19, no. 2 (April 1976): 163.

4   Claude Lévi-Strauss, *Structural Anthropology*, trans. Claire Jacobson and Brooke Grundfest Schoepf, vol. I (New York: Basic Books, 1963), v.

5   Claude Lévi-Strauss, *Tristes Tropiques* (New York: Atheneum, 1975), 59.

6   Lévi-Strauss, 59.

7   Claude Lévi-Strauss, "French Sociology," in *Twentieth-Century Sociology*, ed. Georges Gurvitch and William E. Moore (New York: Philosophical Library, 1945), 508.

8   Lévi-Strauss, 517.

9   Lévi-Strauss, 518.

10   Mauss, "An Intellectual Self-Portrait."

11   Miriam Glucksmann, *Structuralist Analysis in Contemporary Social Thought: A Comparison of the Theories of Claude Lévi-Strauss and Louis Althusser* (London: Routledge, 1974), 69.

12   Émile Durkheim, Marcel Mauss, and Émile Durkheim, *Primitive Classification*, 13. [pr.] (Chicago: University of Chicago Press, 1967), 77f.

13   Émile Durkheim, *The Elementary Forms of the Religious Life: A Study in Religious Sociology*, trans. Joseph Ward Swain (New York: Macmillan, 1915), 122.

14   Durkheim, 122.

15   Durkheim, 101–2.

16   Durkheim, 152.

17   Durkheim, 101, 122.

18   Durkheim, 420.

19   Durkheim, 25f.

20   Durkheim, 49f.

21   Maurice Merleau-Ponty, "De Mauss À Lévi-Strauss," in *Signes* (Paris: Gallimard, 1960), 143–57; Jean Piaget, *Structuralism* (New York: Harper & Row, 1970), 98.

22   Lévi-Strauss, *Tristes Tropiques*, 47.

23   Claude Lévi-Strauss, *The Elementary Structures of Kinship* (Boston: Beacon Press, 1969), xxv.

24   Claude Lévi-Strauss, *Introduction to the Work of Marcel Mauss*, trans. Felicity Baker (London: Routledge, 1987), xxxviii, xxv, xliv.

25   Lévi-Strauss, 10.

26   Georges Vacher de Lapouge, "Old and New Aspects of the Aryan Question," *American Journal of Sociology* 5, no. 3 (November 1899): xxxix.
27   Lévi-Strauss, *The Elementary Structures of Kinship*, chap. 5.
28   Clifford, *Person and Myth*, 181.
29   Lévi-Strauss, *Structural Anthropology*, 1976, vol. II, chap. 5.
30   Lévi-Strauss, II:67.
31   "Introduction [aux Mythes]," *L'Année sociologique* 6 (1901): 243–46; Marcel Mauss and Henri Hubert, "Myths," in *Saints, Heroes, Myths, and Rites: Classical Durkheimian Studies of Religion and Society*, ed. Alexander Riley, Sarah Daynes, and Cyril Isnart (London: Routledge, 2016), 13–16.
32   Henri Hubert, "Conclusion [aux Mythes]," *L'Année sociologique* 6 (1901): 268–71.
33   Berr, "Les progrès de la sociologie religieuse," 25 n3; Berr, "The Expansion of the Celts," 1934, xvi.
34   Marcel Mauss, review of *Religion und Mythologie der Uitoto. (Textaufnahmen und Beobachtungen, etc.). (Quellen der Religionsgeschichte. Gruppe II). — Vol. I (Einführung und Texte Vol. II (Texte und Wörterbuch)*, by Karl Preuss, *L'Année sociologique* 1 (nouvelle série) (1924): 510.
35   Lévi-Strauss, *Introduction to the Work of Marcel Mauss*, xxx–xxxi.
36   Hubert, "Conclusion [aux Mythes]," 271.
37   Mauss, "An Intellectual Self-Portrait," 145.
38   Isambert, "At the Frontier of Folklore and Sociology," 171.
39   Isambert, 154 n9.
40   Henri Hubert, *Divinités Gauloises* (Macon: Protat Frères, 1925).
41   Henri Hubert, *The Rise of the Celts*, ed. Marcel Mauss, Raymond Lantier, and Jean Marx, trans. M. R. Dobie (New York: Knopf, 1934).
42   Littleton, *The New Comparative Mythology*.
43   Mauss, "An Intellectual Self-Portrait," 140f.
44   Mauss, 140f.
45   Mauss, 140f.
46   Mauss, 145f.
47   Bert, *Henri Hubert et la sociologie des religions*; Bert, *Marcel Mauss, Henri Hubert et la sociologie des religions*; Olivier, *La mémoire et le temps*; Hubert, *Essay on Time*; Mauss, Hubert, and Hertz, *Saints, Heroes, Myths, and Rites*.
48   Hubert and Mauss, "Introduction à l'analyse de quelques phénomènes religieux," 17.
49   Hubert and Mauss, 17.
50   Hubert, "Préface," xxxviif; Hubert and Mauss, "Introduction à l'analyse de quelques phénomènes religieux," 17.
51   Henri Hubert, review of *Ephialtes. Eine pathologisch-mythologische Abhandlung über die Alpträume und Alpdämonen des klassischen Altertums (Abhandlungen der philologischhistorischen Classe der Kgl. Sächs. Gesellschaft der Wissenschaften, t. XX, no II)*, by William Henry Roscher, *L'Année sociologique* 6 (1901): 230–36.
52   Henri Hubert, review of *Les légendes hagiographiques*, by Hippolyte Delehaye, *L'Année sociologique* 7 (1902): 344–47.
53   Henri Hubert, review of *Review of L'évangile et l'église (2e éd. augmentée)*, by Alfred Loisy, *L'Année sociologique* 8 (1903): 292.
54   Hubert and Mauss, "Introduction à l'analyse de quelques phénomènes religieux," 17.
55   Hubert, "Préface," xxxviii.

56 Henri Hubert, "Introduction à la traduction française," in *Manuel de l'histoire des religions*, by Pierre Daniel Chantepie de la Saussaye (Paris: Colin, 1904), xliiif.

57 Émile Durkheim, "Individual and Collective Representations," in *Sociology and Philosophy*, trans. D. F. Pocock (New York: Free Press, 1974), 1–34.

58 Hubert, "Préface," xxxix.

59 Hubert, "Conclusion [aux Mythes]," 271.

60 Hubert, "Préface," xlvii.

61 Hubert, "Introduction à la traduction française," xxxviii.

62 Hubert, "Préface," xxxix.

63 "Introduction [aux Mythes]," 244.

64 Hubert, "Préface," xxxix.

65 Hubert, xxxix.

66 Hubert, xlvii.

67 Robin Horton and Ruth H. Finnegan, eds., *Modes of Thought: Essays on Thinking in Western and Non-Western Societies* (London: Faber, 1973).

68 Littleton, *The New Comparative Mythology*, 270.

69 Louis Dumont, *From Mandeville to Marx: The Genesis and Triumph of Economic Ideology* (Chicago: University of Chicago Press, 1977).

70 Marcel Granet, *The Religion of the Chinese People* (New York: Harper & Row, 1975), 54.

71 Granet, 54.

72 Granet, 96.

73 Hubert, "Conclusion [aux Mythes]," 271.

74 Hubert, 271.

75 Granet, *The Religion of the Chinese People*, 53f.

76 Granet, 54.

77 Granet, 56.

78 Lévi-Strauss, *Structural Anthropology*, 1976, II:256.

79 Hubert, "Introduction à la traduction française," xxxviii.

80 Hubert, xxxviii.

81 Hubert, "Conclusion [aux Mythes]," 271.

82 Hubert, "Introduction à la traduction française," xxxviii.

83 Hubert, xxxviii.

84 Hubert, "Conclusion [aux Mythes]," 272.

85 Hubert, 270.

86 Hubert, "Introduction à la traduction française," xliii.

87 Hubert, "Conclusion [aux Mythes]," 271.

88 Hubert, "Introduction à la traduction française," xxxviii.

89 Hubert, "Conclusion [aux Mythes]," 271.

90 Hubert, "Introduction à la traduction française," xxxviii.

91 Hubert and Mauss, "Introduction à l'analyse de quelques phénomènes religieux," 35.

92 Hubert, "Introduction à la traduction française," xxxviii.

93 Hubert, xliii.

94 Hubert, xliii.

95 Hubert, "Conclusion [aux Mythes]," 271.

96 Lévi-Strauss, "French Sociology," 534f.

97 Lévi-Strauss, *Tristes Tropiques*, 57f.

98 Clifford, *Person and Myth*, 202–6.

99 Clifford, 204.

100 Hubert, "Étude sommaire," 1–39.
101 Besnard, "The *Année Sociologique* Team," 22.
102 Ivan Strenski, *Four Theories of Myth in Twentieth-Century History: Cassirer, Eliade, Lévi-Strauss, and Malinowski* (Iowa City: University of Iowa Press, 1987), 359–60.
103 Hubert, *The Rise of the Celts*, 39, 211; Hubert, *Divinités Gauloises*, 9.
104 Marcel Mauss, review of *Mythologie. Archiv für Religionswissenschaft* by H. Usener and *Vorwort zum Siebenten Bande* by A. Dietrich, *L'Année sociologique* 8 (1903): 224.
105 H. Hubert and Marcel Mauss, review of *Astralmythen der Hebräer, Babylonier und Aegypter*, by Eduard Stucken, *L'Année sociologique* 6 (1901): 262.
106 Marcel Mauss, review of *Le festin de l'immortalité. Étude de mythologie comparée Indo-Européenne*, by Georges Dumézil, *L'Année sociologique* 1 (nouvelle série) (1924): 518.
107 Hubert, "Étude sommaire," 3f.
108 Hubert, "Conclusion [aux Mythes]," 269.
109 Lévi-Strauss, *Introduction to the Work of Marcel Mauss*, xlvi.
110 Lévi-Strauss, xlvii.
111 Clifford, *Person and Myth*, 177, 80, 202–6.
112 Clifford, 7, 202–6.
113 Clifford, 177, chap. 6.

Chapter 6

1 Bronislaw Malinowski, "Magic, Science and Religion," in *Magic, Science and Religion and Other Essays*, ed. Robert Redfield (New York: Free Press, 1948), 79.
2 Bronislaw Malinowski, *Argonauts of the Western Pacific* (New York: E. P. Dutton, 1961), 234.
3 Bryan S. Rennie, review of *Theorizing About Myth*, by Robert A. Segal, *Culture and Religion* 1, no. 1 (May 2000): 149–50. https://doi.org/10.1080/01438300008567148
4 Robert A. Segal, "Understanding Myth: A Response to Bryan Rennie," *Culture and Religion* 1, no. 2 (November 2000): 287–89. https://doi.org/10.1080/01438300008567156
5 Malinowski, "Myth in Primitive Psychology," 122.
6 Malinowski, *Argonauts of the Western Pacific*, 311.
7 Segal, *Myth Theorized*, 146–47.
8 Malinowski, *Argonauts of the Western Pacific*, 229.
9 Malinowski, "Myth in Primitive Psychology," 122.
10 Malinowski, *Argonauts of the Western Pacific*, chap. XII, 290–330.
11 Bronislaw Malinowski, "'Psychoanalysis and Anthropology' (1924)," in *Malinowski and the Work of Myth*, ed. Ivan Strenski (Princeton, NJ: Princeton University Press, 1992), 55–57; Bronislaw Malinowski, "Obscenity and Myth," in *Sex and Repression in Savage Society* (London: Kegan Paul, 1927), 104–34; Malinowski, "Myth in Primitive Psychology"; Bronislaw Malinowski, "Myth as a Dramatic Development of Dogma," in *Sex, Culture, and Myth* (New York: Harcourt, 1962), 245–55; Bronislaw Malinowski, "The Foundations of Faith and Morality," in *Sex, Culture, and Myth* (New York: Harcourt, 1962), 295–336.
12 Malinowski, *A Scientific Theory of Culture*, 71.

13   M. F. Ashley Montagu, "Bronislaw Malinowski (1884-1942)," *Isis* 34, no. 2 (October 1942): 148.
14   Bascom, "Malinowski's Contributions to the Study of Folklore," 167.
15   Bronislaw Malinowski, "Magic, Science and Religion," in *Magic, Science and Religion and Other Essays*, ed. Robert Redfield (Prospect Heights, IL: Waveland Press, 1992), 79.
16   Alfred Métraux, "Bronislaw Malinowski: (1884-1942)," *Boletín Bibliográfico de Antropología Americana (1937-1948)* 6, no. 1/3 (1942): 26-29.
17   Bronislaw Malinowski, "'Elementary Forms of Religious Life,' review of *Les formes élémentaire de la vie religieuse, le système totémique en Australie*, by Émile Durkheim," in *Sex, Culture, and Myth* (New York: Harcourt, 1962), 283-88.
18   Robert J. Thornton and Peter Skalnik, "Introduction: Malinowski's Reading, Writing, 1904-1914," in *Early Writings of Bronislaw Malinowski*, ed. Robert J. Thornton and Peter Skalnik (Cambridge: Cambridge University Press, 1993), 47; Bronislaw Malinowski, "Totemism and Exogamy," in *Early Writings of Bronislaw Malinowski*, ed. Robert J. Thornton and Peter Skalnik, trans. Ludwik Krzyzanowski (Cambridge: Cambridge University Press, 1993), 168.
19   Malinowski, "'Elementary Forms of Religious Life,' review of *Les formes élémentaire de la vie religieuse, le système totémique en Australie*, by Émile Durkheim."
20   William Watts Miller, "The anthropological roots of Émile Durkheim's British career," *Sociologie* 8, no. 3 (2017): 309-14. https://doi.org/10.3917/socio.083.0309
21   A. C. Haddon, *Folk-Tales* (Cambridge: Cambridge University Press, 1908), 45.
22   Miller, "The anthropological roots of Émile Durkheim's British career."
23   Raymond Firth, "Seligman's Contributions to Oceanic Anthropology," *Oceania* 45, no. 4 (June 1975): 280.
24   Firth, 280.
25   Malinowski, *Argonauts of the Western Pacific*, 84.
26   Miller, "The anthropological roots of Émile Durkheim's British career," passim.
27   Miller, 311.
28   Bronislaw Malinowski, "Ethnology and the Study of Society," *Economica*, no. 6 (October 1922): 218.
29   B. Malinowski, review of *The Children of the Sun: a Study in the Early History of Civilisation*, by W. K. Perry, *Nature* 113, no. 2835 (March 1924): 299.
30   Malinowski, *Argonauts of the Western Pacific*, 18.
31   Malinowski, "The Children of the Sun," 300.
32   Malinowski, 300.
33   Malinowski, 299.
34   Malinowski, 301.
35   Malinowski, 300.
36   Malinowski, 300.
37   Malinowski, *Argonauts of the Western Pacific*, 406. Emphasis mine.
38   Malinowski, 406.
39   Malinowski, 406.
40   Bronislaw Malinowski, "On the Principle of the Economy of Thought (1906)," in *Early Writings of Bronislaw Malinowski*, ed. Robert J. Thornton and Peter Skalnik, trans. Ludwik Krzyzanowski (Cambridge: Cambridge University Press, 1993), 89-116.

41 Malinowski, *Argonauts of the Western Pacific*, 406.
42 Alfred R. Radcliffe-Brown, *The Andaman Islanders: A Study in Social Anthropology* (Cambridge: Cambridge University Press, 1922), 325; Robert A. Segal, "Durkheim in Britain: The Work of Radcliffe-Brown," *Journal of the Anthropological Society of Oxford* 30, no. 2 (1999): 131–62.
43 Marcell Mauss, review of *Reports of the Cambridge Anthropological Expedition to Torres Straits. Vol. V, Sociology, Magic and Religion of the Western Islanders*, by A. C. Haddon, *L'Année sociologique* 8 (1903): 260.
44 Mauss, 260.
45 Radcliffe-Brown, *The Andaman Islanders*, 234. Emphases mine.
46 Feliks Gross, "Young Malinowski and His Later Years," *American Ethnologist* 13, no. 3 (August 1986): 559.
47 Andrzej K. Paluch, "The Polish Background to Malinowski's Work," *Man* 16, no. 2 (June 1981): 279.
48 Thornton and Skalnik, "Introduction: Malinowski's Reading, Writing, 1904–1914," 13.
49 Malinowski, "On the Principle of the Economy of Thought (1906)."
50 Robert J. Thornton, "The Chains of Reciprocity: The Impact of Nietzsche's 'Genealogy' on Malinowski's 'Crime and Custom in Savage Society,'" *The Polish Sociological Bulletin*, no. 97 (1992): 23.
51 Thornton and Skalnik, "Introduction: Malinowski's Reading, Writing, 1904–1914," 26.
52 Malinowski, "On the Principle of the Economy of Thought (1906)," 91.
53 Malinowski, 91.
54 Malinowski, 91.
55 Malinowski, 94.
56 Malinowski, 97.
57 Malinowski, *A Scientific Theory of Culture*, 159.
58 Malinowski, *Argonauts of the Western Pacific*, 406.
59 Malinowski, "The Children of the Sun," 300. Emphasis mine.
60 Malinowski, "Myth in Primitive Psychology," 82.
61 Malinowski, 105.
62 Malinowski, 82, 105.
63 Michael W. Young, "Young Malinowski," *Canberra Anthropology* 17, no. 2 (October 1994): 117.
64 Malinowski, "Magic, Science and Religion," 1948, 101. My emphases.
65 Friedrich Nietzsche, *The Birth of Tragedy: Or, Hellenism and Pessimism*, trans. William. A. Haussmann (London: George Allen & Unwin, 1910), 21.
66 Nietzsche, 61.
67 Nietzsche, 64.
68 Nietzsche, 85.
69 Bronislaw Malinowski, "Observations on Friedrich Nietzsche's *The Birth of Tragedy* (1904/5)," in *Early Writings of Bronislaw Malinowski*, ed. Robert J. Thornton and Peter Skalnik, trans. Ludwik Krzyzanowski (Cambridge: Cambridge University Press, 1993), 85.
70 Nietzsche, *The Birth of Tragedy*, 46.
71 Nietzsche, 59.
72 Nietzsche, 64.
73 Young, "Young Malinowski," 117.
74 Young, 117.

75 Bronislaw Malinowski, *A Diary in the Strict Sense of the Term*, trans. Norbert Guterman (London: Routledge, 1967), 34.

76 Edmund Leach et al., "Frazer and Malinowski: A CA Discussion [and Comments and Reply]," *Current Anthropology* 7, no. 5 (December 1966): 567.

77 Gross, "Young Malinowski," 560; Sean Ireton, "«Ich Bin Ein Wanderer Und Ein Bergsteiger» — Nietzsche and Zarathustra in the Mountains," *Colloquia Germanica* 42, no. 3 (2009): 193–212.

78 Young, "Young Malinowski," 117.

79 Edmund Leach, "The Epistemological Background to Malinowski's Empiricism," in *Man and Culture: An Evaluation of the Work of Malinowski*, ed. Raymond Firth (London: Routledge, 1957), 133.

80 Jonny Anomaly, "Nietzsche's Critique of Utilitarianism," *The Journal of Nietzsche Studies* 29, no. 1 (April 1, 2005): 1.

81 Fritz Ringer, *The Decline of the German Mandarins: The German Academic Community, 1890–1933* (Cambridge, MA: Harvard University Press, 1969), 185.

82 Ivan Strenski, "Malinowski: Second Positivism, Second Romanticism," *Man* 17, no. 4 (1982): 767–68.

83 Malinowski, *Argonauts of the Western Pacific*, 60.

84 Malinowski, 60.

85 Malinowski, 516; Strenski, "Malinowski," 768.

86 Marcel Mauss, *The Gift: Forms and Functions of Exchange in Archaic Societies*, trans. Ian Gunnison (New York: Norton, 1967).

87 Mauss, 72.

88 Thornton, "The Chains of Reciprocity," 22.

89 Mariola Flis, "Malinowski and Radcliffe-Brown: Two Versions of Functionalism," *The Polish Sociological Bulletin*, no. 97 (1992): 36–38.

90 Alfred R. Radcliffe-Brown, *Structure and Function in Primitive Society: Essays and Addresses* (Aberdeen: Aberdeen University Press, 1952), 188, quoted in Flis, "Malinowski and Radcliffe-Brown," 35.

91 Radcliffe-Brown, 188, quoted in Flis, "Malinowski and Radcliffe-Brown," 35.

92 Flis, "Malinowski and Radcliffe-Brown," 41–42.

93 Flis, 35.

94 Malinowski, *A Scientific Theory of Culture*, 19.

95 Bronislaw Malinowski, *Sex and Repression in Savage Society* (London: Kegan Paul, 1927), 225; Malinowski, *A Scientific Theory of Culture*, 10; Alfred R. Radcliffe-Brown, *Method in Social Anthropology: Selected Essays*, ed. M. N. Srinivas (Chicago: University of Chicago Press, 1958), 62 as cited in Flis, "Malinowski and Radcliffe-Brown," 41.

96 Malinowski, *Argonauts of the Western Pacific*, 210.

97 Malinowski, 214.

98 Malinowski, *A Scientific Theory of Culture*.

99 Thornton, "The Chains of Reciprocity," 26.

100 Malinowski, *A Scientific Theory of Culture*, 23.

101 Malinowski, 23.

102 Malinowski, 171.

103 Malinowski, 24. Emphasis mine.

104 Malinowski, 111. Emphasis mine.

105 J. H. Driberg, review of *Myth in Primitive Psychology*, by Bronislaw Malinowski, *Economica*, no. 19 (March 1927): 35.

106 Malinowski, "Magic, Science and Religion," 1948, 82.
107 Malinowski, 105.
108 Malinowski, *A Scientific Theory of Culture*, 10.
109 Malinowski, "Magic, Science and Religion," 1948, 52.
110 Malinowski, "The Foundations of Faith and Morality," 336.
111 Malinowski, "Magic, Science and Religion," 1948, 90. Emphasis mine.
112 Malinowski, "Myth in Primitive Psychology," 93.
113 Malinowski, "On the Principle of the Economy of Thought (1906)"; Malinowski, "Totemism and Exogamy."
114 Malinowski, "Myth in Primitive Psychology."
115 Malinowski, "On the Principle of the Economy of Thought (1906)."
116 Malinowski, 125.
117 Leach et al., "Frazer and Malinowski," 563.
118 Leach et al., 563.
119 Malinowski, *A Scientific Theory of Culture*, 189.
120 Thornton and Skalnik, "Introduction: Malinowski's Reading, Writing, 1904–1914," 46.
121 Thornton and Skalnik, 48.
122 Malinowski, "On the Principle of the Economy of Thought (1906)," 184.
123 Leach et al., "Frazer and Malinowski," 562.
124 Leach et al., 562.
125 James George Frazer to Bronislaw Malinowski, "Untitled," February 14, 1926, Series I, Box 3, Folder 203, Bronislaw Malinowski papers, Archives at Yale.
126 Leach et al., "Frazer and Malinowski," 564.
127 Thornton and Skalnik, "Introduction: Malinowski's Reading, Writing, 1904–1914," 4. Italics in the original.
128 Michael W. Young, *Malinowski: Odyssey of an Anthropologist, 1884–1920* (New Haven, CT: Yale University Press, 2004), 19.
129 Young, 19.
130 Strenski, *Understanding Theories of Religion*, chap. 11.
131 Malinowski, "'Psychoanalysis and Anthropology' (1924)."
132 Malinowski, 55.
133 Malinowski, 55.
134 Malinowski, 55.
135 Bascom, "Malinowski's Contributions to the Study of Folklore," 168.
136 Bascom, 168.
137 Bascom, 171.
138 Malinowski, "'Psychoanalysis and Anthropology' (1924)," 56.
139 Paluch, "The Polish Background to Malinowski's Work," 278.
140 Thornton and Skalnik, "Introduction: Malinowski's Reading, Writing, 1904–1914," 33.
141 Malinowski, "On the Principle of the Economy of Thought (1906)," 108.
142 Thornton and Skalnik, "Introduction: Malinowski's Reading, Writing, 1904–1914," 30.
143 Thornton and Skalnik, 30.
144 Malinowski, "On the Principle of the Economy of Thought (1906)," 114.
145 Malinowski, 108.
146 Malinowski, 108.
147 Malinowski, 108.
148 Malinowski, 109.

149 Malinowski, 108–9.
150 Malinowski, 110.
151 Malinowski, 110.
152 Malinowski, 114.
153 Paluch, "The Polish Background to Malinowski's Work," 280.
154 Malinowski, *Argonauts of the Western Pacific*, 517.
155 Clifford Geertz, "'From the Native's Point of View': On the Nature of Anthropological Understanding," *Bulletin of the American Academy of Arts and Sciences* 28, no. 1 (October 1974): 43; Pan, Inghai, "Notes on Anthropological Understanding of the Others," *Journal of Group Dynamics* 30 (December 2013): 312–20. https://doi.org/10.11245/jgd.30.312; Strenski, "Malinowski"; Renée Sylvain, "Malinowski the Modern Other: An Indirect Evaluation of Postmodernism," *Anthropologica* 38, no. 1 (1996): 26.
156 Strenski, "Malinowski," 767.
157 Malinowski, *Argonauts of the Western Pacific*, 11.
158 Malinowski, 9.
159 Driberg, "Myth in Primitive Psychology," 125.
160 Paluch, "The Polish Background to Malinowski's Work," 279.
161 Malinowski, *Argonauts of the Western Pacific*, 13.
162 Malinowski, 12–13.
163 Leach et al., "Frazer and Malinowski," 565.
164 Malinowski, quoted in Paluch, "The Polish Background to Malinowski's Work," 280.
165 Marian Kempny, "Malinowski Fifty Years Later," *The Polish Sociological Bulletin*, no. 97 (1992): 15.
166 Kempny, 15.
167 Malinowski, *Argonauts of the Western Pacific*, 17–22.
168 Malinowski, *A Diary*, 114.
169 Malinowski, 114.
170 Raymond Firth, "Bronislaw Malinowski," in *Totems and Teachers: Perspectives on the History of Anthropology*, ed. Sydel Silverman (New York: Columbia University Press, 1981), 10; Leach et al., "Frazer and Malinowski," 565; Malinowski, *Argonauts of the Western Pacific*, 517–22.
171 Malinowski, *Argonauts of the Western Pacific*, 517.
172 Malinowski, 231.
173 Malinowski, 233.
174 Malinowski, "Myth in Primitive Psychology," 84.
175 Paluch, "The Polish Background to Malinowski's Work," 281.
176 Strenski, "Malinowski."
177 Malinowski, "Myth in Primitive Psychology," 108.
178 Malinowski, "Magic, Science and Religion," 1948, 84.
179 Malinowski, *Argonauts of the Western Pacific*, 517.
180 Akiyama Misako and Susumu Egashira, "Ernst Mach and the Origin of the Knowledge Theory in the Former Austrian Empire," *SSRN Electronic Journal*, 2013. https://doi.org/10.2139/ssrn.2224390
181 Misako and Egashira.
182 Misako and Egashira, 10.
183 Misako and Egashira, 10.
184 Malinowski, *Argonauts of the Western Pacific*, 517.
185 Malinowski, "Magic, Science and Religion," 1948, 84.

186 Malinowski, 84–85.
187 Malinowski, *Argonauts of the Western Pacific*, 517.
188 Malinowski, 230.
189 Malinowski, "Magic, Science and Religion," 1948, 84–85.
190 Malinowski, "Myth in Primitive Psychology," 108.
191 Malinowski, 85-86. Emphasis mine.
192 Malinowski, 85-86. Emphasis mine.
193 Malinowski, "Magic, Science and Religion," 1948.
194 Thornton and Skalnik, "Introduction: Malinowski's Reading, Writing, 1904–1914," 20.
195 Liisa Steinby, "The Rehabilitation of Myth: Enlightenment and Romanticism in Johann Gottfried Herder's *Vom Geist Der Ebräischen Poesie*," *Sjuttonhundratal* 6 (October 1, 2009): 54–79. https://doi.org/10.7557/4.2760
196 Malinowski, "Myth in Primitive Psychology," 108.

Chapter 7

1   Segal, *Myth Theorized*, 146f.
2   Lincoln, *Theorizing Myth*, ix.
3   Lucien Lévy-Bruhl, *Primitive Mentality*, trans. Lilian A. Clare (Boston: Beacon Press, 1966); Lucien Lévy-Bruhl, *How Natives Think*, trans. Lilian A. Clare (New York: Washington Square Press, 1966).
4   Lucien Lévy-Bruhl, *How Natives Think*, trans. Lilian A. Clare (New York: Washington Square Press, 1966), passim.
5   Robert Frazer, review of *Theorizing about Myth*, by Robert A. Segal, *Modern Language Review* 96, no. 2 (April 2001): 451–52. https://doi.org/10.1353/mlr.2001.a828780
6   Segal, *Myth Theorized*, 146f.
7   Segal, 147.
8   Richard Rorty, *Philosophy and Social Hope* (New York: Penguin Books, 2000).
9   Marlène Laruelle, "Le néo-eurasisme russe. L'empire après l'empire?," *Cahiers du monde russe* 42, no. 1 (January 1, 2001): 71–94. https://doi.org/10.4000/monderusse.8437; Marlène Laruelle, *Russian Eurasianism: An Ideology of Empire* (Washington, DC: Woodrow Wilson Center Press, 2008); Konstantin Sheiko and Stephen Brown, *History as Therapy: Alternative History and Nationalist Imaginings in Russia, 1991–2014* (Stuttgart: ibidem, 2014).
10 Malinowski, "Magic, Science and Religion," 1948, 84–85.
11 Jacques Faublée and Marcelle Urbain-Faublée, "Notes sur des travaux d'ethnologie et d'anthropologie," *L'Année sociologique* 23 (1972): 108; Malinowski, "Magic, Science and Religion," 1948, 84–85.
12 Lincoln, *Theorizing Myth*, 17.
13 Laruelle, "Le néo-eurasisme russe"; Laruelle, *Russian Eurasianism*; Sheiko and Brown, *History as Therapy*.
14 Sheiko and Brown, *History as Therapy*.
15 Charles Taylor, "Interpretation and the Sciences of Man," in *Philosophical Papers*, by Charles Taylor, vol. 2: Philosophy and the Human Sciences (Cambridge: Cambridge University Press, 1985), 15–57; Charles Taylor, "Understanding and Ethnocentricity," in *Philosophical Papers*, by Charles Taylor, vol. 2: Philosophy and the Human Sciences (Cambridge: Cambridge University Press, 1985), 116–33.

16 James Shapiro, *A Year in the Life of William Shakespeare: 1599* (New York: HarperCollins, 2005).
17 Shapiro, 127–29.
18 Simon Schama, *Citizens: A Chronicle of the French Revolution* (New York: Knopf, 1989), 259; Edith Flamarion, "Brutus ou l'adoption d'un mythe romain par la Révolution française," in *La révolution française et l'antiquité: bicentenaire de la Révolution Française*, ed. Raymond Chevallier (Tours: Centre de Recherches A. Piganiol, 1991), 91–112.
19 Patrice Higonnet, *Goodness beyond Virtue: Jacobins during the French Revolution* (Cambridge, MA: Harvard University Press, 1998), 196.
20 Plutarch, "Brutus," in *Makers of Rome: Nine Lives*, ed. and trans. Ian Scott-Kilvert (New York: Dorset Press, 1985), 223–70.
21 Plutarch.
22 Flamarion, "Brutus ou l'adoption d'un mythe," 91, 98f.
23 Peter France, ed., "Voltaire (Pseud. of François-Marie Arouet)," in *The New Oxford Companion to Literature in French* (Oxford: Oxford University Press, 1995), 844.
24 Emmet Kennedy, *A Cultural History of the French Revolution* (New Haven, CT: Yale University Press, 1989), 363.
25 Flamarion, "Brutus ou l'adoption d'un mythe," 97.
26 William Doyle, *The Oxford History of the French Revolution* (Oxford: Oxford University Press, 1989), 259.
27 Flamarion, "Brutus ou l'adoption d'un mythe," 95.
28 Robert N. Minor, ed., *Modern Indian Interpreters of the Bhagavad Gita* (Albany: State University of New York Press, 1986).
29 Robert N. Minor, ed., *Modern Indian Interpreters of the Bhagavad Gita* (Albany: State University of New York Press, 1986), passim.
30 J. T. F. Jordens, "Gandhi and the *Bhagavadgita*," in *Modern Indian Interpreters of the Bhagavad Gita*, ed. Robert N. Minor (Albany: State University of New York Press, 1986), 99.
31 Jordens, 100–101.
32 Alice Albinia and Tristram Stuart, "India's Epic Struggle," *Guardian*, August 16, 2007, sec. Books. https://www.theguardian.com/books/2007/aug/16/fiction
33 Stephen N. Hay, ed., *Sources of Indian Tradition*, vol. 2, Records of Civilization: Sources and Studies (New York: Columbia University Press, 1958), 166; Robert W. Stevenson, "Tilak and the *Bhagavadgita*'s Doctrine of Karmayoga," in *Modern Indian Interpreters of the Bhagavad Gita*, ed. Robert N. Minor (Albany: State University of New York Press, 1986), 48.
34 Eric J. Hobsbawm, "The Rules of Violence," in *Revolutionaries: Contemporary Essays* (New York: Pantheon, 1973), 209–15.
35 Mithi Mukherjee, "Sedition, Law, and the British Empire in India: The Trial of Tilak (1908)," *Law, Culture and the Humanities* 16, no. 3 (October 2020): 471.
36 Mukherjee, 472.
37 A. C. Niemeijer, "Some General Aspects of Nationalism in India," in *The Khilafat Movement in India 1919–1924* (The Hague: Martinus Nijhoff, 1972), 5.
38 Stevenson, "Tilak and the *Bhagavadgita*'s Doctrine of Karmayoga," 47.
39 Niemeijer, "Some General Aspects of Nationalism in India," 149.
40 Niemeijer, 26.
41 Stevenson, "Tilak and the *Bhagavadgita*'s Doctrine of Karmayoga," 58.
42 Niemeijer, "Some General Aspects of Nationalism in India," 26.

43   Sashi Ahluwalia, "A Sheaf of Anecdotes," in *Shivaji and Indian Nationalism*, ed. B. K. Ahluwalia and Sashi Ahluwalia (Delhi: Cultural Publishing House, 1984), 179f.
44   Ahluwalia, 182.
45   James W. Laine, "Śivāji's Mother," in *Images of Women in Maharashtrian Literature and Religion*, ed. Anne Feldhaus (Albany: State University of New York Press, 1996), 109.
46   Laine, 97.
47   B. G. Bhosale, "Indian Nationalism: Gandhi Vis-a-Vis Tilak and Savarkar," *The Indian Journal of Political Science* 70, no. 2 (2009): 421.
48   Sukeshi Kamra, "Law and Radical Rhetoric in British India: The 1897 Trial of Bal Gangadhar Tilak," *South Asia: Journal of South Asian Studies* 39, no. 3 (July 2, 2016): 550n18.
49   Stevenson, "Tilak and the *Bhagavadgita*'s Doctrine of Karmayoga," 58.
50   Abha Chauhan Khimta, "The Concept of Ends and Means in the Ideals of B.G. Tilak and Sri Aurobindo," *Research Journal of Philosophy & Social Sciences* 47, no. 1 (June 30, 2021): 52.
51   Kamra, "Law and Radical Rhetoric in British India."
52   Arjun Raghvendra Singh, "Sedition: An Insight on History, Evolution, Shortcoming and Relevance of This Law in Post Colonial India," *Supremo Amicus* 28 (February 2022). https://doi-ds.org/doilink/02.2022-67571545/supremoamicus/v28/2022/53
53   Stevenson, "Tilak and the *Bhagavadgita*'s Doctrine of Karmayoga," 46.

Chapter 8

1   Segal, *Myth Theorized*, chap. 2.
2   Segal, 44.
3   Jonathan Z. Smith, "A Matter of Class: Taxonomies of Religion," *Harvard Theological Review* 89, no. 4 (October 1996): 401.
4   Nancy Levene, "Courses and Canons in the Study of Religion (With Continual Reference to Jonathan Z. Smith)," *Journal of the American Academy of Religion* 80, no. 4 (December 1, 2012): 1012.
5   Frazer, "Theorizing about Myth," 451.
6   Segal, *Myth Theorized*, 39.
7   Segal, 146–47.
8   Segal, 39.
9   Segal, 30.
10 Segal, "Understanding Myth," 288.
11 Segal, 288.
12 Rennie, "Theorizing About Myth," 150.
13 Rennie, 150.
14 Segal, "Understanding Myth," 288.
15 Segal, *Myth Theorized*, 40.
16 Segal, 69.
17 Segal, "Understanding Myth," 287.
18 Segal, *Myth Theorized*, 40.
19 Robert A. Segal, email to the author, March 7, 2023.
20 Segal to Strenski.

21 Segal to Strenski.
22 Segal to Strenski.
23 Segal, *Myth Theorized*, 146.
24 Segal, 109.
25 Segal, 40. Emphasis mine.
26 Segal, 109-16.
27 Segal, email to the author, March 7, 2023.
28 Segal, *Myth Theorized*, 146-47. Emphasis mine.
29 Segal, 147.
30 Farhang Erfani, review of *Cinematic Gods? Robert Segal on Myth's Persistence: Review of: Robert Alan Segal, Myth: A Very Short Introduction, Oxford: Oxford University Press, 2004*, by Robert A. Segal, *Jung Journal* 6, no. 3 (Summer 2012): 72.
31 Segal, email message to the author, March 7, 2023.
32 Lincoln, *Theorizing Myth*, 17.
33 Segal, email to the author, March 7, 2023.
34 Segal, "Understanding Myth," 288.
35 Segal, 288.
36 Segal, 288.
37 Segal, email to the author, March 7, 2023.
38 Segal, "Understanding Myth," 288.
39 Max Weber, *The Protestant Ethic and the Spirit of Capitalism*, trans. Talcott Parsons (New York: Scribner, 1976), chap. 2.
40 Richard Herbert Howe, "Max Weber's Elective Affinities: Sociology Within the Bounds of Pure Reason," *American Journal of Sociology* 84, no. 2 (September 1978): 366-85. https://doi.org/10.1086/226788
41 Segal, "Understanding Myth," 288.
42 Frazer, "Theorizing about Myth," 451.
43 Segal, email to the author, March 7, 2023. Emphasis in the original.
44 Segal, *Myth Theorized*, 39.
45 Segal, 31.
46 Segal, 31.
47 Segal, 28.
48 Segal, email to the author, March 7, 2023.
49 Segal to Strenski.
50 Segal, *Myth Theorized*, 151.
51 Segal, "Understanding Myth," 289.
52 Frazer, "Theorizing about Myth," 451.
53 Frazer, 452.
54 Frazer, 451.
55 Robert A. Segal, review of *Classification and Comparison in the Study of Religion: The Work of Jonathan Z. Smith*, by Jonathan Z. Smith, *Journal of the American Academy of Religion* 73, no. 4 (December 1, 2005): 1175-88. https://doi.org/10.1093/jaarel/lfi120
56 Jonathan Z. Smith, "Earth and Gods," *The Journal of Religion* 49, no. 2 (April 1969): 103-27. https://doi.org/10.1086/486164
57 Jonathan Z. Smith, "Birth Upside down or Right Side Up?," *History of Religions* 9, no. 4 (May 1970): 281-303. https://doi.org/10.1086/462610
58 Jonathan Z. Smith, "I Am a Parrot (Red)," *History of Religions* 11, no. 4 (May 1972): 391-413. https://doi.org/10.1086/462661; Jonathan Z. Smith, "When

the Bough Breaks," *History of Religions* 12, no. 4 (May 1973): 342–71. https://doi.org/10.1086/462686

59   Jonathan Z. Smith, "Conjectures on Conjunctures and Other Matters: Three Essays," in *Redescribing the Gospel of Mark*, ed. Barry S. Crawford and Merrill P. Miller (Atlanta: SBL Press, 2017), 17–98; Jonathan Z. Smith, *Drudgery Divine: On the Comparison of Early Christianities and the Religions of Late Antiquity*, Jordan Lectures in Comparative Religion 14 (Chicago: University of Chicago Press, 1990); Jonathan Z. Smith, *To Take Place: Toward Theory in Ritual* (Chicago: University of Chicago Press, 1987).

60   Smith, *Drudgery Divine*; Smith, *To Take Place*.
61   Smith, "Conjectures on Conjunctures," 67.
62   Smith, 67.
63   Smith, "Conjectures on Conjunctures."
64   Strenski, *Four Theories of Myth*, chap. 4; Ivan Strenski, "Love and Anarchy in Romania: A Critical Review of Mircea Eliade's *Autobiography, Volume 1: 1907–37*," in *Religion in Relation: Method, Application, and Moral Location* (Columbia: University of South Carolina Press, 1993), 166–79.

65   Seung Il Kang, "A Comparison of Mircea Eliade's and Jonathan Z. Smith's Views on Dur-an-Ki," *Zeitschrift Für Religions- Und Geistesgeschichte* 64, no. 1 (January 1, 2012): 62; Jonathan Z. Smith, "The Wobbling Pivot," *The Journal of Religion* 52, no. 2 (April 1972): 134–49. https://doi.org/10.1086/486294

66   Kang, "A Comparison of Mircea Eliade's and Jonathan Z. Smith's Views on Dur-an-Ki," 63; Bryan S. Rennie, *Reconstructing Eliade: Making Sense of Religion* (Albany: State University of New York Press, 1996), 189n7.

67   Smith, "Conjectures on Conjunctures," 61n105.
68   Smith, 69.
69   Smith, 66f.
70   Smith, 61n105.
71   Smith, 62.
72   Smith, 62.
73   Smith, 66–67.
74   Claude Lévi-Strauss, *The Savage Mind* (London: Weidenfeld and Lincoln, 1966), 95.
75   Robert A. Segal, "Does Myth Have a Future?," in *Myth and Method*, ed. Laurie L. Patton and Wendy Doniger (Charlottesville: University Press of Virginia, 1996), 82–83.
76   Smith, "Conjectures on Conjunctures," 62.
77   Smith, 67.
78   Smith, 67.
79   Smith, 61.
80   Allan Sun, "Chasing One's Tail: Some Reflections on the Methodologies of Mircea Eliade and Jonathan Z Smith," in "On a Panegyrical Note: Studies in Honour of Garry W Trompf," ed. Victoria Barker and Frances Di Lauro, special issue, *Sydney Studies in Religion*, 2007, 196.
81   Sun, 196.
82   Sun, 196.
83   Smith, "Conjectures on Conjunctures," 60.
84   Smith, 61n105.
85   Smith, 61n105.
86   Smith, 59f.

87 Smith, 61n105.
88 Smith, 61.
89 Smith, 61n105.
90 Smith, 61n105.
91 Smith, 61n105.
92 Smith, 61n105.
93 Smith, 61n105.
94 Smith, 61n105.
95 Claude Lévi-Strauss, "Four Winnebago Myths," in *Structural Anthropology*, vol. 2 (New York: Basic Books, 1976), 203–4.
96 Smith, "Conjectures on Conjunctures," 59f.
97 James George Frazer, *The Golden Bough: A Study in Magic and Religion*, Abridged ed. (New York: Macmillan, 1958), 448.
98 Smith, *Drudgery Divine*, 85.
99 Smith, 87.
100 Smith, 89.
101 Smith, 97.
102 Smith, 99.
103 Smith, 114.
104 Smith, 101.
105 Smith, 101.
106 Smith, 110.
107 Smith, 94.
108 Sun, "Chasing One's Tail," 201.
109 Sun, 201; Walter Burkert, René Girard, and Jonathan Z. Smith, *Violent Origins: Walter Burkert, René Girard and Jonathan Z. Smith on Ritual Killing and Cultural Formation*, ed. Robert G. Hamerton-Kelly (Stanford, CA: Stanford University Press, 1987), 204.
110 Sun, "Chasing One's Tail," 201; Sam Gill, "No Place to Stand: Jonathan Z. Smith as *Homo Ludens*, The Academic Study of Religion *Sub Specie Ludi*," *Journal of the American Academy of Religion* 66, no. 2 (January 1, 1998): 306.
111 Sun, "Chasing One's Tail," 204.
112 Robert A. Segal, "The Life of King Saul as Myth," in *Myth and Scripture: Contemporary Perspectives on Religion, Language, and Imagination*, ed. Dexter E. Callender Jr., 245–79 (Atlanta: SBL Press, 2014).
113 Segal, 255.
114 Segal, *Myth Theorized*, 113.
115 Segal, "The Life of King Saul as Myth," 260.
116 Segal, 113.
117 Segal, 264.
118 Segal, 260.
119 Segal, 245.
120 Segal, 245.
121 Segal, 252.
122 George W. Stocking, "Anthropology and the Science of the Irrational: Malinowski's Encounter with Freudian Psychoanalysis," in *Malinowski, Rivers, Benedict and Others: Essays on Culture and Personality*, ed. George W. Stocking (Madison: University of Wisconsin Press, 1988), 42.
123 Bronislaw Malinowski, *Malinowski and the Work of Myth*, ed. Ivan Strenski (Princeton, NJ: Princeton University Press, 1992), 55–57.

124 Malinowski, 55–57.
125 Michael P. Carroll, *The Cult of the Virgin Mary: Psychological Origins* (Princeton, NJ: Princeton University Press, 1992), chap. 9.

Chapter 9

1   Karady, "The Durkheimians in Academe," 74.
2   Jeffrey C. Alexander, ed., *Durkheimian Sociology: Cultural Studies* (Cambridge: Cambridge University Press, 1988); Émile Durkheim, "The Determination of Moral Facts," in *Sociology and Philosophy*, trans. D. F. Pocock (New York: Free Press, 1974), 35–62; Émile Durkheim, *Professional Ethics and Civic Morals* (Westport, CT: Greenwood, 1958).
3   William Logue, *From Philosophy to Sociology: The Evolution of French Liberalism, 1870–1914* (DeKalb: Northern Illinois University Press, 1983), 182.
4   Émile Durkheim, "Individualism and the Intellectuals," in *Durkheim on Religion: A Selection of Readings with Bibliographies and Introductory Remarks*, ed. W. S. F. Pickering (London: Routledge, 1975), 59–73; Louis Dumont, "The Modern Conception of the Individual: Notes on Its Genesis," *Contributions to Indian Sociology* 8 (1965): 13–61.
5   Pierre Favre, "The Absence of Political Sociology in the Durkheimian Classification of the Social Sciences," in *The Sociological Domain: The Durkheimians and the Founding of French Sociology*, ed. Philippe Besnard (Cambridge: Cambridge University Press, 1983), 212.
6   W. Paul Vogt, "The Politics of Academic Sociology in France, 1890–1914" (PhD diss., Indiana University, 1976), 66, 272.
7   Ivan Strenski, *Contesting Sacrifice: Religion, Nationalism, and Social Thought in France* (Chicago: University of Chicago Press, 2002); Ivan Strenski, "Hubert, Mauss and the Comparative Social History of Religions," in *Religion in Relation: Method, Application, and Moral Location* (Columbia: University of South Carolina Press, 1993), 75–88; Ivan Strenski, *Theology and the First Theory of Sacrifice* (Leiden: Brill, 2003).
8   Bert, *Henri Hubert et la sociologie des religions*; Bert, *Marcel Mauss, Henri Hubert et la sociologie des religions*.
9   Strenski, *Theology and the First Theory of Sacrifice*, 219–27.
10 Strenski, 219–27.
11 Hubert, "Review of L'évangile et l'église (2e éd. augmentée)," 290–92.
12 Hubert, 291.
13 Drouin, "Hubert (Henri)," 46.
14 Lukes, *Emile Durkheim, His Life and Work*, 32n4.
15 For details on Hubert's biography, consult Strenski, *Religion in Relation*, 180-201.
16 Elie Halévy et al., "Symposium: The Problem of Nationality," *Proceedings of the Aristotelian Society* 20, no. 1 (June 1, 1920): 237–65. https://doi.org/10.1093/aristotelian/20.1.237
17 Halévy et al.
18 Steve Fenton, *Durkheim and Modern Sociology* (Cambridge: Cambridge University Press, 1984), 122–24.
19 André Béjin, "Le sang, le sens et le travail: Georges Vacher de Lapouge darwiniste social fondateur de l'anthroposociologie," *Cahiers internationaux de sociologie* 73 (1982): 323–43; W. Paul Vogt, "Durkheimian Sociology Versus Philosophical

Rationalism: The Case of Célestin Bouglé," in *The Sociological Domain: The Durkheimians and the Founding of French Sociology*, ed. Philippe Besnard (Cambridge: Cambridge University Press, 1983), 231–47.

20   For Hubert's treatment of Müller's Aryanism, see Strenski, "The Rise of Ritual and the Hegemony of Myth: Sylvain Lévi, the Durkheimians, and Max Müller," 60–63.

21   Friedrich Max Müller, *Lectures on the Science of Language Delivered at the Royal Institution of Great Britain in April, May, and June, 1861* (New York: Scribner, 1862), 199.

22   Lapouge, "Old and New Aspects of the Aryan Question," 335.

23   Lapouge, 334.

24   Lapouge, 334.

25   Vogt, "Durkheimian Sociology Versus Philosophical Rationalism," 245.

26   Lapouge's son, Claude, directed Darquier de Pellepoix's infamous Institut de l'Anthroposociologie from 1940–1942 under the Vichy Regime. See Marrus and Paxton, *Vichy France and the Jews*, 300.

27   Émile Durkheim, "Préface," *L'Année sociologique* 1 (1898): i–vii.

28   Besnard, "The *Année Sociologique* Team," 21–24, 32, 4, 50.

29   Besnard, 50f.

30   Béjin, "Le sang, le sens et le travail."

31   Josep R. Llobera, "The Fate of Anthroposociology in *L'année Sociologique*," *Journal of the Anthropological Society of Oxford* 27, no. 3 (1996): 235–51.

32   Henri Hubert, review of *L'Aryen: son rôle social*, by Georges Vacher de Lapouge, *L'Année sociologique* 4 (1901): 143.

33   Henri Pierre [Henri Hubert], review of *L'Aryen: son rôle social*, by Georges Vacher de Lapouge, *Revue Historique* 78, no. 1 (1902): 162–64.

34   Hubert, "L'Aryen: son rôle social," 145.

35   Pierre, "L'Aryen: son rôle social."

36   Pierre, 162.

37   Pierre, 163.

38   Pierre, 164, 163.

39   Pierre, 164.

40   Hubert, "L'Aryen: son rôle social," 145.

41   Hubert, 145.

42   Hubert, 144.

43   Hubert, 144.

44   Henri Hubert, *Les Germains* (Paris: Albin Michel, 1952), 83, 159, 99.

45   Hubert, 75.

46   Henri Hubert, "l'Origine des Aryens. À propos des fouilles américaines au Turkestan," *L'Anthropologie* 21 (1910): 519–28.

47   Isambert, "At the Frontier of Folklore and Sociology," 155n11.

48   Henri Hubert, "Introduction [aux Mythes]," *L'Année sociologique* 6 (1901): 243–46; Hubert, "Conclusion [aux Mythes]."

49   Hubert, "Préface," v.

50   Hubert, xv, lxix.

51   Henri Hubert, "Le culte des héros et ses conditions sociales," *Revue de l'histoire des religions* 70 (1914): 1–20.

52   Isambert, "At the Frontier of Folklore and Sociology," 154n9.

53   Ernest Renan, "La poésie des races Celtiques," *Revue des deux Mondes* 5, no. 3 (1854): 473–506.

54   Poliakov, *The Aryan Myth*.
55   Poliakov, 17.
56   Poliakov, chap. 2; Renan, "La poésie des races Celtiques."
57   Poliakov, *The Aryan Myth*, 25.
58   Poliakov, 31f.
59   Henri Hubert, *Les Celtes et l'expansion Celtique jusqu'à l'époque de La Tène* (Paris: Albin Michel, 2012), 28; translation is mine.
60   Hubert, 29; translation is mine.
61   Hubert, 29.
62   Pierre Daniel Chantepie de la Saussaye, *Manuel d'histoire des religions* (Paris: Colin, 1904), 137.
63   Chantepie de la Saussaye, 137.
64   Chantepie de la Saussaye, 133.
65   Henri Berr, "The Expansion of the Celts," foreword to *The Rise of the Celts*, by Henri Hubert, ed. Marcel Mauss, Raymond Lantier, and Jean Marx, trans. M. R. Dobie (New York: Knopf, 1934), xvi.
66   Henri Berr, "The Celtic Genius," foreword to *The Greatness and Decline of the Celts*, by Henri Hubert, ed. Marcel Mauss, Raymond Lantier, and Jean Marx, trans. M. R. Dobie (London: Kegan Paul, 1934).
67   Hubert, "Conclusion [aux Mythes]," 269.

Chapter 10

1   Strenski, *Four Theories of Myth*.
2   Lincoln, *Theorizing Myth*.
3   Segal, *Myth Theorized*, 146ff.
4   Lincoln, *Theorizing Myth*.
5   Lincoln, 17.
6   Maurice Godelier, *The Enigma of the Gift*, trans. Nora Scott (Chicago: University of Chicago Press, 1999).
7   Malinowski, *Argonauts of the Western Pacific*, 231.
8   Ivan Strenski, "Actually, You Can Compare Apples to Oranges: Secrets of Successful Comparison of Myths," in *Religion: Narrating Religion*, ed. Sarah Iles Johnston (New York: Macmillan, 2017), 49–64.
9   "Theory," Wikipedia, accessed August 2, 2015. https://en.wikipedia.org/w/index.php?title=Theory&oldid=673376304; *Dobbs v. Jackson Women's Health Org.*, 597 U.S. 215 (2022).
10   Ivan Strenski, "Henri Hubert, Racial Science and Political Myth," *Journal of the History of the Behavioral Sciences* 23, no. 4 (October 1987): 353–67. https://doi.org/10.1002/1520-6696(198710)23:4%3C353::AID-JHBS2300230405%3E3.0.CO;2-O
11   Johannes Fried, *"Donation of Constantine" and "Constitutum Constantini": The Misinterpretation of a Fiction and Its Original Meaning* (Berlin: De Gruyter, 2007).
12   Wil van Den Bercken, *Holy Russia and Christian Europe: East and West in the Religious Ideology of Russia*, trans. John Bowden (London: SCM, 1999), 143–44.
13   Vladimir Malinin, *Starec Elezarova Monastyrja Filofei I Ego Poslanija*, 1901.
14   Østbø, *The New Third Rome*.
15   Filofei, "Filofei's Concept of the 'Third Rome,'" in *Medieval Russia: A Source Book, 850–1700*, ed. and trans. Basil Dmytryshyn (Fort Worth, TX: Harcourt Brace, 1991), 260–61.

16 Filofei, 260–61.
17 Bercken, *Holy Russia and Christian Europe*, 141; Østbø, *The New Third Rome*, 11.
18 Østbø, *The New Third Rome*, 11.
19 Bercken, *Holy Russia and Christian Europe*, 141.
20 Bercken, 140–41.
21 Bercken, 140.
22 Robert Ponzini, "The Italian 'Invasion' of Russia and Its Key Role in the Emergence of a Unified Russian State," *Economia Aziendale Online* – 12, no. 4 (December 30, 2021): 399–405. https://doi.org/10.13132/2038-5498/12.4.399-405
23 Ponzini.
24 Daniel B. Rowland, "Moscow—The Third Rome or the New Israel?," *Russian Review* 55, no. 4 (October 1996): 591; Donald Ostrowski, "'Moscow the Third Rome' as Historical Ghost," in *Byzantium, Faith and Power (1261 - 1557): Perspectives on Late Byzantine Art and Culture*, ed. Sarah T. Brooks (Exhibition Byzantium: Faith and Power (1261 - 1557), New York: Metropolitan Museum of Art, 2006), 171, 3.
25 Edward L. Keenan, "Muscovite Political Folkways," *Russian Review* 45, no. 2 (April 1986): 18n, 35.
26 Østbø, *The New Third Rome*, 72.
27 Peter John Stuart Duncan, "Russian Messianism: A Historical and Political Analysis" (PhD thesis, University of Glasgow, 1989), 29. https://theses.gla.ac.uk/id/eprint/6873
28 Jean-Pierre Arrignon, "Les relations diplomatiques entre Byzance et la Russie de 860 à 1043," *Revue des études slaves* 55, no. 1 (1983): 130.
29 Arrignon, 133.
30 Arrignon, 134.
31 Arrignon, 135.
32 Nicholas V. Riasanovsky and Mark D. Steinberg, *A History of Russia*, 7th ed. (New York: Oxford University Press, 2005), 95f.
33 Duncan, "Russian Messianism," 31.
34 Riasanovsky and Steinberg, *A History of Russia*, 99f.
35 Keenan, "Muscovite Political Folkways," 118n35.
36 Judith E. Kalb, *Russia's Rome: Imperial Visions, Messianic Dreams, 1890–1940* (Madison: University of Wisconsin Press, 2008), 10.
37 Kalb, 11.
38 Kalb, 4n2.
39 Pål Kolstø, Foreword to *The New Third Rome: Readings of a Russian Nationalist Myth*, by Jardar Østbø (Stuttgart: ibidem, 2016), xiii.
40 Kalb, *Russia's Rome*, chap. 1.
41 Østbø, *The New Third Rome*, 12.
42 Østbø, 12.
43 Østbø, 12.
44 Østbø, 12.
45 Kolstø, "Foreword," xiv.
46 Marshall Poe, "Moscow, the Third Rome: The Origins and Transformations of a 'Pivotal Moment,'" *Jahrbücher Für Geschichte Osteuropas* 49, no. 3 (2001): 425.
47 Dmitrii Sidorov, "Post-Imperial Third Romes: Resurrections of a Russian Orthodox Geopolitical Metaphor," *Geopolitics* 11, no. 2 (July 2006): 324.
48 Østbø, *The New Third Rome*, 23.
49 Østbø, 20.

50 Østbø, 22.
51 Østbø, 16.
52 Østbø, 18; Sidorov, "Post-Imperial Third Romes," 328–31.
53 Østbø, *The New Third Rome*, 5.
54 Sidorov, "Post-Imperial Third Romes," 332–34.
55 Sidorov, 323; Østbø, *The New Third Rome*, 18.
56 Sidorov, "Post-Imperial Third Romes," 335.
57 Østbø, *The New Third Rome*, 18.
58 Egor Kholmogorov, "Tretii Rim," *Spetsnaz Rossii* 63, no. 12 (December 2001): 197.
59 Kalb, *Russia's Rome*, 197n2; Ostrowski, "'Moscow the Third Rome' as Historical Ghost," 177n12.
60 Yulia Latynina, "Византия: Идеальная Катастрофа," *Novaya Gazeta*, February 7, 2015. http://www.novayagazeta.ru/arts/67159.html; Niels Drost and Beatrice de Graaf, "Putin and the Third Rome: Imperial-Eschatological Motives as a Usable Past," *Journal of Applied History* 4, no. 1–2 (December 12, 2022): 28–45. https://doi.org/10.1163/25895893-bja10032
61 Vladimir Putin, "On the Historical Unity of Russians and Ukrainians," Kremlin, July 12, 2021. http://en.kremlin.ru/events/president/news/66181
62 Personal correspondence, 11 August 2015.
63 Putin, "On the Historical Unity of Russians and Ukrainians."
64 Putin.
65 Charles Clover, "Putin and the Monk: How Much Influence Does Father Tikhon Shevkunov Have over the Russian President?," *Financial Times*, January 25, 2013, sec. Life & Arts. https://www.ft.com/content/f2fcba3e-65be-11e2-a3db-00144feab49a; Irina Papkova, "Saving the Third Rome. 'Fall of the Empire', Byzantium and Putin's Russia," in *IWM Junior Visiting Fellows' Conference Proceedings*, vol. XXIV: Reconciling the Irreconcilable (Vienna: IWM, 2009).
66 Clover, "Putin and the Monk."
67 Drost and Graaf, "Putin and the Third Rome," 34.
68 Bercken, *Holy Russia and Christian Europe*, 198.
69 Sidorov, "Post-Imperial Third Romes," 320.
70 Bercken, *Holy Russia and Christian Europe*, 145.
71 Kholmogorov, "Tretii Rim"; Kalb, *Russia's Rome*.
72 Putin, "On the Historical Unity of Russians and Ukrainians"; Drost and Graaf, "Putin and the Third Rome."
73 Sidorov, "Post-Imperial Third Romes," 319.
74 Marcel de Haas, *Russia's Foreign Security Policy in the 21st Century: Putin, Medvedev and Beyond*, 1. issued in paperback (London: Routledge, 2011), 3.
75 Drost and Graaf, "Putin and the Third Rome," 31.
76 Roy Aleksandrovich Medvedev, *Post-Soviet Russia: A Journey through the Yeltsin Era* (New York: Columbia University Press, 2000), 239.
77 Gennady Zyuganov, *Derzhava* [The Great Power], trans. Roy Aleksandrovich Medvedev (Moscow: Informpechat, 1994), 179n2.
78 Zyuganov, 15n2.
79 Kenneth Scott, "Mussolini and the Roman Empire," *The Classical Journal* 27, no. 9 (1932): 645–57.
80 Bercken, *Holy Russia and Christian Europe*, 133f.
81 Peter Baker, "Russian Dissident Opens New Chapter in His Anti-Putin Movement," *New York Times*, October 2, 2014, sec. World. https://www.nytimes.

com/2014/10/03/world/europe/mikhail-khodorkovsky-ex-oil-tycoon-plans-to-lead-political-movement.html

82 Baker.
83 Bercken, *Holy Russia and Christian Europe*, 197.
84 Kalb, *Russia's Rome*, 197; Paul Bushkovitch, review of *Tretii Rim: Istoki i evoliutsiia russkoi srednevekovoi kontseptsii (XV–XVI vv.)*, by Nina V. Sinitsyna, *Kritika: Explorations in Russian and Eurasian History* 1, no. 2 (March 2000): 391–99. https://doi.org/10.1353/kri.2008.0083
85 Keenan, "Muscovite Political Folkways," 118.
86 Ronald Bergan, *Eisenstein: A Life in Conflict* (Woodstock, NY: Overlook Press, 1999), 305.
87 Sidorov, "Post-Imperial Third Romes," 324.
88 Lincoln, *Theorizing Myth*, chap. 11.
89 "Theory," Wikipedia, accessed August 2, 2015. https://en.wikipedia.org/w/index.php?title=Theory&oldid=673376304
90 Keenan, "Muscovite Political Folkways," 118n35.

Bibliography

Ahluwalia, Sashi. "A Sheaf of Anecdotes." In *Shivaji and Indian Nationalism*, edited by B. K. Ahluwalia and Sashi Ahluwalia. Delhi: Cultural Publishing House, 1984.

Albinia, Alice, and Tristram Stuart. "India's Epic Struggle." *Guardian*, August 16, 2007, sec. Books. https://www.theguardian.com/books/2007/aug/16/fiction

Alexander, Jeffrey C., ed. *Durkheimian Sociology: Cultural Studies*. Cambridge: Cambridge University Press, 1988.

Alphandéry, Philippe. "Albert Réville." *Revue de l'histoire des religions* 54 (1906): 401–23.

Anomaly, Jonny. "Nietzsche's Critique of Utilitarianism." *The Journal of Nietzsche Studies* 29, no. 1 (April 1, 2005): 1–15. https://doi.org/10.2307/20717848

Arrignon, Jean-Pierre. "Les relations diplomatiques entre Byzance et la Russie de 860 à 1043." *Revue des études slaves* 55, no. 1 (1983): 129–37. https://doi.org/10.3406/slave.1983.5310

Baker, Peter. "Russian Dissident Opens New Chapter in His Anti-Putin Movement." *New York Times*, October 2, 2014, sec. World. https://www.nytimes.com/2014/10/03/world/europe/mikhail-khodorkovsky-ex-oil-tycoon-plans-to-lead-political-movement.html

Barnette, Sarah. "Friedrich Max Müller and George Eliot: Affinities, *Einfühlung*, and the Science of Religion." *Publications of the English Goethe Society* 85, no. 2–3 (September 2016): 191–203. https://doi.org/10.1080/09593683.2016.1224490

Bascom, William. "Malinowski's Contributions to the Study of Folklore." *Folklore* 94, no. 2 (January 1983): 163–72. https://doi.org/10.1080/0015587X.1983.9716274

Béjin, André. "Le sang, le sens et le travail: Georges Vacher de Lapouge darwiniste social fondateur de l'anthroposociologie." *Cahiers internationaux de sociologie* 73 (1982): 323–43.

Bercken, Wil van Den. *Holy Russia and Christian Europe: East and West in the Religious Ideology of Russia*. Translated by John Bowden. London: SCM, 1999.

Bergaigne, Abel. *Abel Bergaigne's Vedic Religion*. Translated by V. G. Paranjpe. Vol. 3. Delhi: Motilal Banarsidass, 1978.

Bergan, Ronald. *Eisenstein: A Life in Conflict*. Woodstock, NY: Overlook Press, 1999.

Berr, Henri. "The Expansion of the Celts." Foreword to *The Rise of the Celts*, by Henri Hubert, ix–xx. Edited and brought up to date by Marcel Mauss, Raymond Lantier, and Jean Marx, translated by M. R. Dobie. New York: Knopf, 1934.

Berr, Henri. "The Celtic Genius." Foreword to *The Greatness and Decline of the Celts*, by Henri Hubert, edited by Marcel Mauss, Raymond Lantier, and Jean Marx, translated by M. R. Dobie. London: Kegan Paul, 1934.

Berr, Henri. "Les progrès de la sociologie religieuse." *Revue de synthèse historique* 34 (1906): 16–43.

Bert, Jean-François, ed. *Henri Hubert et la sociologie des religions: sacré, temps, héros, magie*. Liège: Presses Universitaires de Liège, 2015.

Berr, Henri, ed. *Marcel Mauss, Henri Hubert et la sociologie des religions: Penser et écrire à deux*. Paris: La Cause des Livres, 2012.

Besnard, Philippe. "The *Année Sociologique* Team." In *The Sociological Domain: The Durkheimians and the Founding of French Sociology*, edited by Philippe Besnard, 11–70. Cambridge: Cambridge University Press, 1983.

Bhosale, B. G. "Indian Nationalism: Gandhi Vis-a-Vis Tilak and Savarkar." *The Indian Journal of Political Science* 70, no. 2 (2009): 419–27.

Burkert, Walter, René Girard, and Jonathan Z. Smith. *Violent Origins: Walter Burkert, René Girard and Jonathan Z. Smith on Ritual Killing and Cultural Formation*. Edited by Robert G. Hamerton-Kelly. Stanford, CA: Stanford University Press, 1987.

Bushkovitch, Paul. Review of *Tretii Rim: Istoki i evoliutsiia russkoi srednevekovoi kontseptsii (XV–XVI vv.)*, by Nina V. Sinitsyna. *Kritika: Explorations in Russian and Eurasian History* 1, no. 2 (March 2000): 391–99. https://doi.org/10.1353/kri.2008.0083

Carroll, Michael P. *The Cult of the Virgin Mary: Psychological Origins*. Princeton, NJ: Princeton University Press, 1992.

Chantepie de la Saussaye, Pierre Daniel. *Manuel d'histoire des religions*. Paris: Colin, 1904.

Chaudhuri, Nirad C. *Scholar Extraordinary: The Life of Professor the Rt. Hon. Friedrich Max Müller, P.C.* London: Chatto & Windus, 1974.

Clifford, James. *Person and Myth: Maurice Leenhardt in the Melanesian World*. Berkeley: University of California Press, 1982.

Clifford, James. "Power and Dialogue in Ethnography: Marcel Griaule's Initiation." In *Observers Observed: Essays on Ethnographic Fieldwork*, edited by George W. Stocking Jr., 121–56. Madison: University of Wisconsin Press, 1985.

Clover, Charles. "Putin and the Monk: How Much Influence Does Father Tikhon Shevkunov Have over the Russian President?" *Financial Times*, January 25, 2013, sec. Life & Arts. https://www.ft.com/content/f2fcba3e-65be-11e2-a3db-00144feab49a

Darmesteter, James. "The Prophets of Israel." In *Selected Essays of James Darmesteter*, edited by Morris Jastrow Jr., translated by Helen B. Jastrow, 16–104. Boston: Houghton and Mifflin, 1895.

Davenport, R. Dean. "Patriarchy and Politics: A Comparative Evaluation of the Religious, Political and Social Thought of Sir Robert Filmer and Robert Lewis Dabney." PhD diss., Baylor University, 2006.

Desmond, Jane. "Ethnography as Ethics and Epistemology: Why American Studies Should Embrace Fieldwork, and Why It Hasn't." *American Studies* 53, no. 1 (2014): 27–56. https://doi.org/10.1353/ams.2014.0034

Dorson, Richard M. *The British Folklorists: A History*. Chicago: Chicago University Press, 1968.

Doyle, William. *The Oxford History of the French Revolution*. Oxford: Oxford University Press, 1989.

Driberg, J. H. Review of *Myth in Primitive Psychology*, by Bronislaw Malinowski. *Economica*, no. 19 (March 1927): 124–25. https://doi.org/10.2307/2548371

Drost, Niels, and Beatrice de Graaf. "Putin and the Third Rome: Imperial-Eschatological Motives as a Usable Past." *Journal of Applied History* 4, no. 1–2 (December 12, 2022): 28–45. https://doi.org/10.1163/25895893-bja10032

Drouin, Marcel. "Hubert (Henri)." In *Annuaire*, 45–51. Paris: Association des anciens élèves, élèves et amis de l'École normale supérieure, 1929.

Duchesne, Louis. *Christian Worship: Its Origin and Evolution*. Translated by M. L. McClure. 2nd English ed. London: Society for Promoting Christian Knowledge, 1903.

Duchesne, Louis. *Origines du culte chrétien: étude sur la liturgie latine avant Charlemagne*. 5e éd. rev. et augm. Paris: Éditions de Bocard, 1920.

Dumont, Louis. "A Modified View of Our Origins: The Christian Beginnings of Modern Individualism." *Religion* 12, no. 1 (January 1982): 1–27. https://doi.org/10.1016/0048-721X(82)90013-6

Dumont, Louis. *From Mandeville to Marx: The Genesis and Triumph of Economic Ideology*. Chicago: University of Chicago Press, 1977.

Dumont, Louis. "The Modern Conception of the Individual: Notes on Its Genesis." *Contributions to Indian Sociology* 8 (1965): 13–61.

Duncan, Peter John Stuart. "Russian Messianism: A Historical and Political Analysis." PhD thesis, University of Glasgow, 1989. https://theses.gla.ac.uk/id/eprint/6873

Durkheim, Émile. "Individual and Collective Representations." In *Sociology and Philosophy*, translated by D. F. Pocock, 1–34. New York: Free Press, 1974.

Durkheim, Émile. "Individualism and the Intellectuals." In *Durkheim on Religion: A Selection of Readings with Bibliographies and Introductory Remarks*, edited by W. S. F. Pickering, 59–73. London: Routledge, 1975.

Durkheim, Émile. *Lettres à Marcel Mauss*. Edited by Philippe Besnard and Marcel Fournier. Sociologies. Paris: Presses Universitaires de France, 1998.

Durkheim, Émile. "Préface." *L'Année sociologique* 1 (1898): i–vii.

Durkheim, Émile. *Professional Ethics and Civic Morals*. Westport, CT: Greenwood, 1958.

Durkheim, Émile. "Review. 'Guyau—*L'Irréligion de L'avenir*'." In *Durkheim on Religion: A Selection of Readings with Bibliographies and Introductory Remarks*, edited by W. S. F. Pickering, 24–38. London: Routledge, 1975.

Durkheim, Émile. *Sociology and Philosophy*. Translated by D. F. Pocock. New York: Free Press, 1974.

Durkheim, Émile. "The Determination of Moral Facts." In *Sociology and Philosophy*, translated by D. F. Pocock, 35–62. New York: Free Press, 1974.

Durkheim, Émile. *The Elementary Forms of Religious Life*. Translated by Karen E. Fields. New York: Free Press, 1995.

Durkheim, Émile. *The Elementary Forms of the Religious Life: A Study in Religious Sociology*. Translated by Joseph Ward Swain. New York: Macmillan, 1915.

Durkheim, Émile, and Marcel Mauss. *Primitive Classification*. 13th ed. Chicago: University of Chicago Press, 1967.

Eliot, George. *Middlemarch*. New York: New American Library, 1964.

Erfani, Farhang. Review of *Cinematic Gods? Robert Segal on Myth's Persistence: Review of: Robert Alan Segal, Myth: A Very Short Introduction, Oxford: Oxford University Press, 2004*, by Robert A. Segal. *Jung Journal* 6, no. 3 (Summer 2012): 72–75. https://doi.org/10.1525/jung.2012.6.3.72

Faublée, Jacques, and Marcelle Urbain-Faublée. "Notes sur des travaux d'ethnologie et d'anthropologie." *L'Année sociologique* 23 (1972): 303–15.

Favre, Pierre. "The Absence of Political Sociology in the Durkheimian Classification of the Social Sciences." In *The Sociological Domain: The Durkheimians and the Founding of French Sociology*, edited by Philippe Besnard, 199–216. Cambridge: Cambridge University Press, 1983.

Félice, Philippe de. *Poisons sacrés, ivresses divines. Essai sur quelques formes inférieures de la mystique*. Paris: Albin Michel, 1936.

Fenton, Steve. *Durkheim and Modern Sociology*. Cambridge: Cambridge University Press, 1984.

Filofei. "Filofei's Concept of the 'Third Rome.'" In *Medieval Russia: A Source Book, 850–1700*, edited and translated by Basil Dmytryshyn, 259–61. Fort Worth, TX: Harcourt Brace, 1991.

Firth, Raymond. "Bronislaw Malinowski." In *Totems and Teachers: Perspectives on the History of Anthropology*, edited by Sydel Silverman, 101–40. New York: Columbia University Press, 1981.

Firth, Raymond. "Seligman's Contributions to Oceanic Anthropology." *Oceania* 45, no. 4 (June 1975): 272–82. https://doi.org/10.1002/j.1834-4461.1975.tb01870.x

Flamarion, Edith. "Brutus ou l'adoption d'un mythe romain par la Révolution française." In *La révolution française et l'antiquité: bicentenaire de la Révolution Française*, edited by Raymond Chevallier, 91–112. Tours: Centre de Recherches A. Piganiol, 1991.

Flis, Mariola. "Malinowski and Radcliffe-Brown: Two Versions of Functionalism." *The Polish Sociological Bulletin*, no. 97 (1992): 35–43.

Fournier, Marcel. *Marcel Mauss: A Biography*. Princeton, NJ: Princeton University Press, 2006.

France, Peter, ed. "Voltaire (Pseud. of François–Marie Arouet)." In *The New Oxford Companion to Literature in French*. Oxford: Oxford University Press, 1995.

Frazer, James George. *The Golden Bough: A Study in Magic and Religion*. Abridged ed. New York: Macmillan, 1958.

Frazer, James George. Letter to Bronislaw Malinowski. "Untitled," February 14, 1926. Series I, Box 3, Folder 203. Bronislaw Malinowski papers, Archives at Yale.

Frazer, Robert. Review of *Theorizing about Myth*, by Robert A. Segal. *Modern Language Review* 96, no. 2 (April 2001): 451–52. https://doi.org/10.1353/mlr.2001.a828780

Fried, Johannes. *"Donation of Constantine" and "Constitutum Constantini": The Misinterpretation of a Fiction and Its Original Meaning*. Berlin: De Gruyter, 2007.

Geertz, Clifford. "'From the Native's Point of View': On the Nature of Anthropological Understanding." *Bulletin of the American Academy of Arts and Sciences* 28, no. 1 (October 1974): 26. https://doi.org/10.2307/3822971

Gill, Sam. "No Place to Stand: Jonathan Z. Smith as *Homo Ludens*, The Academic Study of Religion *Sub Specie Ludi*." *Journal of the American Academy of Religion* 66, no. 2 (January 1, 1998): 283–312. https://doi.org/10.1093/jaarel/66.2.283

Glucksmann, Miriam. *Structuralist Analysis in Contemporary Social Thought: A Comparison of the Theories of Claude Lévi-Strauss and Louis Althusser*. London: Routledge, 1974.

Godelier, Maurice. *The Enigma of the Gift*. Translated by Nora Scott. Chicago: University of Chicago Press, 1999.

Granet, Marcel. *The Religion of the Chinese People*. New York: Harper & Row, 1975.

Gross, Feliks. "Young Malinowski and His Later Years." *American Ethnologist* 13, no. 3 (August 1986): 556–70. https://doi.org/10.1525/ae.1986.13.3.02a00110

Haas, Marcel de. *Russia's Foreign Security Policy in the 21st Century: Putin, Medvedev and Beyond*. 1. issued in paperback. London: Routledge, 2011.

Haddon, A. C. *Folk-Tales*. Cambridge: Cambridge University Press, 1908.

Halévy, Elie, Marcel Mauss, Théodore Ruyssen, René Johannet, Gilbert Murray, and Frederick Pollock. "Symposium: The Problem of Nationality." *Proceedings of the Aristotelian Society* 20, no. 1 (June 1, 1920): 237–65. https://doi.org/10.1093/aristotelian/20.1.237

Hay, Stephen N., ed. *Sources of Indian Tradition*. Vol. 2. Records of Civilization: Sources and Studies. New York: Columbia University Press, 1958.

Higonnet, Patrice. *Goodness beyond Virtue: Jacobins during the French Revolution*. Cambridge, MA: Harvard University Press, 1998.

Hobsbawm, Eric J. "The Rules of Violence." In *Revolutionaries: Contemporary Essays*, 209–15. New York: Pantheon, 1973.

Hofstadter, Richard. *Social Darwinism in American Thought*. Boston: Beacon Press, 1955.

Horton, Robin, and Ruth H. Finnegan, eds. *Modes of Thought: Essays on Thinking in Western and Non-Western Societies*. London: Faber, 1973.

Howe, Richard Herbert. "Max Weber's Elective Affinities: Sociology Within the Bounds of Pure Reason." *American Journal of Sociology* 84, no. 2 (September 1978): 366–85. https://doi.org/10.1086/226788

Hubert, Henri. "Conclusion [aux Mythes]." *L'Année sociologique* 6 (1901): 268–71.

Hubert, Henri. Review of *Cultes, Mythes et Religions, tome IV*, by Salomon Reinach. *L'Année sociologique* 12 (1909): 80–82.

Hubert, Henri. *Divinités Gauloises*. Macon: Protat Frères, 1925.

Hubert, Henri. Review of *Ephialtes. Eine pathologisch-mythologische Abhandlung über die Alpträume und Alpdämonen des klassischen Altertums (Abhandlungen der philologischhistorischen Classe der Kgl. Sächs. Gesellschaft der Wissenschaften, t. XX, no II)*, by William Henry Roscher. *L'Année sociologique* 6 (1901): 230–36.

Hubert, Henri. *Essay on Time: A Brief Study of the Representation of Time in Religion and Magic*. Edited by Robert Parkin. Translated by Jacqueline Redding and Robert Parkin. Oxford: Durkheim Press, 1999.

Hubert, Henri. "Étude sommaire de la représentation du temps dans la religion et la magie." *Annuaire de l'École pratique des hautes études, section des sciences religieuses* 18, no. 14 (1904): 1–39. https://doi.org/10.3406/ephe.1904.19635

Hubert, Henri. "Introduction à la traduction française." In *Manuel de l'histoire des religions*, by Pierre Daniel Chantepie de la Saussaye, v–xlviii. Paris: Colin, 1904.

Hubert, Henri. "Introduction [aux Mythes]." *L'Année sociologique* 6 (1901): 243–46.

Hubert, Henri. Review of *L'Aryen: son rôle social*, by Georges Vacher de Lapouge. *L'Année sociologique* 4 (1901): 145–47.

Hubert, Henri. "Le culte des héros et ses conditions sociales." *Revue de l'histoire des religions* 70 (1914): 1–20.

Hubert, Henri. "Le rituel: Introduction." *L'Année sociologique* 5 (1900): 247–48.

Hubert, Henri. *Leçons. St Germain-en-Laye: Archives*. Saint-Germain-en-Laye: Musée des Antiquités nationales, 1924.

Hubert, Henri. *Les Celtes et l'expansion Celtique jusqu'à l'époque de La Tène*. Paris: Albin Michel, 2012.

Hubert, Henri. *Les Germains*. Paris: Albin Michel, 1952.

Hubert, Henri. Review of *Les légendes hagiographiques*, by Hippolyte Delehaye. *L'Année sociologique* 7 (1902): 344–47.

Hubert, Henri. "l'Origine des Aryens. À propos des fouilles américaines au Turkestan." *L'Anthropologie* 21 (1910): 519–28.

Hubert, Henri. Préface to *Le culte des héros et ses conditions sociales: Saint Patrick, héros national de l'Irlande*, by Stefan Czarnowski, i–xciv. Paris: Alcan, 1919.

Hubert, Henri. Review of *Review of L'évangile et l'église (2e éd. augmentée)*, by Alfred Loisy. *L'Année sociologique* 8 (1903): 290–92.

Hubert, Henri. Review of *Steinzeit Kunst und Moderne Kunst: Ein Vergleich*, by Wilhelm Paulcke. *L'Année sociologique* 1 (nouvelle série) (1924): 960–61.

Hubert, Henri. Review of *The Jew in London: A Study of Racial Character and Present-Day Conditions*, by G. Russel and H. S. Lewis. *Notes critiques. Sciences sociales* 1, no. 20 (n.d.): 310–11.

Hubert, Henri. *The Rise of the Celts*. Edited and brought up to date by Marcel Mauss, Raymond Lantier, and Jean Marx. Translated by M. R. Dobie. New York: Knopf, 1934.

Hubert, Henri, and Marcel Mauss. "Introduction à l'analyse de quelques phénomènes religieux." In *Oeuvres*, edited by Victor Karady, 1: Les fonctions sociales du sacré: 3–39. Paris: Éditions de Minuit, 1968.

Hubert, Henri, and Marcel Mauss. *Mélanges d'histoire des religions*. Paris: Librorium, 2021.

Hubert, Henri, and Marcel Mauss. Review of *Astralmythen der Hebräer, Babylonier und Aegypter*, by Eduard Stucken. *L'Année sociologique* 6 (1901): 261–63.

Hubert, Henri, and Marcel Mauss. *Sacrifice: Its Nature and Function*. Translated by W. D. Halls. Chicago: University of Chicago Press, 1964.

"Introduction [aux Mythes]." *L'Année sociologique* 6 (1901): 243–46.

Ireton, Sean. "«Ich Bin Ein Wanderer Und Ein Bergsteiger» — Nietzsche and Zarathustra in the Mountains." *Colloquia Germanica* 42, no. 3 (2009): 193-212.
Isambert, François A. "At the Frontier of Folklore and Sociology: Hubert, Hertz and Czarnowski, Founders of a Sociology of Folk Religion." In *The Sociological Domain: The Durkheimians and the Founding of French Sociology*, edited by Philippe Besnard, 152-76. Cambridge: Cambridge University Press, 1983.
Jones, Robert Alun. "Robertson Smith, Durkheim, and Sacrifice: An Historical Context for the Elementary Forms of the Religious Life." *Journal of the History of the Behavioral Sciences* 17, no. 2 (April 1981): 184-205. https://doi.org/10.1002/1520-6696(198104)17:2<184::AID-JHBS2300170205>3.0.CO;2-J
Jordens, J. T. F. "Gandhi and the *Bhagavadgita*." In *Modern Indian Interpreters of the Bhagavad Gita*, edited by Robert N. Minor, 98-109. Albany: State University of New York Press, 1986.
Kalb, Judith E. *Russia's Rome: Imperial Visions, Messianic Dreams, 1890-1940*. Madison: University of Wisconsin Press, 2008.
Kamra, Sukeshi. "Law and Radical Rhetoric in British India: The 1897 Trial of Bal Gangadhar Tilak." *South Asia: Journal of South Asian Studies* 39, no. 3 (July 2, 2016): 546-59. https://doi.org/10.1080/00856401.2016.1196529
Kando, Thomas M. "L'Annee Sociologique: From Durkheim to Today." *The Pacific Sociological Review* 19, no. 2 (April 1976): 147-74. https://doi.org/10.2307/1388781
Kang, Seung Il. "A Comparison of Mircea Eliade's and Jonathan Z. Smith's Views on Dur-an-Ki." *Zeitschrift Für Religions- Und Geistesgeschichte* 64, no. 1 (January 1, 2012): 62-65. https://doi.org/10.1163/157007312800211633
Karady, Victor. "The Durkheimians in Academe: A Reconsideration." In *The Sociological Domain: The Durkheimians and the Founding of French Sociology*, edited by Philippe Besnard, 71-89. Cambridge: Cambridge University Press, 1983.
Keenan, Edward L. "Muscovite Political Folkways." *Russian Review* 45, no. 2 (April 1986): 115-81. https://doi.org/10.2307/130423
Kempny, Marian. "Malinowski Fifty Years Later." *The Polish Sociological Bulletin*, no. 97 (1992): 7-17.
Kennedy, Emmet. *A Cultural History of the French Revolution*. New Haven, CT: Yale University Press, 1989.
Keylor, William R. *Academy and Community: The Foundation of the French Historical Profession*. Cambridge, MA: Harvard University Press, 1975.
Khimta, Abha Chauhan. "The Concept of Ends and Means in the Ideals of B.G. Tilak and Sri Aurobindo." *Research Journal of Philosophy & Social Sciences* 47, no. 1 (June 30, 2021): 49-53. https://doi.org/10.31995/rjpsss.2021v47i01.07
Kholmogorov, Egor. "Tretii Rim." *Spetsnaz Rossii* 63, no. 12 (December 2001).
Kolstø, Pål. Foreword to *The New Third Rome: Readings of a Russian Nationalist Myth*, by Jardar Østbø, xiii-xvii. Stuttgart: ibidem, 2016.
Laine, James W. "Śivājī's Mother." In *Images of Women in Maharashtrian Literature and Religion*, edited by Anne Feldhaus, 97-113. Albany: State University of New York Press, 1996.

Lapouge, Georges Vacher de. "Old and New Aspects of the Aryan Question." *American Journal of Sociology* 5, no. 3 (November 1899): 329–46. https://doi.org/10.1086/210895

Laruelle, Marlène. "Le néo-eurasisme russe. L'empire après l'empire?" *Cahiers du monde russe* 42, no. 1 (January 1, 2001): 71–94. https://doi.org/10.4000/monderusse.8437

Laruelle, Marlène. *Russian Eurasianism: An Ideology of Empire*. Washington, DC: Woodrow Wilson Center Press, 2008.

Latynina, Yulia. "Византия: Идеальная Катастрофа." *Novaya Gazeta*, February 7, 2015. http://www.novayagazeta.ru/arts/67159.html

Leach, Edmund. "The Epistemological Background to Malinowski's Empiricism." In *Man and Culture: An Evaluation of the Work of Malinowski*, edited by Raymond Firth, 119–38. London: Routledge, 1957.

Leach, Edmund, I. C. Jarvie, Edwin Ardener, J. H. M. Beattie, Ernest Gellner, and K. S. Kathur. "Frazer and Malinowski: A CA Discussion [and Comments and Reply]." *Current Anthropology* 7, no. 5 (December 1966): 560–76. https://doi.org/10.1086/200773

Levene, Nancy. "Courses and Canons in the Study of Religion (With Continual Reference to Jonathan Z. Smith)." *Journal of the American Academy of Religion* 80, no. 4 (December 1, 2012): 998–1024. https://doi.org/10.1093/jaarel/lfs084

Lévi, Sylvain. "Abel Bergaigne et l'indianisme [1890]." In *Mémorial Sylvain Lévi*, edited by Jacques Bacot. Paris: Paul Hartmann, 1937.

Lévi, Sylvain. *La doctrine du sacrifice dans les Brāhmaṇas*. Paris: Leroux, 1898.

Lévi, Sylvain. *Une renaissance juive en Judée*. Ligue des Amis du Sionisme, Tract no. 5. Paris: Driay-Cahen, 1918.

Lévi-Strauss, Claude. "Four Winnebago Myths." In *Structural Anthropology*, 2:198–210. New York: Basic Books, 1976.

Lévi-Strauss, Claude. "French Sociology." In *Twentieth-Century Sociology*, edited by Georges Gurvitch and William E. Moore, 503–37. New York: Philosophical Library, 1945.

Lévi-Strauss, Claude. *Introduction to the Work of Marcel Mauss*. Translated by Felicity Baker. London: Routledge, 1987.

Lévi-Strauss, Claude. *Structural Anthropology*. Translated by Claire Jacobson and Brooke Grundfest Schoepf. Vol. I. New York: Basic Books, 1963.

Lévi-Strauss, Claude. *Structural Anthropology*. Translated by Monique Layton. Vol. II. New York: Basic Books, 1976.

Lévi-Strauss, Claude. *The Elementary Structures of Kinship*. Boston: Beacon Press, 1969.

Lévi-Strauss, Claude. *The Savage Mind*. London: Weidenfeld and Lincoln, 1966.

Lévi-Strauss, Claude. *Tristes Tropiques*. New York: Atheneum, 1975.

Lévy-Bruhl, Lucien. *How Natives Think*. Translated by Lilian A. Clare. New York: Washington Square Press, 1966.

Lévi-Strauss, Claude. *Primitive Mentality*. Translated by Lilian A. Clare. Boston: Beacon Press, 1966.

Lincoln, Bruce. *Theorizing Myth: Narrative, Ideology, and Scholarship*. Chicago: University of Chicago Press, 1999.

Littleton, C. Scott. *The New Comparative Mythology: An Anthropological Assessment of the Theories of Georges Dumézil*. 3rd ed. Berkeley: University of California Press, 1982.

Llobera, Josep R. "The Fate of Anthroposociology in *L'année Sociologique*." *Journal of the Anthropological Society of Oxford* 27, no. 3 (1996): 235-51.

Logue, William. *From Philosophy to Sociology: The Evolution of French Liberalism, 1870-1914*. DeKalb: Northern Illinois University Press, 1983.

Lukes, Steven. *Emile Durkheim, His Life and Work: A Historical and Critical Study*. New York: Harper & Row, 1973.

Malinin, Vladimir. *Starec Elezarova Monastyrja Filofei I Ego Poslanija*, 1901.

Malinowski, Bronislaw. Review of *The Children of the Sun: A Study in the Early History of Civilisation*, by W. K. Perry. *Nature* 113, no. 2835 (March 1924): 299-301. https://doi.org/10.1038/113299a0

Malinowski, Bronislaw. *A Diary in the Strict Sense of the Term*. Translated by Norbert Guterman. London: Routledge, 1967.

Malinowski, Bronislaw. *A Scientific Theory of Culture and Other Essays*. Oxford: Oxford University Press, 1944.

Malinowski, Bronislaw. *Argonauts of the Western Pacific*. New York: E. P. Dutton, 1961.

Malinowski, Bronislaw. "'Elementary Forms of Religious Life,' review of *Les formes élémentaire de la vie religieuse, le système totémique en Australie*, by Émile Durkheim." In *Sex, Culture, and Myth*, 283-88. New York: Harcourt, 1962.

Malinowski, Bronislaw. "Ethnology and the Study of Society." *Economica*, no. 6 (October 1922): 208-19. https://doi.org/10.2307/2548314

Malinowski, Bronislaw. "Magic, Science and Religion." In *Magic, Science and Religion and Other Essays*, edited by Robert Redfield. New York: Free Press, 1948.

Malinowski, Bronislaw. "Magic, Science and Religion." In *Magic, Science and Religion and Other Essays*, edited by Robert Redfield, 17-92. Prospect Heights, IL: Waveland Press, 1992.

Malinowski, Bronislaw. *Malinowski and the Work of Myth*. Edited by Ivan Strenski. Princeton, NJ: Princeton University Press, 1992.

Malinowski, Bronislaw. "Myth as a Dramatic Development of Dogma." In *Sex, Culture, and Myth*, 245-55. New York: Harcourt, 1962.

Malinowski, Bronislaw. "Myth in Primitive Psychology." In *Magic, Science and Religion and Other Essays*, edited by Robert Redfield, 93-148. New York: Free Press, 1948.

Malinowski, Bronislaw. "Obscenity and Myth." In *Sex and Repression in Savage Society*, 104-34. London: Kegan Paul, 1927.

Malinowski, Bronislaw. "Observations on Friedrich Nietzsche's *The Birth of Tragedy* (1904/5)." In *Early Writings of Bronislaw Malinowski*, edited by Robert J. Thornton and Peter Skalnik, translated by Ludwik Krzyzanowski, 67-88. Cambridge: Cambridge University Press, 1993.

Malinowski, Bronislaw. "On the Principle of the Economy of Thought (1906)." In *Early Writings of Bronislaw Malinowski*, edited by Robert J. Thornton and Peter Skalnik, translated by Ludwik Krzyzanowski, 89-116. Cambridge: Cambridge University Press, 1993.

Malinowski, Bronislaw. "'Psychoanalysis and Anthropology' (1924)." In *Malinowski and the Work of Myth*, edited by Ivan Strenski, 55–57. Princeton, NJ: Princeton University Press, 1992.

Malinowski, Bronislaw. *Sex and Repression in Savage Society*. London: Kegan Paul, 1927.

Malinowski, Bronislaw. "The Foundations of Faith and Morality." In *Sex, Culture, and Myth*, 295–336. New York: Harcourt, 1962.

Malinowski, Bronislaw. "Totemism and Exogamy." In *Early Writings of Bronislaw Malinowski*, edited by Robert J. Thornton and Peter Skalnik, translated by Ludwik Krzyzanowski, 123–201. Cambridge: Cambridge University Press, 1993.

Marrus, Michael R., and Robert O. Paxton. *Vichy France and the Jews*. New York: Basic Books, 1981.

Masuzawa, Tomoko. *In Search of Dreamtime: The Quest for the Origin of Religion*. Religion and Postmodernism. Chicago: University of Chicago Press, 1993.

Mauss, Marcel. *A General Theory of Magic*. Translated by Robert Brain. London: Routledge and K. Paul, 1972.

Mauss, Marcel. "An Intellectual Self-Portrait." In *The Sociological Domain: The Durkheimians and the Founding of French Sociology*, edited by Philippe Besnard, 139–51. Cambridge: Cambridge University Press, 1983.

Mauss, Marcel. Review of "Introduction à la traduction française" in *Manuel de l'histoire des religions* by Pierre Daniel Chantepie de la Saussaye, by Henri Hubert. *Notes critiques. Sciences sociales* 5 (1904): 177.

Mauss, Marcel. Review of *Le festin de l'immortalité. Étude de mythologie comparée Indo-Européenne*, by Georges Dumézil. *L'Année sociologique* 1 (nouvelle série) (1924): 517–20.

Mauss, Marcel. *On Prayer*. Edited by W. S. F. Pickering. Translated by Susan Leslie. Reprint. New York: Durkheim Press, 2003.

Mauss, Marcel. Review of *Religion und Mythologie der Uitoto. (Textaufnahmen und Beobachtungen, etc.). (Quellen der Religionsgeschichte. Gruppe II). – Vol. I (Einführung und Texte Vol. II (Texte und Wörterbuch)*, by Karl Preuss. *L'Année sociologique* 1 (nouvelle série) (1924): 509–12.

Mauss, Marcel. "Review of *La doctrine du sacrifice dans les Brâhmanas*, by Sylvain Lévi." In *Oeuvres*, edited by Victor Karady, 1: Les fonctions sociales du sacré: 352–54. Paris: Éditions de Minuit, 1968.

Mauss, Marcel. "Sylvain Lévi." In *Oeuvres*, edited by Victor Karady, 3: Cohésion sociale et divisions de la sociologie: 535–47. Paris: Éditions de Minuit, 1969.

Mauss, Marcel. *The Gift: Forms and Functions of Exchange in Archaic Societies*. Translated by Ian Gunnison. New York: Norton, 1967.

Mauss, Marcel. Review of *Mythologie. Archiv für Religionswissenschaft* by Hermann Usener, and Vorwort zum Siebenten Bande, by Albrecht Dietrich. *L'Année sociologique* 8 (1903): 224–25.

Mauss, Marcel. Review of *Reports of the Cambridge Anthropological Expedition to Torres Straits. Vol. V, Sociology, Magic and Religion of the Western Islanders*, by A. C. Haddon. *L'Année sociologique* 8 (1903): 256–61.

Mauss, Marcel, and Henri Hubert. "Myths." In *Saints, Heroes, Myths, and Rites: Classical Durkheimian Studies of Religion and Society*, edited by Alexander Riley, Sarah Daynes, and Cyril Isnart, 13–16. London: Routledge, 2016.

Mauss, Marcel, Henri Hubert, and Robert Hertz. *Saints, Heroes, Myths, and Rites: Classical Durkheimian Studies of Religion and Society*. Edited by Alexander Riley, Sarah Daynes, and Cyril Isnart. London: Routledge, 2016.

Medvedev, Roy Aleksandrovich. *Post-Soviet Russia: A Journey through the Yeltsin Era*. New York: Columbia University Press, 2000.

Merleau-Ponty, Maurice. "De Mauss À Lévi-Strauss." In *Signes*, 143–57. Paris: Gallimard, 1960.

Métraux, Alfred. "Bronislaw Malinowski: (1884–1942)." *Boletín Bibliográfico de Antropología Americana (1937–1948)* 6, no. 1/3 (1942): 26–29.

Miller, William Watts. "The anthropological roots of Émile Durkheim's British career." *Sociologie* 8, no. 3 (2017): 309–14. https://doi.org/10.3917/socio.083.0309

Minor, Robert N., ed. *Modern Indian Interpreters of the Bhagavad Gita*. Albany: State University of New York Press, 1986.

Misako, Akiyama, and Susumu Egashira. "Ernst Mach and the Origin of the Knowledge Theory in the Former Austrian Empire." *SSRN Electronic Journal*, 2013. https://doi.org/10.2139/ssrn.2224390

Momigliano, Arnaldo. "Georges Dumézil and the Trifunctional Approach to Roman Civilization." *History and Theory* 23, no. 3 (October 1984): 312–30. https://doi.org/10.2307/2505078

Monod, Gabriel. "James Darmesteter." In *Portraits et souvenirs*, 155–74. Paris: Calmann Levy, 1897.

Montagu, M. F. Ashley. "Bronislaw Malinowski (1884–1942)." *Isis* 34, no. 2 (October 1942): 146–50. https://doi.org/10.1086/347767

Mukherjee, Mithi. "Sedition, Law, and the British Empire in India: The Trial of Tilak (1908)." *Law, Culture and the Humanities* 16, no. 3 (October 2020): 454–76. https://doi.org/10.1177/1743872116685034

Müller, Friedrich Max. *Auld Lang Syne*. New York: Scribner, 1899.

Müller, Friedrich Max. *Chips from a German Workshop*. Vol. 1. London: Longman, 1867.

Müller, Friedrich Max. *Chips from a German Workshop*. Vol. 2. London: Longman, 1867.

Müller, Friedrich Max. "Comparative Mythology (*Oxford Essays*, 1856)." In *Selected Essays on Language, Mythology and Religion*, I:299–451. London: Longman, 1881.

Müller, Friedrich Max. "Forgotten Bibles." In *Last Essays: Essays on the Science of Religion*, I:1–35. Collected Works of the Right Honorable F. Max Müller. New York: Longman, 1901.

Müller, Friedrich Max. *Introduction to the Science of Religion: Four Lectures Delivered at the Royal Institution, in February and May 1870*. London: Spottiswoode, 1870.

Müller, Friedrich Max. "Lecture on the Vedas or the Sacred Books of the Brahmans (March 1865)." In *Last Essays: Essays on the Science of Religion*, II:109–59. Collected Works of the Right Honorable F. Max Müller. London: Longman, 1881.

Müller, Friedrich Max. *Lectures on the Science of Language Delivered at the Royal Institution of Great Britain in April, May, and June, 1861*. New York: Scribner, 1862.

Müller, Friedrich Max. *My Autobiography*. New Delhi: Scribner, 2002.
Müller, Friedrich Max. *Natural Religion*. London: Longman, 1889.
Müller, Friedrich Max. "On the Philosophy of Mythology (Lecture at the Royal Institute, 1871)." In *Chips from a German Workshop*, 5:53–97. New York: Scribner, 1890.
Müller, Friedrich Max. *Physical Religion*. London: Longman, 1891.
Mus, Paul. "La mythologie primitive et la penseé de l'Inde." *Bulletin de la Société Française de philosophie* 37 (Mai-Juin 1937): 83–126.
Niemeijer, A. C. "Some General Aspects of Nationalism in India." In *The Khilafat Movement in India 1919–1924*, 1–21. The Hague: Martinus Nijhoff, 1972.
Nietzsche, Friedrich. *The Birth of Tragedy: Or, Hellenism and Pessimism*. Translated by William. A. Haussmann. London: George Allen & Unwin, 1910.
Olivier, Laurent, ed. *La mémoire et le temps: l'œuvre transdisciplinaire d'Henri Hubert (1872–1927)*. Paris: Éditions Demopolis, 2017.
Østbø, Jardar. *The New Third Rome: Readings of a Russian Nationalist Myth*. Stuttgart: ibidem, 2016.
Ostrowski, Donald. "'Moscow the Third Rome' as Historical Ghost." In *Byzantium, Faith and Power (1261–1557): Perspectives on Late Byzantine Art and Culture*, edited by Sarah T. Brooks. New York: Metropolitan Museum of Art, 2006.
Paluch, Andrzej K. "The Polish Background to Malinowski's Work." *Man* 16, no. 2 (June 1981): 276–85. https://doi.org/10.2307/2801400
Pan, Inghai. "Notes on Anthropological Understanding of the Others." *Journal of Group Dynamics* 30 (December 2013): 312–20. https://doi.org/10.11245/jgd.30.312
Papkova, Irina. "Saving the Third Rome. 'Fall of the Empire', Byzantium and Putin's Russia." In *IWM Junior Visiting Fellows' Conference Proceedings*, Vol. XXIV: Reconciling the Irreconcilable. Vienna: IWM, 2009.
Piaget, Jean. *Structuralism*. New York: Harper & Row, 1970.
Pickering, W. S. F. *Durkheim's Sociology of Religion: Themes and Theories*. London: Routledge & Kegan Paul, 1984.
Pierre, Henri [Henri Hubert]. Review of *L'Aryen: son rôle social*, by Georges Vacher de Lapouge. *Revue Historique* 78, no. 1 (1902): 162–64.
Plutarch. "Brutus." In *Makers of Rome: Nine Lives*, edited and translated by Ian Scott-Kilvert, 223–70. New York: Dorset Press, 1985.
Poe, Marshall. "Moscow, the Third Rome: The Origins and Transformations of a 'Pivotal Moment.'" *Jahrbücher Für Geschichte Osteuropas* 49, no. 3 (2001): 412–29.
Poliakov, Léon. *The Aryan Myth: A History of Racist and Nationalist Ideas in Europe*. New York: Basic Books, 1974.
Ponzini, Robert. "The Italian 'Invasion' of Russia and Its Key Role in the Emergence of a Unified Russian State." *Economia Aziendale Online* 12, no. 4 (December 30, 2021): 399–405. https://doi.org/10.13132/2038-5498/12.4.399-405
Poulat, Émile. *Histoire, dogme et critique dans la crise moderniste*. Paris: Casterman, 1979.
Putin, Vladimir. "On the Historical Unity of Russians and Ukrainians." Kremlin, July 12, 2021. http://en.kremlin.ru/events/president/news/66181

Radcliffe-Brown, Alfred R. *Method in Social Anthropology: Selected Essays*. Edited by M. N. Srinivas. Chicago: University of Chicago Press, 1958.

Radcliffe-Brown, Alfred R. *Structure and Function in Primitive Society: Essays and Addresses*. Aberdeen: Aberdeen University Press, 1952.

Radcliffe-Brown, Alfred R. *The Andaman Islanders: A Study in Social Anthropology*. Cambridge: Cambridge University Press, 1922.

Radcliffe-Brown, Alfred R. *Orpheus: A History of Religions*. Translated by Florence Simmonds. Rev. ed. New York: Liveright, 1930.

Reinach, Salomon. "Henri Hubert." *Revue archéologique* 26 (1927): 176–78.

Renan, Ernest. "La poésie des races Celtiques." *Revue des deux Mondes* 5, no. 3 (1854): 473–506.

Rennie, Bryan S. *Reconstructing Eliade: Making Sense of Religion*. Albany: State University of New York Press, 1996.

Rennie, Bryan S. Review of *Theorizing About Myth*, by Robert A. Segal. *Culture and Religion* 1, no. 1 (May 2000): 149–50. https://doi.org/10.1080/01438300008567148

Renou, Louis. "Préface." In *La doctrine du sacrifice dans les Brâhmanas*, by Sylvain Lévi, 2nd ed. Paris: Presses Universitaires de France, 1966.

Renou, Louis. "Sylvain Lévi et son œuvre scientifique." In *Mémorial Sylvain Lévi*, edited by Jacques Bacot, xi–li. Paris: Paul Hartmann, 1937.

Réville, Albert. "Contemporary Materialism in Religion: The Sacred Heart." *Theological Review* 44 (January 1874): 138–56.

Réville, Albert. *Les religions des peuples non-civilisés*. Vol. 1. Paris: Fischbacher, 1883.

Riasanovsky, Nicholas V., and Mark D. Steinberg. *A History of Russia*. 7th ed. New York: Oxford University Press, 2005.

Ringer, Fritz. *The Decline of the German Mandarins: The German Academic Community, 1890–1933*. Cambridge, MA: Harvard University Press, 1969.

Rorty, Richard. *Philosophy and Social Hope*. New York: Penguin Books, 2000.

Rowland, Daniel B. "Moscow—The Third Rome or the New Israel?" *Russian Review* 55, no. 4 (October 1996): 591–614. https://doi.org/10.2307/131866

Savart, Claude. *Les catholiques en France au XIXe siècle. Le témoignage du livres religieux*. Paris: Beauchesne, 1985.

Schama, Simon. *Citizens: A Chronicle of the French Revolution*. New York: Knopf, 1989.

Scott, Kenneth. "Mussolini and the Roman Empire." *The Classical Journal* 27, no. 9 (1932): 645–57.

Segal, Robert A. Review of *Classification and Comparison in the Study of Religion: The Work of Jonathan Z. Smith*, by Jonathan Z. Smith. *Journal of the American Academy of Religion* 73, no. 4 (December 1, 2005): 1175–88. https://doi.org/10.1093/jaarel/lfi120

Segal, Robert A. "Does Myth Have a Future?" In *Myth and Method*, edited by Laurie L. Patton and Wendy Doniger, 82–106. Charlottesville: University Press of Virginia, 1996.

Segal, Robert A. "Durkheim in Britain: The Work of Radcliffe-Brown." *Journal of the Anthropological Society of Oxford* 30, no. 2 (1999): 131–62.

Segal, Robert A. "Myth." In *The Wiley Blackwell Companion to the Study of Religion*, edited by Robert Alan Segal and Nickolas P. Roubekas, 2nd ed., 348-60. Hoboken, NJ: Wiley-Blackwell, 2021.

Segal, Robert A. *Myth: A Very Short Introduction*. Oxford: Oxford University Press, 2004.

Segal, Robert A. *Myth Theorized*. Sheffield: Equinox, 2023.

Segal, Robert A. "The Life of King Saul as Myth." In *Myth and Scripture: Contemporary Perspectives on Religion, Language, and Imagination*, edited by Dexter E. Callender Jr. 245-79. Atlanta: SBL Press, 2014.

Segal, Robert A., ed. *The Myth and Ritual: An Anthology*. Malden, MA: Blackwell, 1998.

Segal, Robert A. *Theorizing about Myth*. Amherst: University of Massachusetts Press, 1999.

Segal, Robert A. "Understanding Myth: A Response to Bryan Rennie." *Culture and Religion* 1, no. 2 (November 2000): 287-89. https://doi.org/10.1080/01438300008567156

Shapiro, James. *A Year in the Life of William Shakespeare: 1599*. New York: HarperCollins, 2005.

Sheiko, Konstantin, and Stephen Brown. *History as Therapy: Alternative History and Nationalist Imaginings in Russia, 1991-2014*. Stuttgart: ibidem, 2014.

Sidorov, Dmitrii. "Post-Imperial Third Romes: Resurrections of a Russian Orthodox Geopolitical Metaphor." *Geopolitics* 11, no. 2 (July 2006): 317-47. https://doi.org/10.1080/14650040600598585

Singh, Arjun Raghvendra. "Sedition: An Insight on History, Evolution, Shortcoming and Relevance of This Law in Post Colonial India." *Supremo Amicus* 28 (February 2022). https://doi-ds.org/doilink/02.2022-67571545/supremoamicus/v28/2022/53

Smith, Jonathan Z. "A Matter of Class: Taxonomies of Religion." *Harvard Theological Review* 89, no. 4 (October 1996): 387-403. https://doi.org/10.1017/S0017816000006118

Smith, Jonathan Z. "Birth Upside down or Right Side Up?" *History of Religions* 9, no. 4 (May 1970): 281-303. https://doi.org/10.1086/462610

Smith, Jonathan Z. "Conjectures on Conjunctures and Other Matters: Three Essays." In *Redescribing the Gospel of Mark*, edited by Barry S. Crawford and Merrill P. Miller, 17-98. Atlanta: SBL Press, 2017.

Smith, Jonathan Z. *Drudgery Divine: On the Comparison of Early Christianities and the Religions of Late Antiquity*. Jordan Lectures in Comparative Religion 14. Chicago: University of Chicago Press, 1990.

Smith, Jonathan Z. "Earth and Gods." *The Journal of Religion* 49, no. 2 (April 1969): 103-27. https://doi.org/10.1086/486164

Smith, Jonathan Z. "I Am a Parrot (Red)." *History of Religions* 11, no. 4 (May 1972): 391-413. https://doi.org/10.1086/462661

Smith, Jonathan Z. "The Wobbling Pivot." *The Journal of Religion* 52, no. 2 (April 1972): 134-49. https://doi.org/10.1086/486294

Smith, Jonathan Z. *To Take Place: Toward Theory in Ritual*. Chicago: University of Chicago Press, 1987.

Smith, Jonathan Z. "When the Bough Breaks." *History of Religions* 12, no. 4 (May 1973): 342-71. https://doi.org/10.1086/462686

Smith, William Robertson. *Lectures on the Religion of the Semites: Fundamental Institutions. First Series*. 2nd ed. London: Black, 1894.
Smith, William Robertson. "The Place of Theology in the Work and Growth of the Church (March 1875)." In *Lectures and Essays of William Robertson Smith*, edited by John Sutherland Black and George Chrystal, 309–40. London: Black, 1912.
Smith, William Robertson. "What History Teaches Us to Seek in the Bible (November 1870)." In *Lectures and Essays of William Robertson Smith*, edited by John Sutherland Black and George Chrystal, 207–34. London: Black, 1912.
Sorlin, Pierre. *«La Croix» et les Juifs (1880–1899), contribution à l'histoire de l'antisémitisme contemporain*. Paris: Grasset, 1967.
Steinby, Liisa. "The Rehabilitation of Myth: Enlightenment and Romanticism in Johann Gottfried Herder's *Vom Geist Der Ebräischen Poesie*." *Sjuttonhundratal* 6 (October 1, 2009): 54–79. https://doi.org/10.7557/4.2760
Stern, Fritz. *The Politics of Cultural Despair: A Study in the Rise of the Germanic Ideology*. Berkeley: University of California Press, 1961.
Stevenson, Robert W. "Tilak and the *Bhagavadgita*'s Doctrine of Karmayoga." In *Modern Indian Interpreters of the Bhagavad Gita*, edited by Robert N. Minor, 44–60. Albany: State University of New York Press, 1986.
Stocking, George W. "Anthropology and the Science of the Irrational: Malinowski's Encounter with Freudian Psychoanalysis." In *Malinowski, Rivers, Benedict and Others: Essays on Culture and Personality*, edited by George W. Stocking, 13–49. Madison: University of Wisconsin Press, 1988.
Storne, Franck. "Le protestantisme libéral français au 19e siècle à travers l'engagement des Révilles, pasteurs réformés." Diplôme d'études approfondies, Université de Reims, 1985.
Strenski, Ivan. "Actually, You Can Compare Apples to Oranges: Secrets of Successful Comparison of Myths." In *Religion: Narrating Religion*, edited by Sarah Iles Johnston, 49–64. New York: Macmillan, 2017.
Strenski, Ivan. *Contesting Sacrifice: Religion, Nationalism, and Social Thought in France*. Chicago: University of Chicago Press, 2002.
Strenski, Ivan. *Durkheim and the Jews of France*. Chicago Studies in the History of Judaism. Chicago: University of Chicago Press, 1997.
Strenski, Ivan. *Four Theories of Myth in Twentieth-Century History: Cassirer, Eliade, Lévi-Strauss, and Malinowski*. Iowa City: University of Iowa Press, 1987.
Strenski, Ivan. "Henri Hubert, Racial Science and Political Myth." *Journal of the History of the Behavioral Sciences* 23, no. 4 (October 1987): 353–67. https://doi.org/10.1002/1520-6696(198710)23:4%3C353::AID-JHBS2300230405%3E3.0.CO;2-O
Strenski, Ivan. "Hubert, Mauss and the Comparative Social History of Religions." In *Religion in Relation: Method, Application, and Moral Location*, 75–88. Columbia: University of South Carolina Press, 1993.
Strenski, Ivan. "Love and Anarchy in Romania: A Critical Review of Mircea Eliade's *Autobiography, Volume 1: 1907–37*." In *Religion in Relation: Method, Application, and Moral Location*, 166–79. Columbia: University of South Carolina Press, 1993.
Strenski, Ivan. "Malinowski: Second Positivism, Second Romanticism." *Man* 17, no. 4 (1982): 766–71.

Strenski, Ivan. "Misreading Max Müller." *Method & Theory in the Study of Religion* 8, no. 3 (1996): 291-96.
Strenski, Ivan. *Religion in Relation: Method, Application, and Moral Location.* Columbia: University of South Carolina Press, 1993.
Strenski, Ivan. "The Rise of Ritual and the Hegemony of Myth: Sylvain Lévi, the Durkheimians, and Max Müller." In *Myth and Method*, edited by Laurie L. Patton and Wendy Doniger, 52-81. Charlottesville: University Press of Virginia, 1996.
Strenski, Ivan. *Theology and the First Theory of Sacrifice.* Leiden: Brill, 2003.
Strenski, Ivan. *Thinking about Religion: An Historical Introduction to Theories of Religion.* Oxford: Blackwell, 2006.
Strenski, Ivan. *Understanding Theories of Religion: An Introduction.* 2nd ed. Malden, MA: Wiley-Blackwell, 2015.
Sun, Allan. "Chasing One's Tail: Some Reflections on the Methodologies of Mircea Eliade and Jonathan Z Smith." In "On a Panegyrical Note: Studies in Honour of Garry W Trompf," edited by Victoria Barker and Frances Di Lauro. Special issue, *Sydney Studies in Religion*, 2007, 189-204.
Sylvain, Renée. "Malinowski the Modern Other: An Indirect Evaluation of Postmodernism." *Anthropologica* 38, no. 1 (1996): 21-45. https://doi.org/10.2307/25605818
Taylor, Charles. "Interpretation and the Sciences of Man." In *Philosophical Papers*, by Charles Taylor, 15-57. Cambridge: Cambridge University Press, 1985.
Taylor, Charles. "Understanding and Ethnocentricity." In *Philosophical Papers*, by Charles Taylor, 116-33. Cambridge: Cambridge University Press, 1985.
Thornton, Robert J. "The Chains of Reciprocity: The Impact of Nietzsche's 'Genealogy' on Malinowski's 'Crime and Custom in Savage Society.'" *The Polish Sociological Bulletin*, no. 97 (1992): 19-33.
Thornton, Robert J., and Peter Skalnik. "Introduction: Malinowski's Reading, Writing, 1904-1914." In *Early Writings of Bronislaw Malinowski*, edited by Robert J. Thornton and Peter Skalnik, 1-64. Cambridge: Cambridge University Press, 1993.
Vidler, Alec R. *A Variety of Catholic Modernists.* Cambridge: Cambridge University Press, 1970.
Vogt, W. Paul. "Durkheimian Sociology Versus Philosophical Rationalism: The Case of Célestin Bouglé." In *The Sociological Domain: The Durkheimians and the Founding of French Sociology*, edited by Philippe Besnard, 231-47. Cambridge: Cambridge University Press, 1983.
Vogt, W. Paul. "The Politics of Academic Sociology in France, 1890-1914." PhD diss., Indiana University, 1976.
Voigt, Johannes. *Max Mueller: The Man and His Ideas.* Calcutta: Firma KLM, 1967.
Weber, Max. *The Protestant Ethic and the Spirit of Capitalism.* Translated by Talcott Parsons. New York: Scribner, 1976.
Wikimedia Foundation. "Theory." *Wikipedia.* Accessed August 2, 2015. https://en.wikipedia.org/w/index.php?title=Theory&oldid=673376304
Young, Michael W. *Malinowski: Odyssey of an Anthropologist, 1884-1920.* New Haven, CT: Yale University Press, 2004.

Young, Michael W. "Young Malinowski." *Canberra Anthropology* 17, no. 2 (October 1994): 103–22. https://doi.org/10.1080/03149099409508423

Zyuganov, Gennady. *Derzhava* [The Great Power]. Translated by Roy Aleksandrovich Medvedev. Moscow: Informpechat, 1994.

Index

affaire Dreyfus *See* Dreyfus affair
anthroposociology
 (L'Anthroposociologie) 177,
 179ff, 230, 243
anti-Semitism 35ff, 47ff
Aryanism 32ff, 39, 48, 123, 172, 179,
 230
Austin, J. L. 1, 9

Barnette, Sarah 19, 208f, 235
Bercken, Wil van den 192, 199, 231ff
Berdyaev, Nikolai 197f
Bible 4f, 26f, 34ff, 42f, 52, 152, 156,
 162f, 171, 207ff, 246, 249
Boas, Franz 25, 69f, 157f, 162, 177,
 205
Brāhmanas 49
Brothers Grimm 22
Byzantium 191ff, 194ff, 198f, 202f,
 206, 232f, 246

Calvinism 41ff, 154
Campbell, Joseph 18, 130, 150, 153,
 156f, 164
Casaubon, Edward 17, 19f
Celts, Celtism (*Celtisme*) 56, 60, 63ff,
 75f, 84f, 176, 184ff, 202, 215, 218,
 230f, 236, 240, 246
Charles I (Stuart king) 8, 190
Constantinople *See* Byzantium
Czarnowski, Stefan 54, 64, 182f, 185f,
 211f, 240f

Davenport, R. Dean 8, 207, 236
Desmond, Jane 2f, 207, 210, 237
disease of language 22f, 28, 30, 98,
 104
Dreyfus affair 40, 52, 57, 65, 77, 174f,
 177, 179

Duchesne, Abbé Louis 55, 58, 61,
 174, 213, 237
Dugin, Alexander 198
Durkheim, Émile 6f, 10f, 14ff, 26,
 39f, 42-8, 55-68, 71-81, 86-91,
 92, 95-7, 102f, 123, 156, 162,
 173-7, 178-80, 181-7, 209ff,
 212-9, 235f, 238, 240, 243f, 246
Durkheimians *See* Durkheim, Émile

Eliade, Mircea 155, 161f, 217, 241,
 247, 249f
Eliot, George 25, 27f, 36, 216f, 243
evolution 6, 43, 47f, 59, 62, 93f 140,
 153, 177, 185, 226, 229, 242

Fifth Section, École Pratique des
 Hautes Études (EPHE) 2, 21,
 41-5, 73
Filofei 191, 194-201, 203, 206, 231ff,
 238, 243
Fioravanti, Rodolfo 'Aristotele' 193
Franks, Frankish 34, 56, 104, 184f,
 190
Frazer, James George 91, 104-7, 148,
 155-60, 162f, 220-5, 228, 238, 242
Freud, Sigmund 10, 18, 38, 69, 83, 91,
 107-11, 148,156f, 158, 164f, 166,
 168, 170-2, 228, 249

Germany, Germans 6, 20-2, 25-36,
 42, 48, 51f, 56, 60, 63-5, 67, 76,
 84, 123, 128, 160, 176, 181, 184ff,
 187, 192, 210, 241, 245-7, 249
Grimm, Jacob and Wilhelm *See*
 Brothers Grimm

*histoire historisant, historiens
 historisants* 61

Index

Hubert, Henri ('Henri Pierre') chs. 4, 5, 9 *passim*, 10f, 13f, 21f, 39f, 42, 44-7, 50, 190, 207-17, 241, 244-9

imagination 14, 141f, 165, 169, 175, 182, 185f, 200, 228, 248
India 4-6, 13, 18, 20f, 29f, 32-4, 48f, 50, 56, 128, 139-45, 164, 198, 204, 211, 224f, 229, 235-7, 239-42, 245f, 248-50
Indo-European/Indo-German/*Indogermanisch* 21, 23, 34, 36, 54, 66, 80, 181
Ireland 182f, 186
Israel 51, 165-7, 168, 193, 212, 232, 236, 248
Ivan III (tsar) 192-95, 206

Jews 35f, 41, 43, 50f, 57, 128, 180, 185, 230, 244, 249
Jung, Carl 18, 38, 156f, 164

Kalb, Judith 195, 229, 232-4, 241
Kerry, John (U.S. Senator) 204-6
Kholmogorov, Egor 198, 200, 233, 241
Kiev 194-6, 199, 201f
Kolstø, Pål 195, 232, 241

Lapouge, Georges Vacher de 169-72
Lagarde, Paul de 48, 51
laïcité 60
Latynina, Yulia 198, 233, 242
Leenhardt, Maurice 11, 54, 68f, 73f, 81, 83-5, 213, 236
Legend of the White Cowl 190f
Levada Opinion Research 199
Levene, Nancy 147, 225, 242
Lévi-Strauss, Claude 10f, 14f, 19, 54f, ch. 5 *passim*, 154-60, 214-7, 227, 239, 242, 245, 249
Lévi, Israel 42, 57, 175
Lévi, Sylvain 6, 42, 48-53, 57, 211f, 222, 230, 242, 244, 247, 250
Lévy, Isidore 57f, 83, 125, 175, 223, 229, 239, 242
Ligue des Amis du Sionisme 52, 212, 242

lili'u 12, 114f, 122, 132, 189
Lincoln, Bruce 12, 122f, 134f, 152, 156, 188f, 200, 203, 207, 223-7, 231, 234, 242
Loisy, Alfred 61, 78, 174f, 215, 240
Luther, Martin/Lutheranism 3-5, 27, 29f, 40, 42, 127

magic 8, 40, 42f, 90, 105, 125f, 176, 206, 210, 214, 217-9, 221-3, 228, 238, 240, 243f
Malinowski, Bronislaw 1f, 4, 7, 10-2, 37f, 50, 54, ch. 6 *passim*, 122, 131-4, 165f, 169f, 189, 207, 210, 218-23, 229, 231, 235, 237f, 239, 241-6, 249-51
Marian cult 170
Martin, Henri 30,185, 224, 245
Mary (mother of Jesus) 170f
Masuzawa, Tomoko 17-9, 28, 208f, 244
Mauss, Marcel 7, 11, 14f, 22, 39f, 156, 174-6, 182, 202f, 207-20, 229, 231, 236-40, 242, 244f
Michelet, Jules 76, 185
Middlemarch 25, 27, 216, 246
Moscow, Myth of Third Rome (MMTR) 190-201, 203-206, 232f
modernism, modernists 52, 60f, 78f, 86, 100, 174, 212, 222, 246, 250
Monod, Gabriel 58, 61, 180, 192, 245
Muffang, Henri 179
Müller, Friedrich Max 4-6, 9-13, 16-42, 47-54, 88-91, 88, 116, 118, 120, 146-9, 156f, 159, 164f, 177, 184, 207-9, 255f, 250
Mussolini, Benito 201, 233, 247

Narochnitskaia, Natalia 198
Novaya Gazeta 198, 233, 242
Novgorod 191

Orthodox Church, Russian 13, 26, 43, 126, 187, 191, 193-201, 213, 232, 248
Østbø, Jardar 8f, 192, 197, 209, 231-3, 241, 246
Ottomans 136, 191, 192, 195

Our Lady of Kazan Cathedral 192, 196

Paleologos, Zoe 193
Pamiat 198
pan-Slavism 196-8
Patrick, Saint 63f, 182-6, 211, 240
Paul I of Russia (emperor) 196
Péguy, Charles 57
Peter the Great 195f
Pfleiderer, Otto 163
Poland 64, 100, 183, 185
Poliakov, Léon 36, 209, 211f, 231, 246
Popper, Karl 157
post-modernism 19, 28, 86
pragmatism 1f, 4-6, 10-2, 16, 37f, 54, 79, 88-91, 94, 96-106, 130f, 134, 147f, 168f
Principle of the Two Swords 202
Putin, Vladimir 137, 197-9, 203, 233, 235-8, 239, 246

Radcliffe-Brown, Alfred Reginald 11, 92, 95, 102
Reinach, Salomon 47, 59, 212f, 239, 247
Renan, Ernest 36, 61, 184f, 230f, 247
Rennie, Brian 88, 149f, 159, 217, 225, 227, 247, 250
ritual, ritualism 6f, 10, 16, 20, 24, 27-30, 3f, 41-53, 62, 64, 78-81, 90-2, 103-7, 135, 148 160, 165, 230, 236, 248, 250
Romania 159, 227, 249
Romanos II (emperor) 194
Romantic, romanticism 21, 25, 21-32, 49, 102f, 112, 118f, 150, 161, 194, 220, 223, 249
Rome, Second Rome, Third Rome 5, 13, 26, 136f, 172, 188-201, 203, 205-7, 224, 131-4, 236, 237-9, 241, 246-8
Romism 192f, 200
Ruffo, Marco 193
Russia ch. 10 *passim*
Russia-Ukraine War 201

Russian Special Forces (*Spetsnaz Rossii*) 198, 203, 241
Rzeczpospolita Polska (Polish-Lithuanian Commonwealth) 201

sacrifice 6, 24, 29, 33, 45-50, 58, 66, 139, 210-2, 229, 240-2, 244, 250
Saul (Biblical king) 10, 31, 148, 157, 164-72, 204, 248
Segal, Robert A. 9f, 17f, 20f, 29, 37f, 88f, 120, 129f, ch. 8 *passim*, 189, 207-10, 219, 223, 225, 227f, 231, 238, 247f
Shevkunov, Father Tikhon 199, 233, 236
Smith, Jonathan Z. 9f, ch. 8 *passim*, 225-8, 236, 239, 241f, 247f
Smith, William Robertson 43, 46, 47-51, 210, 241, 249
Solari, Pietro 193
Solovyov, Vladimir 197
Spasskaya Tower 193
Stalin, Josef 195, 197, 203
Stalinism 195
Strenski, Ivan 207, 208, 211, 217, 220, 221, 222, 2526, 227, 238, 239, 230, 231, 249f
Sun, Allan 161, 163f
Swift Boat Veterans for Truth 203-6,
Sylvester I (pope) 190

Talmud 51f
Thomas, Albert 65, 176
Trobriand Islands 12, 100f 106, 109, 114f, 116-21, 131-3, 189
Tylor, Edward Burnett 18, 151, 156

Ukraine 198-201, 206

Vasilij I (prince) 202
Vedas 5f, 20f, 25, 27, 31-6, 48-53, 123, 209, 245
Virgin Mary *See* Mary (mother of Jesus)
Vogt, W. Paul 174, 229, 250
Voldomar I (Kievan Rus) 194-6

Weber, Max 127f, 135, 153f, 226, 239, 250

Zhirinovsky, Vladimir 209

Zionism (*Sionisme*) 60
Zosima, Metropolitan 193
Zyuganov, Gennady 198, 233, 251

www.ingramcontent.com/pod-product-compliance
Lightning Source LLC
Chambersburg PA
CBHW070336240426
43665CB00045B/2101